THE LONDON SCOTTISH
IN THE GREAT WAR

THE LONDON SCOTTISH

IN THE GREAT WAR

Mark Lloyd

LEO COOPER

Here's tae us
Wha's like us
Damned few
An'the're died.

Written to the memory of the fallen Highlanders at Culloden, and since adopted by Scottish Regiments everywhere. No greater toast can truly be drunk to the memory of the 1st Battalion The London Scottish who, in late 1914, prepared peacefully for summer camp, and yet who, by late 1915, were mostly dead.

'Strike Sure'

First published in Great Britain in 2001 by Leo Cooper
an imprint of Pen & Sword Books Limited
47 Church Street, Barnsley, South Yorkshire S70 2AS

Copyright © Mark Lloyd, 2001

For up to date information on other titles produced under the Pen & Sword imprint, please telephone or write to:
Pen & Sword Books Limited
FREEPOST
47 Church Street
Barnsley
South Yorkshire
S70 2BR

Telephone (24 hours): 01226 734555

ISBN 0-85052-713-9

British Library Cataloguing in Publication Data

Printed by CPI UK

Contents

Notes and Acknowledgements

The spelling of certain fundamental words and place names has changed in the last century. To preserve continuity between the text and the many original sources from which I have quoted I have, where necessary, reverted to the spelling-style prevailing during the Great War.

In particular, the modern rank of 'sergeant' appears throughout as 'serjeant', more commonly applied at the time. Equally, towns in Flemish-speaking Belgium are identified by their French names, then universally employed by the British soldiers on the ground.

I would like to pay tribute to Bob Harman, Clem Webb, Alan Morris and those at the London Scottish whose help and knowledge have been so invaluable to me over the years. I would also like to thank Susan Ottaway and the long-suffering Brigadier Henry Wilson for their advice and patience throughout the preparation of this book.

Preface

Few regiments have better served the Territorial Army than the London Scottish. At the beginning of the twentieth century they sent troops to the service of the Crown in the Second Boer War. Today they have officers and men serving with the regular forces in the Balkans and elsewhere.

The professionalism and fighting ability of the London Scottish was perfectly recognized in 1914 when they became one of the first Territorial Force battalions ordered to France and the first to see action. On the night of Hallowe'en 1914 they fought the cream of the German Army to a standstill and destroyed, forever, the myth that Territorial soldiers were somehow inferior to their regular brethren.

For the next four years the 1st and 2nd Battalions fought in every major campaign other than Gallipoli. They served in France and Belgium, Salonica and Palestine, the 2nd Battalion finishing the war no more than a few miles from Messines where the 1st Battalion had brought such honour to the regiment four bloody years earlier.

Today the London Scottish lives on as part of the recently reconstituted London Regiment. May its survival be assured for another hundred years.

Mark Lloyd
May, 2001.

Introduction

For two centuries the officers and men of the London Scottish have faithfully served their country, never more so than during the terrible years of the Great War. Initially with the 1st Guards Brigade, and later with the 56th (London) Division, the 1st Battalion served in France and Flanders throughout the war. They were the first Territorial soldiers to be committed to battle, at Messines in 1914 when they suffered one-third casualties, and were among the last to disengage. So dedicated was the 1st Battalion to the prosecution of its cause that by November 1918 its numbers included only three survivors of the original Battle of Messines.

The 2nd Battalion saw action in campaigns as diverse as France and Flanders, Ireland, the Balkans and Palestine where it won two Victoria Crosses.

The London Scottish in the Great War does not set out to recite the oft-told details of famous battles fought and won. Rather it employs a wealth of previously unpublished war journals, diaries and photographs to provide a unique insight into this most auspicious Regiment. It demonstrates as no history of the Scottish has before the hopes, sufferings and aspirations of the volunteers who filled its ranks, so many of whom in the process made the supreme sacrifice.

Chapter One

Early Days

The Highland Armed Association, the original processor of the London
Scottish, was formed on 14 June 1798 when, at a committee meeting of the
Highland Society of London, William Ogilvie proposed and Colonel Allan
Cameron seconded that a General Meeting should be called to form a
'Corps of Highlanders in the Highland uniform from the Highlanders and
other natives of Scotland resident in London.' In a letter to the Marquis of
Titchfield, Lord Lieutenant of Middlesex, the Association offered to form
itself into a Highland Corps distinguished by the national dress and music.
It would march to any part of Great Britain in the case of invasion by
Napoleon Bonaparte and would serve without pay, everything being found
from within except for arms and ammunition. The Battalion was to be 800
strong with officers of its own choosing; subscriptions were to be one guinea
entrance and one guinea annually.

The Corps was readily accepted by a desperate British Government, but
disbanded on the signing of the Peace of Amiens in 1802. After a year of
uneasy peace, Britain once again declared war on France. On 18 May 1803
a group of former Volunteers met together in Covent Garden and resolved
once again to offer their services. It was decided that the new organization

Canterbury, 1894

Items of Uniform worn by Colonel the Earl of Wemyss

would be known as the Loyal North Britons, thus cutting out the emphasis on 'Highland' which had proved a brake on earlier recruiting. Their services were accepted on 15 July 1803 after which the Company began drilling on several sites in London. The initial membership ceiling of 200 was quickly reached and permission granted for an increase, until by March 1806 the official complement had reached 324. However, the victory at Trafalgar in October 1805 drastically reduced the fear of invasion. There being no coercion or absenteeism numbers steadily dropped until, by the time of the final parade of the Loyal North Britons on 20 June 1814, the unit could hardly raise 150 on parade.

The Panics

In March 1856, after two years of particularly chaotic and incompetent warfare, the armies of Britain and France forced Russia to the negotiating table. Yet within three years the alliance which had won the Crimean War had already dissolved into mutual distrust. Emperor Napoleon III was steadily rearming, conspicuously building an ironclad squadron in the port of Cherbourg. Despite French protestations of peace, many in England became thoroughly alarmed. The British wooden-walled fleet was almost obsolete, her army backward-looking and wholly incapable of frustrating the hostile intentions of a sophisticated European adversary.

In the face of Government lethargy the populace as a whole reacted positively. In virtually every major town and city steps were taken to raise, equip, arm and train a new volunteer defence force. In a few weeks, more than 100,000 Volunteers, many of them ex-Regulars, had been

Drum Major Alfred Goodman, Queens Victoria's Silver Jubilee, 1897.

Queen Victoria's Silver Jubilee, 1897.

Queen Victoria's Silver Jubilee, 1897.

enrolled. Even when General Peel, the then Secretary for War, gave the Volunteers reluctant recognition it constituted little more than a begrudging and wholly gratuitous acknowledgement of the new force. Units remained unpaid, responsible for the provision of their own arms, uniforms and instructors and without training grounds.

It is not known precisely who first suggested the formation of a London Scottish Volunteer Corps. What is known is that when Lord Elcho, later the Earl of Wemyss, was approached by Dr Halley, an eminent London Scot, and asked to command the Regiment once formed, he readily concurred. The first public announcement was made on 21 May 1859, at a meeting of the Highland Society of London. The Society had been responsible in 1793 for the formation of 'the Highland Armed Association of London', subsequently reformed as the Loyal North Britons and disbanded in 1816, and boasted many of the wealthiest and most influential of expatriate Scottish society.

On 4 July 1859 a meeting of Scottish residents was convened jointly by the Highland Society and Caledonian Society at the Freemason's Tavern.

With Lord Elcho in the chair a motion was proposed by Sir John Heron-Maxwell, seconded by Sir Charles Forbes and adopted unanimously:

'That as the present condition of affairs on the Continent of Europe may lead to complications that will render it impossible for Great Britain, with due regard to her

Winners of the first year of the Competition for Vanishing Targets at 200 yards, National Rifle Association, Wimbledon 1888.
J. Monro, H.M. White, J. McRobbie, W. Scott, H.J. Billie, K.B. Brown.

Lord Wemyss VD, ADC and Lieutenant Colonel E.J. Balfour at Gosford House at the end of the Scottish March, 1897.

> *material interests and high station among the nations, to maintain a neutrality, it is expedient that Scottish residents in London and its neighbourhood be invited to participate in strengthening the defensive resources of the country, by forming a Volunteer Rifle Corps, to be designated the London Scottish Rifle Volunteers.'*

A committee was formed and enrolments at once began. Drilling began in October in a number of different centres. The Corps was formally accepted by the Government on 2 November 1859 and a few days later the first two officers were gazetted; Lord Elcho as Major in command and Mr George Mackenzie as Captain. In January 1860 the Corps was formally granted battalion status and designated the 15th Middlesex (London Scottish) Rifle Volunteer Corps, with an establishment of six companies, each 100 strong. A month later Lord Elcho was promoted to Lieutenant Colonel.

At first the Volunteers were largely aided by the subscriptions of

The London Scottish Band, 1885.

Wimbledon, 1864

Scotsmen in London, and had a large number of honorary members. The entrance fee was fixed at £1 and the annual subscription at £1, members providing their own uniform and equipment; but of the 600 men originally recruited, 340 were 'artisans,' who paid no entrance-fee and only 5s. (25 pence) a year subscription. Of these only fifty provided their own uniforms, the rest being equipped from regimental funds. From the outset the Volunteers thus comprised a broad cross-section of Scots in London, with two of the companies found almost entirely from the ranks of the 'artisans.'

As if in anticipation of the wars ahead several of the volunteer battalions elected for a grey uniform, shunning the red of the Regular line battalions. Lord Elcho was a firm exponent of the new fashion, claiming that,

'a soldier is a man hunter, neither more nor less; as a deer stalker chooses the least visible of colours, so ought a soldier to be clad.'

True to his word he clothed his battalion in hodden grey, relieved by facings of royal blue. Initially only No 1, the Highland Company was kilted. However, the others gradually followed suit, until by the turn of the century the entire regiment had abandoned trews in favour of the hodden grey kilt.

In 1862 the entrance-fee was abolished, but Scottish nationality remained a prerequisite. This may have proved an impediment to recruiting as, although the battalion was expanded to ten companies in November 1860, the increase was not fully implemented until 1884.

Lieutenant General Colin Campbell, Lord Clyde, was appointed the first honorary colonel in 1861. After his death in 1863 he was succeeded by another distinguished Scottish officer, Lieutenant General Sir James Hope Grant, who held the post until his death in 1875. Several volunteer battalions proved less durable than the Scottish and quickly folded. Consequently, on 3 September 1880, it was announced in The *London Gazette* that the battalion was to be elevated in seniority and renumbered the 7th Middlesex (London Scottish) Rifle Volunteers.

In the twenty years that followed, the Battalion continued to consolidate, moving into its new headquarters in Buckingham Gate in 1896. It held the first of a series of marches through Scotland in 1898 and, a year later, in the company of 30,000 London Volunteers, was reviewed on Horse Guards Parade by the Prince of Wales.

The Boer War

In 1898 the growing tension between Britain and the South African Boer republics erupted into open conflict. Three months before the formal declaration of war Colonel Balfour, then commanding the London Scottish, wrote to the War Office offering the services of a complete company of *selected* officers and men. Other battalions quickly followed suit, until it became obvious that London alone would be in a position to provide a substantial independent force both of infantry and mounted infantry. This placed the War Office in a dilemma, and caused considerable controversy within the ranks of the Volunteer movement. No one seriously considered that the Regular Army was inferior to the task ahead of it, and all assumed a speedy and relatively bloodless victory. Many therefore feared that in seeking to take part in operations abroad where their services were not required, the Volunteers, inherently a home defence force, would run the very real risk of earning the distrust rather than support of the military hierarchy.

Over half the British casualties in the Boer war died from disease. In Memorium Private Paton Menzies who died of dysentery in South Africa on 28 May 1900.

The dark days which closed the month of December 1899 changed matters considerably. In one 'Black Week' Buller was checked at Colenso, Methuen at Magersfontein, and Gatacre at Stormberg. It quickly became clear that the Regular Army would not be able to bring the Boers to their knees unaided. The War Office did not ask for help directly, but instead indicated that offers of service would be favourably considered.

The Court of Common Council of the City of London met on 20 December, and announced that the Commander-in-Chief had agreed to the City equipping and sending to the front a force of 1,000 carefully chosen officers and men. Within days the Court, which also offered the Freedom of the City to every volunteer, subscribed £25,000 to the cause, the major City Companies a further £34,000 and various patriotic citizens a staggering £55,000. On 11 January 1900 it was announced that the total sum required had been raised, and that permission had been granted by the War Office to increase the establishment of the regiment to 1,500 all ranks. That day the City Imperial Volunteers were placed on the establishment of the Army by Royal Warrant, command was passed to Colonel W.M. Mackinnon, and the officers and men became regular soldiers for the period of one year or for the duration of hostilities.

The standard of qualification laid down by the War Office was exceedingly stringent. Beside passing the Army medical examination the men were required to be between the ages of twenty-five and thirty-five, to be unmarried, and to have qualified as marksmen for the previous two years. This final proviso implied a minimum of three years' prior service in the Volunteers, as recruits did not normally fire their marksmanship course during their period of initial training.

The first contingent of 500 officers and men of the CIV embarked on board the *Briton* and the *Garth Castle* on 13 January, the remainder on board the *Ariosto*, the *Gaul* and *Kinfauns Castle* a week later. All arrived in Cape Town on 19 February. The Mounted Infantry Company, including a number of London Scots, was in action almost at once, taking part in the capture of Jacobsdaal on 15 February.

The Infantry Battalion, however, remained camped on the Orange River until early April when it started for the front, reaching Bloemfontein by route march three weeks later. As part of 21st Brigade it took part in the advance on Pretoria and was in action at Houtnek Poort, Zand River, Doornkop and Irene Station. It was present at the entry of Lord Roberts into Pretoria, and was

Lieutenant B.C. Green CIV South Africa 1901.

The CIV Detachment, South Africa 1900.

The London Scottish Detachment, The Volunteer Company The 2nd Battalion The Gordon Highlanders.

later in action in the Battle of Diamond Hill. By now the Boer will was broken. The enemy was driven back to Komati Poort and forced to abandon its heavy artillery. There followed a period of attrition and guerrilla warfare entailing a series of long and trying marches but little action. The role of the CIV was considered at an end, even though the war was destined to drag on for a further eight months. It was reviewed by Lord Roberts on 2 October, and on 11 October embarked for home.

One officer and forty-five soldiers of the London Scottish served with the CIV. Of these, Lieutenant B. C. Green, Serjeant Major T. Smith, Armourer Serjeant E. A. H. Gordon and Serjeant J. T. Hutchinson were mentioned in dispatches, while Serjeant Major Smith and Serjeant Hutchinson received the medal for distinguished conduct.

London Scots serving with the CIV

CIV Number		London Scottish Company
	Lieutenant Green B.C.	C
654	Brook W.B.	D
655	Glover J.A.	I
656	Robertson T.	G
657	Everall H.F.	I
658	Duguid E.	H
659	Ginger A.S.	F
660	Earle A.W.	I
661	Fraser M	K
662	Johnston W.	K
663	Wilson W.S.	F

664	Tattershall T.H.	K
665	Barrett F.B.	G
666	Gordon E.A.H.	F
667	Forbes L.	G
668	Willows G.W.	A
669	Findlay E.J.	B
670	McNally J.C.	A
671	Robertson H.C.	F
672	Flood-Page A.	G
673	Budd P.J.	K
674	Budd H.G.	K
675	Mansbridge C.	F
676	Wailes J.M.	E
677	Walker R.D.	F
678	Hunter S.M.	B
679	Mollett H.B.	D
680	McDonnell F.	B
681	Macdonald J.	D
682	Drummond A.	E
683	Calder G.J.	C
684	Lane H.W.	D
685	Airey W.M.	E
686	Greig L.G.	F
687	Hutchison J.T.	B
688	McLean T.N.	A
1409	McDonell G.L.	B
1410	Nesham H.P.	G
1411	Murray H.E.S.	F
1412	Duncan J.L.	H
1413	Mumford W.B.	B
1414	Donald A.P.	E
1415	Burn A.K.	A
1416	Dunsmore R.	E
	Smith T (Serjeant Major) Staff	

Even before the formation of the CIV, the London Scottish announced that it had been invited to send a full company to the Gordon Highlanders. Volunteers flocked to both calls, with perhaps an inevitable preference for the Gordon Company. However, after the CIV was full, there was an inexplicable announcement that the Gordon contingent would be halved, causing the residue, among them some of the finest soldiers to volunteer, to be left behind. The London Scottish contingent comprised its Officer Commanding, Captain A. W. Buckingham, and fifty-six other ranks, the remainder of the Company being made up from the 5th and 6th Volunteer Battalions Gordon Highlanders.

London Scots Half-Company Attached to the Gordon Highlanders

Company	Rank	Name
A	*Captain*	Buckingham A.W.
A	*Private*	Buchanan H.S.
A	*Private*	McBean D.R.
B	*Private*	Cooper A.J.
B	*Private*	Geggie F.J.
B	*Private*	Hopping D.M.
B	*Private*	Kerr G.F.
B	*Bugler*	Smith F.M.
C	*Private*	Bailey H.G.C.
C	*Private*	Cunningham T.C.
C	*Private*	Hoy L.C.
C	*Private*	Stewart C.J.
C	*Private*	Tucker W.J.
D	*Serjeant*	Aitchison J.G.
D	*Lance Corporal*	Scott A.T.
D	*Piper*	Keith A.R.
D	*Private*	Langhorne W.A.
D	*Private*	Richardson A.F.
D	*Private*	Sharp E.F.
E	*Lance Serjeant*	Kidd W.H.
E	*Corporal*	Murray E.B.M.
E	*Bugler*	McNab R.C.
E	*Private*	Browne S.W.
E	*Private*	Ferguson A.G.
E	*Private*	Fraser C.F.
E	*Private*	Maxwell A.D.
E	*Private*	Rait W.
E	*Private*	Russell H.
E	*Private*	Smeall J.F.
E	*Private*	Way H.
F	*Lance Corporal*	Whyte R.
F	*Private*	Fiddes W.C.
F	*Private*	Syer H.L.
F	*Private*	Thomson D.E.
G	*Corporal*	Thorn F.C.
G	*Lance Corporal*	Fleming E.G.
G	*Lance Corporal*	Mitchell J.D.A.
G	*Private*	Hoey H.G.
G	*Private*	Menzies T.P.
G	*Private*	Redding J.H.
G	*Private*	Smith W.S.C.

G	Private	Wilson G.R.
H	Serjeant	Budgett W.F.
H	Serjeant	Routledge F.J.
H	Serjeant	Turner J.S.
H	Lance Corporal	Southgate G.M.
H	Private	Hunter H.
H	Private	Reid G.A.
H	Private	Smeaton T.A.
I	Lance Serjeant	Carter W.L.
I	Private	Colquhoun P.
K	Serjeant	Gavin E.
K	Serjeant	Anderson F.B.
K	Corporal	Saunders E.S.
K	Private	Greenfield A.J.
K	Private	Menzies T.A.
K	Private	Showler G.W.

The Company left Aberdeen on 23 February, and joined the 2nd Battalion Gordon Highlanders at Ladysmith on 25 March. The Gordons had suffered grievously during the siege of Ladysmith and remained unfit for active operations until June. The long period of inaction in camp in bad weather told heavily on the unacclimatized Volunteers, several of whom fell ill and died in hospital. When at last the advance into the Transvaal began, Captain Buckingham himself was invalided, his place being taken by Captain A. E. Rogers, a fellow London Scot. Rogers had not been selected for the original contingent, but instead had made his own way out to South Africa where he had volunteered his services. Irritated by this irregularity, the War Office refused to pay him, and when shortly afterwards he was wounded in action, made him pay for his passage home.

The Gordon contingent suffered far more heavily than their colleagues in the CIV. Corporal E. B. M. Murray was mortally wounded at Rooikopjes on 24 July. On 8 September, while marching along an open road near Lydenburg, the company lost three killed and sixteen wounded when a shell burst overhead; of these Serjeant W. F. Budgett, killed, and ten wounded belonged to the London Scottish. During the campaign Serjeant W. H. Kidd, Private D. E. Thomson and Private T. P. Menzies died of disease. The company returned to Aberdeen on 3 May.

Early in 1901 the 3rd Volunteer Service Company, Gordon Highlanders was formed to relieve the original Company on completion of its year of service. As the war was nearly over there was not the same keenness to volunteer. Nonetheless the London Scottish provided the Officer Commanding, Captain B. C. Green who had earlier served with the CIV, a subaltern and twenty-six other ranks, of whom Serjeant W. Steven was mentioned for gallantry on 10 August, when a derailed train was attacked.

As the Boer war drew to a close and the full extent of British and Imperial losses became apparent, steps were taken to apportion the blame. Why, for instance, were British strategists so often out-manoeuvred, and why were a staggering half of deaths ascribed to disease? At one stage the high injury rate among the Highlanders was attributed to the kilt, the sporran allegedly offering far too convenient a target for well-trained marksmen. The Scottish press rallied to 'the garb of old Gaul'. In a spirited leader, the *Glasgow Evening News* reminded its readers of the dangers of allowing Whitehall economists to exploit the losses sustained by the Gordons in particular, to scrap what it conceded was an expensive mode of military dress. '*We are not yet prepared*,' it warned, '*to sacrifice the one sartorial feature which has for a century and a half made Scots regiments different*.' Fortunately common sense, and public opinion, prevailed and the kilt remained.

The Haldane Reforms

The years after the South African War brought first an enquiry into the whole operation and subsequently a series of fundamental reforms. In 1908 the Volunteers were transformed into the Territorial Force. In theory their function was not changed, but in practice it was now accepted that Territorials might, *with their agreement*, serve abroad.

The London Scottish was redesignated the Fourteenth Battalion, County of London Regiment (London Scottish). At the same time its ten companies were reduced to eight and a new badge adopted, showing the Lion of Scotland superimposed over a Saint Andrew's Cross, surrounded by a border of thistles, with the words 'LONDON SCOTTISH - STRIKE SURE - SOUTH AFRICA, 1900-02.'

Warrant Officers and Serjeants of the 1st Battalion Gordon Highlanders and London Scottish at Maida Barracks, Aldershot: Easter 1910.

The London Scottish route march from Oban to Glasgow: 1911.

Although theoretically a rifle regiment, the London Scottish had for years drawn its regular staff from the Gordon Highlanders to whom it had effectively held its allegiance. The Regiment remained, although a London organization, strictly Scottish in character. It also remained socially elite. Its ranks remained filled largely by public school and university men, many with the capacity to seek a commission elsewhere but with an overriding desire to serve with the Scottish.

Motorcycle scouts at Abergavenny Camp, 1913. The six men made the journey to camp by road on the four machines.

D Company, Dover, Easter 1901.

During the years leading to the Great War the Regiment evolved a cadre of highly disciplined and motivated NCOs and soldiers, as well as a more transient population of young Scots who served with the Regiment for two or three years before leaving London and often moving abroad. Initially, so large a turnover was disadvantageous. However, in 1914 it proved to be most fortunate, for it was these men who, on the outbreak of war, returned from the ends of the earth to serve with their chosen regiment.

The Scottish March, 1901.

Crucially, the London Scottish selected its officers from the ranks. Those felt suitable for a commission inevitably enjoyed positions of responsibility in their civilian lives and were natural and authoritative leaders. The Scottish also adopted a simplified system of drill which, although frowned upon and forbidden when first introduced, was in 1905 substantially adopted by the British regular army. Responsibility for post-recruit training devolved upon the companies and was left largely to the discretion of the Officers Commanding. Thus it was that individual company commanders were forced to work closely with their men, attaining levels of marksmanship and field training sadly lacking in other Territorial Force battalions. This was to prove crucial when, in the autumn of 1914, the Regiment was precipitated into war.

The Scottish March from Oban to Glasgow, 1911.

Chapter Two

Mobilization

Organized Chaos at Buckingham Gate

By late July 1914 all but the most optimistic feared the imminence of war. No attempts were made to mobilize the Territorial Force, which instead dispersed to its various annual camps. The London Scottish were allocated Ludgershall Camp on Salisbury Plain. The advance party arrived on 29 July and began the onerous task of preparing the tented camp for occupation. Rumours quickly replaced fact as the main currency of conversation. In the words of an NCO forming part of the advance party, *'All ready for the Battalion, but wars and rumours of war continue. News comes that the Battalion has arrived at Ludgershall. Heavy showers come on, in one of which the Battalion is caught. Hear the pipes along the road, and break out the flag, "the ruddy lion ramped in gold," as the head of the column comes into sight.'*

The Battalion settled down as best it could in its rain swept environs, but was destined to enjoy little rest. A quarter of an hour after lights out bugles roused the camp. A telegram had been received from the War Office ordering the Scottish to return to London. The Battalion mustered in confusion, many a volunteer inevitably wearing his tent mates' kit and, in time honoured fashion waited in the pouring rain. The Battalion was dismissed, fell in again, waited a further hour, and at last marched off to the station. The men were dismissed upon reaching London, with a warning that mobilization might come at any moment. There followed two days of waiting until, on 3 August, Sir Edward Grey made a statement to the House of Commons. An ultimatum was delivered to Berlin on the next day and ignored. At midnight, Berlin time, 11.00p.m. London time, on Tuesday, 4 August 1914, Britain declared war.

Mobilization papers were issued by

During the early days medicals were both rigorous and exacting; yet still the London Scottish was able to fill the ranks of a second battalion within a week.

25

Marching to Watford Station, 15 September 1914.

telegram and post the next morning. However, men began streaming in long before their receipt. With them came members of the Reserve and potential recruits by the hundred. The headquarters at Buckingham Gate quickly became the scene of organized chaos, made bearable only by the high degree of preparation undertaken by the regular cadre during the preceding few days. As volunteers arrived they were shepherded along a slow but carefully prepared route which began with a medical inspection and ended with the drawing of rifle, ammunition and identity disc. Even so the building proved inadequate for the task, and it quickly became necessary to requisition Caxton Hall as an annexe.

At first the volunteers, once equipped, were sent home. However an early, and wholly unwarranted fear of invasion led to a direction that units remain at their headquarters. Routine was broken by an early morning march to Westminster Baths and later, as the officers began to free themselves from administration, by a series of gradually lengthening company road and route marches in which increasingly heavy weights were carried, until full packs and pouches became the norm. Arthur Davidson, who was later commissioned into the 4th Battalion Gordon Highlanders and killed in September 1917, recalled the routine for 8 October.

En route to war, Watford Station September 1914.

'*Bathing parade for E and F Companies 7.30a.m. at Gt. Smith St. baths. Whole battalion go to Wimbledon Common in two specials from St James's Street - Putney Bridge on underground. March up through Putney to Wimbledon Common, and drill, then lunch, more drill and march back to HQ without halt in two hours with full kit.*'

Two days later he remembered;

'*Bathing parade. 100 rounds of ammunition issued to each man. March to Clapham Common by Vauxhall Bridge in 1hr 20min. Half hours rest at Common, march back to HQ via Chelsea Bridge in 1hr 15min.*'

By 15 August all battalions of the 4th London Brigade including the London Scottish were able to report their mobilization complete. That day they were inspected in Hyde Park by Major General Morland commanding the Division, and ordered to begin their march north to their training stations in the Watford area. Next morning the Scottish left Headquarters, rendezvousing with the Brigade at Hyde Park for the march north. The Brigade bivouacked that night in Canons Park, not a great distance from base yet far enough to cause consternation to those not yet hardened to boots and heavy weights. After an uneventful, and thankfully dry night the battalion continued its march northwards, onto Watford where it dispersed.

In the words of *Glenworple*, the pseudonym of an NCO writing in the Regimental journal, the battalion set off;

'carrying about 56lbs of kit of various sorts, through crowds of people who request us to bring them a present from Potsdam when we return....Bivouac somewhere, and find the Canteen cart has arrived. Loud cheers. Sleep under the stars, and dream of spiders crawling down my neck. Wake, and find that my dream has come true. Sleep again, using my pack as a little tent for my head. Good idea; spiders sitting round with a puzzled air, hear them tapping on the roof. Think of putting up notice saying "for Tartan spiders only".'

The next night the weary NCO arrived at his destination to find, not for the last time, that the cooks had taken the wrong turning, were lost and that there was nothing to eat. In his words, *'the grousing season was now commenced.'*

One fortunate company found itself billeted in the confines of a lunatic asylum. The padded cells, it is reported, proved particularly popular lodgings.

Training

Despite the valiant efforts of the CIV and others less than fifteen years earlier, few initially expected the Territorial Force to see action abroad. Rather, it was felt that the volunteers would be held in reserve against the contingency of invasion. Given that such a threat would not occur for some time, even were the British Expeditionary Force to be sent abroad at once, it was assumed that the volunteer battalions would have at least six months to bring themselves to battle readiness.

Notwithstanding this, officers and men were almost immediately asked to volunteer for foreign service. Spurred on by the undertaking, all too soon broken, that any battalion which provided seventy-five percent volunteers would be allowed to remain together, most agreed. However, some 200 of the Scottish did not, their places being taken by former members and recruits still eagerly thronging the Regimental headquarters in London. Initial training was dedicated to the mundane arts of elementary squad drill and deployment at section level; in the absence of suitable ranges there was no musketry practice, nor did the officers or senior ranks exercise field command. Thus the battalion that went to war only one month later, learned little of practical use when in base camp. The skills which it later demonstrated in abundance may therefore be said to pay true testimony to the skills and dedication of the pre-war Territorial Force.

Formation of the Second Battalion

On 26 August the War Office gave permission for Territorial units which had volunteered for foreign service to raise second battalions.

Recruiting within the London Scottish began five days later. Colonel Greig CB MP, who had retired from command four years before, assumed command and at once began to process applicants at the rate of 160 volunteers per day. In the words of the Regimental Archives,

> 'The new men are enrolled on exactly the same conditions as the old. Four years service, usual subscription, Scottish nationality. Four out of five have volunteered for general service. For absolute physique, the Second Battalion bids fair to compete favourably with our existing First Battalion.'

Within three days the Battalion was fully constituted. Even then volunteers still came forward, so much so that 1,200 recruits were passed to the Highland Division then training at Bedford.

As with a number of reserve units the Second Battalion was originally armed with the outdated Lee-Metford rifle. In 1915 it was re-equipped with the Japanese Meiji 38 rifle, before receiving the Lee-Enfield SMLE Mk III prior to embarkation for France.

'Leave Cancelled, Return at Once'

By early September the Schlieffen Plan lay in ruins; early German advances had been checked, leaving her armies to reform and reflect on the Aisne. Yet even so the War Office, chastened by French complaints of the lack of British commitment, prepared to send the best Territorial units to the Continent. On the night of Saturday, 12 September, Colonel Malcolm received orders that on the following Tuesday the Battalion was to march to Watford and there entrain for Southampton en route for Le Havre. Those enjoying weekend leave received a stark telegram, 'Leave cancelled, return at once.' On the Monday, the Scottish paraded to receive the new short rifle and thereafter was inspected by General Sir Ian Hamilton. Lord Esher, Chairman of the Territorial Association, telegrammed:

> 'Colonel Malcolm, I congratulate you and your splendid Battalion on the high honour conferred on you as being the first chosen from the whole territorial Force to go to the front. Give my hearty greetings to your officers and men for auld lang syne - Esher, Territorial Force Association.'

Inevitably confusion compounded into administrative chaos as the Battalion readied itself for France, so much so that no time was set aside to zero the new weapons. Had it been, the awful realization that the Mk 1 rifle was not compatible with the new Mk VII ammunition might have become apparent. Instead the Battalion went to war, wholly oblivious of the fact that the rifle feeder spring was too weak to force the ammunition into the chamber, causing the weapon to jam when fired at any speed.

On 15 September the London Scottish marched to Watford to entrain for Southampton, the first half of the battalion arriving at about

8.00a.m. Embarkation took place in the converted, and far from clean, Argentinean cattle ship SS *Winifredian* that afternoon, and as night fell the voyage began. As the transport steamed through Southampton Water and on to Spithead, searchlight after eager searchlight illuminated her on her way. Ship after ship saluted with their steam whistles, the last greeting, a prophetic 'Good luck!', coming from the signal station on the hill above the eastern headland of the Isle of Wight.

Fortunately for its cargo of young soldiers, few of whom were accustomed to the sea, the crossing was relatively calm and without incident. The Battalion reached the recently reoccupied port of Havre in the early hours of the morning and at about 6.30a.m. marched through the town, its pipers playing the *Marseillaise* to the vociferous approval of the local population. Early hopes that the Scottish would quickly see action were dashed when Colonel Malcolm received orders to scatter his eight companies to various line-of-communication duties throughout northern France. F, G and H Companies, under the command of Major Green, were ordered to Le Mans, a journey of seventeen hours undertaken in cattle trucks. All, however, was not discomfort. In the words of Private George Wilson:

> *'All the way down the line the country people gave us bread, wine,*
> *eggs, apples, peaches, coffee and cognac, etc. but all asked for*
> *souvenirs. When arriving at stations the general cry from us was "Vive*
> *La France," which would be answered at once with a shower of grub.'*

Those lucky enough to get leave in Le Mans drank fully, and literally, of French hospitality. The eighteen year-old Private Wilson was offered a bath in 'the ladies quarters' and, innocent that he still was, expressed his nervousness when the adjoining cubicle, separated as it was by nothing

Somewhere in France between September and October 1914. The Highland dress was somewhat of an amusement for the French locals.

more than a small petition, was occupied by an apparently wholly unconcerned local female!

Initially many of the other companies fared less well. Corporal Robson of B Company, en route for Villeneuvre St Georges, a fortified railway station on the banks of the Seine, recalled that,

> 'We crowded into little third-class carriages, where our equipment seemed to take up most of the space. Our kit bags had been left on the quay at Southampton, and we had only our webb equipment with us, but this was quite enough to promise an uncomfortable night. Just outside the harbour the train stopped. A crowd of gamins scrambled on to some railings and shouted, "Vive l'Angleterre! Vive la France! Kaiser no bon!" and, of course, "Souvenir! Souvenir!" The war was then young and this was our first night in France, so we yelled back and threw biscuits, which we could ill spare. The business went on at each halt till we were clear of the town. Little did we know how soon only the cry of "Souvenir!" would remain and how sick of it we would become.'

When Robson and his colleagues reached their destination their principal work became that of attending to the many hospital trains that arrived by day and night at the station. Their first sight of the wounded left the young with a lasting impression of the realities of war.

> 'They (the trains) were not swagger shows with beds, nurses, and red crosses,' he wrote, 'but ordinary "chevaux huit-hommes quarante" trucks. The wounded were jumbled together, and many of them had not had their wounds seen to since leaving the field. They still had on their first field dressings, and were plastered with dried mud and blood.'

Private Alex Moffat of F Company was less charitable.

> 'RAMC men should be shot,' he complained in a diary entry of 20 October, 'our wounded and dying travelling five days in train from the front and they don't even look after them and give them water to drink.'

Not all duties were so onerous. Later Robson recalled how, as Corporal of the guard he would inspect the sentries at night before calling on the Army Service Corps for a smoke and a feed of stewed apples.

> 'The French,' he noted, 'also mounted a guard at the station, found by the quaint old Territorials. About midnight their sentry would creep into an empty carriage, and it was the unofficial duty of our man to rouse him at the approach of an officer. These Frenchmen were armed with the same rifles they had used in 1870. One of them handed his over to us to examine. The breech would not open, so we handed it back to him to show us how it worked. He tried hard to open it, shook his head and said that it must be rusty, admitting that not even curiosity had made him open it for over forty years.'

A few detachments of the Scottish were sent close enough to the front to hear the guns and see their flashes in the night. German stragglers were constantly reported by the local villagers and patrols regularly dispatched to tackle them, but there are no recorded instances of weapons being fired in anger. One detachment had the honour of forming the guard for Sir John French's Headquarters at La Fere-en-Tardenois while two others were sent to Orleans to organize a railhead and reception camp for the Indian troops of the Lahore and Meerut Divisions. Other small parties were told to escort prisoners to the rear and stragglers to the front. A small detachment, for which a knowledge of French was a qualification, were sent to Paris for military police duties.

In the words of Private Wilson,

> 'Some of our fellows are Paris Police just now, with swank canes and new jackets and spats. They have to see that none of our British soldiers are in picture palaces, etc. Of course, with such a long fighting line we have thousands of stragglers, but mostly genuine cases, bad feet, or cut off from main body, miss their trains by relieving themselves when train stops, etc. They simply re-equip them and send them back, of course they all have the same uniform of khaki and all their badges they have given away as souvenirs so you can't tell one from the other.'

In early October, Colonel Malcolm received orders which would ultimately bring the London Scottish into the front line. He was directed to send a company to St Omer, and later another to Abbeville, to assist the railway authorities in detraining troops and stores. Recent attempts by the French to blunt and ultimately turn the Germans right by a push up the Oise Valley had been countered when the enemy extended his line from Noyon northwards towards the Somme. In response the Allies extended their line to the left. As part of the 'race to the sea' the British Expeditionary Force was moved from the Aisne front to the extreme left of the Allied line in an attempt to shorten its extended lines of communication with England. St Omer and Abbeville became the points where the troops were to detrain after their move northwards by rail.

In the second week of October the Germans captured Antwerp and began pouring troops into western Belgium, threatening to turn the Allied left, seize the channel ports, and invade France by way of Lille. Before the Allies could react, German cavalry supported by Jäger battalions crossed the frontier of northern France and captured Lille. The British hurriedly closed the gap between the French left and the remnants of the Belgian right, by occupying the Ypres position and the line of the River Lys. On 20 October the First Battle of Ypres began. In three weeks of often bitter fighting the line generally held, although in a few places ground had to be abandoned. A dangerous crisis occurred to the south of Ypres when the weak force of dismounted cavalry holding the line was threatened by a vastly superior German force.

Chapter Three

The Road to Messines

On 25 October Colonel Malcolm was ordered to collect his scattered detachments and concentrate the Battalion at St Omer with a view, at last, to engaging the enemy. By 28 October the concentration of the London Scottish was virtually complete. Save for two sections of E Company the Battalion reached St Omer where they were quartered in a dilapated old Cavalry barracks, made all the worse by the pillaging exploits of its recent occupants. A day later, at approximately 5.00p.m., Colonel Malcolm marched the Scottish out of town. Writing some years later, Baxter Milne graphically recalled the move:

> 'On October 29, our orders came through and we had to pack up and clear off. Those few words, "Pack up and clear off", are soon said, but please remember that in those days there was no such thing as "Battle Order", only "Marching Order." This entailed full kit in the shoulder pack, ordinarily about fifty rounds of small arms ammunition, but, on this occasion, two hundred and fifty rounds, great coat, waterproof sheet, two blankets, and emergency, or iron, rations. My recollection is that my pack at that time weighed about ninety pounds.'

The Scottish marched to the outskirts of St Omer in a steady downpour of rain, without transport wagons or machine guns. After a mile the battalion was met by about forty-five London buses, still with their civilian drivers, with orders to rush the unit to Ypres. The journey was miserable, especially

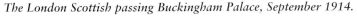

The London Scottish passing Buckingham Palace, September 1914.

SS **Winifredian.**

for those forced to ride on the open tops. As Milne recalls:

> 'the road was abominable and we travelled without lights. Our
> particular bus was ditched four times, which meant that we all got out
> and pushed. The other buses did not fare much better, but we all
> helped each other.'

At 3.00a.m. on Friday, 30 October, after a nine hours' journey, the convoy
of buses reached Ypres. The town had as yet suffered little damage and the
battalion was able to rest in and around the famous Cloth Hall. A few
snatched a little sleep before orders were received to breakfast at six and
parade at eight. At first light the Germans began a cannonade of intense and
rapid fire. The battle, which had raged on for days, was reaching a critical
point. On the right flank, the French held von Bulow in check, further north
the British 2nd Corps under Smith-Dorrien gave ground before standing
firm on a line by Laventine and Festubert. On the flats along the Lys,
Pulteney with the 3rd Corps held the river line and woods to the north of it.
On the extreme left the battered remnants of the Belgian Army, supported
by the French and with the help of naval guns, held on. In the centre the full
fury of the German offensive was directed against Ypres. Here Haig, with
the 1st Corps, and Byng's 3rd Cavalry Division, held the salient against a
series of frontal assaults. The right flank from Ypres to the Lys, running
along a spur crowned by the little towns of Wytschaete and Messines, was
held by Allenby with two weak divisions of dismounted cavalry reinforced
by an Indian Brigade and supported by the 13-pounders of the Royal Horse
Artillery and a single battery of 60-pounders.

The Kaiser had come to witness the hoped-for capture of Ypres, which
was to be undertaken by combining an attack to the east at Gheluvert with
a drive over the Wytschaete-Messines ridge and on into the flats to the west.
Had the operation succeeded, not only would Ypres have fallen, and with it
the final vestiges of Belgian resistance, but the whole Allied force from Ypres
to the sea would have been placed in peril.

The battalion began its march from Ypres in easy stages, crossing the
moat at the Menin Gate before continuing east along the Menin Road past
the crossroads soon to become infamous as Hellfire Corner. Colonel

The Cloth Hall at Ypres before the war

and same view of Cloth Hall as it is today.

Lieutenant Stebbing, Serjeant Finlay (lying down) and Private Morrison, B Company 1st Battalion on the Hooge Road, 30 October 1914.

Malcom reported to Haig at his headquarters at White Chateau, and received orders to continue forward to the woods near Hooge, later to become know as Sanctuary Wood. Once in the wood, the men were allowed to remove their packs and rest at ease. Their respite was to be short-lived, however. Soon after arriving they were ordered to pass their blankets and unwanted baggage to the 1st Coldstream Guards transport, although they were not told that the Coldstreamers had been virtually annihilated and that their transport was now surplus. Later that day the Scottish were ordered to Hooge Chateau to act as 2nd Division reserve. There they met General Munro, the former commander of the 2nd London Territorial Division and an old friend, who welcomed and inspected them and expressed the hope that they would be permanently attached to his Division. This was not to be. Remaining only long enough to eat the remains of their rations, the unit was ordered to return to Ypres, this time by bus; a journey which it completed in the early hours of the morning.

The first day in the front line ended without casualties or actual fighting. However, it had been trying enough, compounded by the long journey and lack of sleep. As Milne remembers:

> *'Our exhaustion on returning to Ypres, with visions of a good meal and a night's rest fading away like a mirage on the desert, forced on our minds the fact that there was a war going on. We had eaten our haversack rations, and had, therefore, to draw more. After doing so we embarked, or should I say "embussed" for a new destination.'*

After a journey of some two hours the unit arrived at St Eloi at about 7.00p.m. on the night of 30 October. A hot meal was provided, after which those who could find shelter slept until aroused for a parade at about midnight. As they paraded, a column of mounted troops, some French cuirassiers and the Scots Greys, passed through St Eloi. The meeting of brother Scots at such a moment was an inspiring incident, as each cheered the other as they passed. General Gough, under whom the Scottish now served, had originally intended to commit them to battle shortly after midnight, but representations from Colonel Malcom as to their exhaustion caused him to change his mind. Instead they were ordered to return to their improvised billets and to parade for action at dawn.

Sandy Innes, then a signaller and later a medical orderly with the Battalion, recalled the confusion then prevailing,

> *'Spent ten hours of last night on bus in rain and finally at Ypres and slept in the Town Hall. At 10.00a.m. we parade and march out to north-east to within 400 yards of firing line. Lie there for four hours and after seeing lots of wounded return we march back to Ypres and mount our buses again. Ride to St Eloi and finally bunk down in a house only to be called out at 11.00p.m. and sent back to bed.'*

Messines

Shortly after 4.00 a.m. on the morning of 31 October, Hallowe'en, the London Scottish paraded along the St Eloi road, for what was destined to be a very memorable day. The day began quietly enough, with a march of about one mile to a wood to the south-east of St Eloi, after which the order was given to dig-in. A fairly heavy bombardment was going on all the time, the noise of bursting shells being interspersed with the crack of rifles and the whining of machine-gun bullets. Many decided to lighten their loads, changing into clean clothes and discarding those which they had been wearing for several days. Even so, Milne recounts that his pack remained formidable:

> *'I suppose I reduced my pack and haversack by about twenty pounds in all. Actually I went into the firing line carrying a pack, a haversack, water bottle, overcoat, and entrenching tool, totalling about seventy pounds weight, two hundred and fifty rounds of ammunition, a rifle, bayonet and a pickaxe.'*

At about 8.00a.m. the Battalion received orders to move to Wytschaete to reinforce General Bingham's 4th Cavalry Brigade, by now fighting as dismounted troops and struggling to hold the Wytschaete-Messines Ridge. As Private J.O. Robson of B Company recalls:

> *'In half an hour we were off again, and marched up the road into Wytschaete. Gendarmes were turning the inhabitants out of the town,*

B Company on the morning of Messines. Colour Serjeant T. Jackson and Serjeant W. Anderson in the forefront.

Eric Millward Wilkins. Wounded at Messines, his brother, L.G.M. Wilkins, was killed there. Eric was commissioned into the Royal Garrison Artillery and won the MC in 1918.

and we met a pitiful procession of refugees - mothers with babies in their arms, little boys carrying huge loads, old grannies pushing dilapidated perambulators full of clothes, sheets and all sorts of odds and ends. At the door of a convent on the right stood a group of nuns - all, I believe, killed by a shell shortly afterwards.'

Initially the Scottish advanced in columns of four by companies, but quickly broke into artillery formation when the enemy guns began to register hits. As they passed through their own gun lines Milne remembers a shell hitting the limber of an 18-pounder, blowing it to pieces and killing several gunners. As soon as practical, the Battalion left the road and moved along the hollow of the Steenbeek until orders were received to halt in the comparative protection of an area of dead ground known as Enfer Wood.

The situation was precarious when, at approximately 10.00a.m. Colonel Malcolm held his Orders Group at the corner of the wood and gave directions for the advance into the fighting line. Messines, by now infiltrated by the Germans, was being held in hand-to-hand fighting by British infantry who had been hurried into the line. To the north, with their line running roughly parallel and approximately 100 yards to the east of the Wytschaete road, were the 4th Dragoon Guards. They were flanked on their left by the 6th Dragoon Guards (Carabineers) forming the right of the 4th Cavalry Brigade, which held the road towards Wytschaete. An Indian regiment, the 57th Wilde's Rifles, had been ordered into the line the day before and had given a good account of itself, but with its European officers killed or wounded and having sustained heavy casualties, it had been forced to withdraw.

The London Scottish were sent in to consolidate a dangerous gap in the line and to help the Carabineers hold the right centre. The position was marked by two farms, later known as Hun's Farm and Middle Farm just west of the road, and by a windmill, which had already sustained severe damage, near the latter.

The Battalion advanced under heavy fire in columns of half-companies with the men extended at five paces interval. Several casualties were

An idealized rendition of the battle of Messines Ridge, 31 October 1914.

sustained before the company positions were reached and the men were able to dig in, with H, D and A Companies from left to right in the first line a little beyond the road and G and B Companies in the second line in close support to the west. These positions were held under sustained artillery fire until dusk, when half of C Company, and elements of D and G Companies, were ordered to join E and F Companies on the heights east of Enfer Wood where they were to form a reserve.

An unknown non-commissioned officer, in an unfinished letter written four months later, perfectly encapsulated the fears and confusion of the ordinary soldier at that time.

'We go on, shells coming over us, and pass behind our own guns. Then into a field and up to a wood, where we lied down.' Later he was ordered to advance. 'Then all of a sudden we're in it, and bolt like rabbits along a wet ditch besides a road. God knows what's happening. My half company are supports, not firing line. I'm on the right, nestling against the bank with my feet in water, sweating with terror, and the shells shrieking over me, and bursting close behind. It's like being tied down on the railway track with the express coming at you; and when they burst the universe falls in on top of you. Mostly they burst four at a time and then a lull. Presently we get wise to this, and when the lull comes, we mount our trenching tools, and dig feverishly into the bank. I look at my watch. Three hours till dark, or three and a half. Damn it, they must get me before then. What's left of me will be a nasty sight, down in the dirty water..., hope it's over quickly..., why can't we go forward?'

The Battle of Messines. Note the soldier in the centre loading his rifle with single rounds after its mechanism had jammed.

Private Eric Wilkins also remembered the carnage as he left the comparative shelter of the woods.

'Then, about midday I should say it was, we left the cover of the woods and extended to eight paces over the country in readiness to advance down to the trenches. We advanced up an incline at the top of which was some barbed wire. As soon as we reached this bullets began to whistle past and some of our men were immediately bowled over. Once through this wire all we had to do was get down to the trenches. I say "all we had to do" but you will see what this meant when I tell you that it was broad daylight, and that we had to advance over an open ploughed field with no cover. In a perfectly straight line, and extended to eight paces, we commenced to make for the trenches at a double. The day was clear and the enemy must have had a fine

view of us. They just waited until we got nicely out into the field, when they suddenly trained machine guns, rifles and artillery onto us. Our men kept their line until the machine guns practically wipe it out.'

Private Moffat recorded vividly the fate of F Company, in reserve.

'Advance over the crest of the hill, and lay down in the open where we are shelled all day. Hell. This continues till dark when we entrench ourselves, but we are suddenly attacked. An awful din going on and can hear the German Imperial Band playing the Austrian National Anthem. Whistles are being blown by the Huns, in the darkness all over the place in order to rally their men.'

The enemy attacked in a dense mass, cheering loudly and with bands playing, at about 9.00p.m. The shooting prowess of the Scottish proved itself, causing severe casualties among the advancing Bavarians. Enemy losses would have been heavier still had the Scottish been better armed. The SMLE Mk 1 rifles, which had been issued immediately before the Battalion left England and had never been tested, proved incapable of taking the new Mk VII ammunition causing the rifles to jam unless loaded singly. Nonetheless the attack was beaten off. As Private Sid Maxwell remembered in a letter to his father, Serjeant Maxwell, late of F Coy:

'The glare from burning farm houses enabled us to continue to shoot, and we did our best. Suddenly we found the Germans had got round our left flank and about thirty-five of us got out of our trenches and charged them - they were about ten to one, but we didn't seem to notice that; we broke them temporarily, but their numbers were too much for us to follow, and we had to retire as best we could.'

The bombardment began again at about midnight, when in the glare of the full moon and by now blazing windmill, the Germans attacked again. For more than an hour they were held at bay, rush after rush being repelled by sustained fire from the Scottish forward positions, until it seemed that the attack was spent. However, at about 2.00a.m. the Germans came on again in even greater numbers, and this time pushed home the attack at the point of the bayonet. By sheer weight of numbers the forward elements were pushed back across the road as the Bavarians forced a gap between the Scottish right flank and the cavalry. However, a spirited counter attack by part of the reserve regained the lost ground enabling the line to be plugged and contact to be regained.

Private Wilkins later recalled,

'A blazing barn in their (the German) rear enabled us to see them very plainly, so we opened fire, being able to use our sights fairly well.

The roll call after Messines. After the battle many soldiers abandoned their rifles in favour of weapons taken from dead and injured Germans and British regulars.

We brought a lot of them down in front of this barn. Soon they began to get very close, for by sheer weight of numbers they had evidently broken through the trench in front. An officer ordered us to cease fire and to wait till the Germans got quite close to us. ...We soon found the enemy quite close, about thirty yards away I should say. Then the order came to fire and we simply poured lead into them. One could not very well miss them for they were just in front, in a great black mass. They seemed to be all talking to each other as hard as they could and we could plainly hear their officers urging them on from behind.'

Lance Corporal Walter Black, with F Company in reserve, even found a few minutes, as the battle raged, to write down his experiences.

'I write this under most peculiar circumstances. Shells are shrieking over our heads while rifle and maxim fire is continuous in front of us. It is simply hellish. It is the only word I can get for it.'

His writings were interrupted when F Company was ordered to dig in and then go forward in support.

'Just managed to start rewriting this after a perfect nightmare of circumstances. I had to stop to take a fellow down who was wounded in both legs and the back by shrapnel. When I got back we were

*ordered to retire and dig ourselves in. We did so and lay there for
hours in the cold listening to the rifle fire and howls and yells of our
chaps keeping the Germans off. Cowper Mackie and I then went out
on patrol and were sniped at all night. About 12 o'clock we got orders
to advance, and did so through a hail of bullets, to the trenches where
we were comparatively safe.'*

Eventually Colonel Malcom was forced to order a retirement across the
Steenbeek Valley towards Wulverghem, having first arranged for the
evacuation of the wounded. Hard close-quarter fighting ensued, with A
Company initially cut off, as individual elements sought to disengage and
withdraw. However, the enemy had been so badly mauled that they were in
no mood to molest the retirement, and instead used the lull in fighting to
consolidate and bring in their wounded.

When the roll call was taken near Wulvergham, no more than 150
officers and men answered. But as the Battalion moved to Kemmel and
thence to La Clytte, where it rested for the night, it was joined by a steady
stream of survivors including the remnants of A Company. Total losses were
subsequently assessed at 394 officers and men. With no preparatory
training, ignorant of the ground and without maps, with defective rifles and
without their machine guns, the London Scottish had met the enemy in
overwhelming numbers and denied them the road to Ypres.

Individual recollections are fragmented and inevitably subjective. Private
George Wilson, in a letter home to his mother, questioned the initial advance
across open ground:

*'The commencement of the whole thing was bad enough though,
fancy advancing over a hill in broad daylight, being shelled and with
bullets flying like hail.'*

*The roll call after Messines. The Battalion numbers increased as the stragglers managed to
disengage and fight their way back to the lines.*

The next day, 1 November, he recorded in his diary:

'We are formed up to march back and take up positions in trenches already dug. Still no grub or sleep. Hang on here all day with a few "coal boxes" dropping, but are relieved in the evening by cavalry. March back to Le Clytte with Mr Grant, where the remainder of battalion are forming up. Drop asleep on the wet field after finding a blanket, and sleep through rain, etc.'

Praise for the London Scottish, the first Territorial Force troops to see action, was as fulsome as it was generous. Within hours of the engagement, Field Marshal Sir John French, Commander-in-Chief of British Forces, telegrammed to Colonel Malcom:

'I wish you and your splendid regiment to accept my warmest congratulations and thanks for the fine work you did yesterday at Messines. You have given glorious lead and example to all Territorial troops who are fighting in France.'

In a letter written to Haig a few hours later, Major General Allenby was fulsome in his praise.

'I wish to tell you how magnificent the London Scottish have behaved. In discipline and tactical efficiency they have been up to the standard of the best Regular Troops. Last night they took their place in the trenches after a hard day of marching and fighting, as I had not enough strength to keep them in reserve. In the small hours of the morning, my front was broken and the brunt of the attack came on that section, held by the London Scottish. Not a man left his trench, until the trenches were overrun by the enemy. They made a great fight, and accounted for hundreds of Germans. The losses were I fear very great, but their staunchness enabled us to maintain the important position at Wytschaete, until the arrival of reinforcements. The Cavalry Corps and the Army owe them a debt of great gratitude. I regret deeply the loss of so many brave men.'

The British press was no less enthusiastic, carrying a series of highly accurate first-hand accounts of the battle. In some the hint of the brutal reality of unconditional warfare was made apparent. On 12 November *The Times* carried two accounts of the bayoneting of Dr Angus McNab, the Regimental Officer who, although injured himself, was tending a wounded man when killed. According to a letter written by a former pupil to the Headmaster of the High School for Boys, Croydon and published in *The Times*:

'The behaviour of the Germans was awful; the whole time they were shouting orders in English, such as "Scottish are to retire", and we really did not know whether we were shooting our own men. All our wounded at hand were bayoneted, and they actually bayoneted a medical officer while he was bandaging a wounded man. He was found afterwards quite dead.'

Fact or exaggeration, it is known that the Germans, by now battered and disillusioned, indulged in unusual brutality along the entire front that night. It is testament to the ferocity and uncompromising nature of the battle for the Wytschaete-Messines ridge throughout the final days of October, that when the French infantry took over the line a few days later they counted bodies of no less than 3,500 Bavarian dead.

The survivors marched back to prepared positions on 1 November, before retiring to La Clytte en route to billets near Bailleul. Although the accommodation was variable, F Company found itself in a series of recently-vacated pig stys, it was at least safe and gave an opportunity for steps to be taken for the bulk of the Battalion to re-equip itself with working rifles. On Thursday, 5 November the Battalion feasted on tinned haggis, intended for Halloween, and less happily learned that fifty-two mail bags containing a large back-log of incoming letters had been destroyed in the Ypres shelling. That day it was ordered to join the 1st Guards Brigade, an otherwise wholly regular unit comprising the 1st Coldstream Guards, 1st Scots Guards, 1st Black Watch and 1st Cameron Highlanders, but was diverted almost immediately to the 4th Guards Brigade under Lord Cavan, then desperately trying to hold the line to the south of the Menin Road. With their depleted numbers the Scottish could only man at the rate of one rifle per six yards, yet exhausted and hungry as they were, they gave such a good account of themselves that they were quickly able to collect sufficient abandoned rifles and ammunition from the enemy to restock those as yet unable to replace their defective weapons.

Muster of the 1st Guards Brigade, November 1914 after the first Battle of Ypres. 1st Scots Guards, 1st Coldstream Guards, 1st Black Watch, 1st Cameron Highlanders, 1st London Scottish (in front). Total Brigade strength about 420 all ranks, Scottish just over 200. Coldstreams 27 (mostly transport and as such were attached to L.S.)

With the Guards at Givenchy and Cuinchy

The Scottish were destined to spend the next month undertaking primitive trench duties in and around the Hazebrouck area. Casualties, both from shelling and sniping, were unrelenting. Lance Corporal Black complained after three days in the trenches that,

'My head aches with the concussion of the earth. I am about three feet down and two or three feet in, so I feel every thud. It is marvellous how one spends the time. I found myself busily filling a spent cartridge case with earth. I was packing it carefully and methodically; evidently the mind has to find some relaxation.'

Private Wilson was wounded on 10 November, and the next days was evacuated to Boulogne where he *'was given a clean shirt to sleep in and a good bed.'* The nurses, he relished;

'were all from Edinburgh, from the Infirmary. They were awfully kind.'

Within three days he was in Aberdeen and safe.

A trench at French Farm, Givenchy, Christmas morning 1914.

Battalion snipers at Hurionville, 1915.

46

Those remaining in the trenches were less fortunate.

'*What a night we had,*' complained Private Moffat writing on the morning of 13 November.

'*Soaked to the skin, and when you lay down, lying in mud. I put my waterproof down, and in the morning cannot find it. I suppose buried in the mud.*'

A welcome draft of five officers and 189 men arrived from the 2nd Battalion on 28 November. Despite the privations of that month, during which the majority of the Battalion suffered from dysentery due to cold food and suspect water, and all suffered from the almost daily route marches from billet to billet, the reinforcements acclimatized quickly with only fifty forced to drop out. Ironically, the 'regular' battalion reserves, many of whom were less than fit, had left the Colours years before and in some cases were decidedly old by the standards of the day, suffered far worse, several battalions losing half their numbers with the first fortnight.

Serjeant L. E. Hall sniping from buildings in the front line breastwork at Festubert, 1915.

On 15 November the 1st Guards Brigade was relieved and marched to Pradelles. Despite the arrival of its reinforcements, in two weeks constant fighting the Scottish had been reduced to a strength of less than 300 and the entire Brigade to a strength of less than half a battalion. The men bore their hardships with stoicism in the field, but in the billets adverse reaction occasionally set in. Private Moffat complained of seeing six different doctors in as many visits, yet remained on the active list. Colonel Malcolm, upon whom much of the strain of the previous month had fallen, was less fortunate. He was forced to return to England seriously ill, after which command passed to Major Sandilands of the Cameron Highlanders.

The Brigade remained for more than a month at Pradelles resting, training and, in the case of the Scottish, reorganizing from eight companies to four, each of four platoons. Lance Corporal Black noted with some satisfaction on 26 November that;

'*We have not much to do in the billets; route march in the morning, then usually a fatigue or two in the afternoon. The frost has gone and with it the snow, but it is still cold and very damp. Today we have had*

Machine-gun practice, 1915.

our fur coats served out and they should be very warm.'

Black was killed at Givenchy less than a month later. More importantly for the Scottish it replaced its wholly inadequate shoes and spats, many of which had by now disintegrated in the Flanders mud, with boots. Hopes that the Brigade would remain at Pradelles for Christmas were dashed on 20 December when the 1st Guards Brigade was ordered forward to help stem a strong German attack at Givenchy, near the point of junction of the British and French Armies.

Church service had been cancelled that morning, a Sunday, as the padre was elsewhere. The time had been taken up instead with a short route march, after which the Scottish had been given permission to play football. During the game, orders were received to move at once. In the words of Private Moffat;

'Game stopped like lightning and place soon deserted, reach our

billets, pack up, roll and give in blankets, etc,etc, and all ready under the hour.'

The Battalion left Pradelles at about 4.30p.m., marching for nine hours until it reached Bethune in the early hours, where it was allowed to rest and reorganize until noon. From there it marched to the trenches at Cuinchy which it occupied in the face of growing German pressure. Private Wright remembered the thirty mile march, during which twenty-three casualties were sustained, as *'quite awful,'* with *'mud over our ankles the whole way'* and *'everybody terrified'*.

What neither soldier knew was that the 1st Guards Brigade had been thrown into the line to prevent a German breakthrough. The Indian Corps had been pushed back around Givenchy which had been lost and retaken at the point of the bayonet. The Brigade remained in the line for a month, missing both Christmas and New Year celebrations in the process and suffering losses throughout.

Despite the complete lack of a truce in this sector, the spirit of Christmas was occasionally allowed to pervade. In a letter to his secretary, published in the *Evening News*, an unknown officer told of how he and two colleagues crawled out into no man's land to rescue a wounded soldier whose cries of agony he had heard for the past three days. The Germans made no serious attempt to impede the party which returned safely to the British trenches.

> *'The poor fellow wept like a baby when I told him it was Christmas Day,'* reported the officer. *'I shall not easily forget how he bit at my piece of bread and jam and emptied my water bottle. I presented him as a Christmas present to his regiment...It is the best present I ever expect to give anyone.'*

During the fighting Corporal Sanderson, a Battalion scout, when out collecting straw for an officers' dugout, distinguished himself by capturing two enemy snipers hiding in a hayrick. Although unarmed, he pointed a pair of 'wire-clippers' at the enemy, causing them to surrender and return with him to the Scottish lines. He was awarded the DCM.

The Winter of 1915

The 1st Guards Brigade spent nearly four weeks in the line, suffering the privations of mud, frost, thaw and constant enemy attack, only slightly ameliorated by the arrival of mail from home, some of it more than a month old. As Private Munro later recalled;

> *'Have not had my boots off for nearly a month now. Have had the opportunity when in reserve but do not believe in taking them off, only to put them on again still wet, and with no opportunity for washing.*
> *My feet are practically numbed, but do not hurt so shall let well alone.'*

Perhaps inevitably, trench foot became a major problem. Sergeant Hall of F Company in his war diary recorded the rather melancholy passage of New Year's Eve.

> *'Still in the trenches, wet at intervals. Captain Low suggests try*

sniping from a little barn at the back. Go and have a look at it. Just don't like the idea as there is no protection either from view or fire and bullets keep whizzing through the building. In the afternoon go up in it twice for half an hour in order to salve my conscience but do not fire as I am quite sure I should have been hit had I done so. New Year's Eve we celebrate by singing "Auld Lang Syne" at 12.00 and then fire three rounds rapid. How different is this from last year's New Year's Eve. There is a big shout from the direction of the German trenches about the same time so suppose there is the same sort of thing going on across the way.'

The Brigade was relieved on 17 January, but in less than a week returned to the front, this time to the Cuinchy sector, on the extreme right of the British line. On 27 January, the Kaiser's birthday, despite the warnings of a German deserter, the enemy launched a surprise attack against the Coldstream and Scots Guards, capturing their forward positions. The London Scottish were ordered out of reserve and were able to inflict considerable casualties on the enemy, forcing them to halt their advance. That afternoon the Black Watch were ordered to make a frontal assault to recapture the lost positions and, although partially successful in their objective, were virtually annihilated.

On 27 January Lieutenant Colonel B.C. Green rejoined the Battalion and took command. The next day, after further hard fighting, the Brigade was relieved and went into reserve. The Scottish were allowed a month to rest, re-equip and to assimilate the latest batch of reinforcements. The period was marred somewhat by a serious outbreak of meningitis and by a growing feeling among the other ranks, many of whom had not enjoyed leave in six months, that their officers were receiving decidedly preferential treatment. The positions was ably expressed by Private Lawrie Inkster in a letter of 2 March 1915 to his sister, Gladys:

'Just a few lines to let you know I am going on all right. We are back in action rather sooner than expected. But for my part I find it rather a relief, as the firing in some ways is more restful than the rest camp...Except for the guns it is quite peaceful here, and the birds are singing outside. One great point is that we do not have to hurry up in the morning, as we do at rest camp.'

Shortly afterwards Inkster was wounded and evacuated to Rouen, from where he again wrote to his sister, setting out graphically the somewhat ad hoc system of returning to the line.

'There are some of our fellows here who have never returned after our first action, and others who although wounded quite recently are already able to return. We find lots of fellows, who we expected had got home, still in this country after all. At these bases all the various odd men from all the various hospitals turn up eventually and join the little crowd of their own fellows, pass the MO when fit, get equipment etc, and when there are sufficient of them, or a draft arrive, up they go.'

Neuve Chapelle

During their stay in reserve, preparations were made for the long-expected offensive. Under pressure from the French, who not unnaturally wished to rid their land of the enemy, the British agreed to mount an attack on the enemy positions around the village of Neuve Chapelle with a view to breaking through to the Aubers Ridge to the south-west of La Bassée. On the morning of 10 March a thunderous cannonade to the Scottish left heralded the beginning of the battle. At 6.00p.m. the 1st Guards Brigade was ordered up to Richebourg in support of the Meerut Division, but soon after their arrival it was discovered that the Indians had taken their objective and that they were not required. The general consensus among the Scottish was that the British had won a great victory. Private Moffat, in his diary, recorded that;

'it is rumoured that there were thousands of enemy dead, after our bombardment, and many prisoners, many of which passed us on our way up last night.'

In reality Neuve Chapelle was at best a partial and incomplete success. The enemy trenches were flattened and the village stormed, but the British attempt to advance further was frustrated. The London Scottish found itself billeted close behind the lines in support of the Camerons. Casualties were inevitably taken from long-range German artillery, although their numbers were quickly made up from fresh drafts from the 2nd Battalion.

Trench life between battles was neither comfortable nor safe. In a letter home, published in a local newspaper, a member of the London Scottish wrote:

'We've been in the firing line again. We had five days and nights in the trenches and are now out of the firing line again and having a rest at this our new billet, where the sound of the artillery is only very distant and intermittent. Our line of trenches ran through a pine wood, and it was eerie work (especially at night, as the moon rose late) keeping guard one hour on and one hour off, two men at a time, with the enemy's trenches only thirty-five yards away and none of us managed to get much sleep for the five days. It was very dark and at times I could not see my hand before my face, and I had some bad moments occasionally, as you may imagine. Owing to the trenches running through a wood there was plenty of ground cover, and the favourite time for the German attacks was either just after dark or just before dawn. We had one very wet night too, thunder and torrential rain; we most of us were soaked through, and I haven't had my feet properly dry and warm from that day about a week ago.'

Private Moffat noted that, 'the fortunes of war' were well demonstrated when the Serjeants' Mess took a direct hit with none of its inhabitants sustaining injury.

'The billet selected by the sergeants because of its weatherproof roof became', he noted, *'probably the least weatherproof of the lot.*

Had it rained the best would have become the worst and the rank and file have scored for once.'

On 15 April the London Scottish were sent to Hingette to train for a new offensive in the following month. The period between then and 2 May, when the Battalion returned to the line, was taken up by administration, the inevitable route marches and periods of rest. An anonymous soldier writing for the *Regimental Gazette*, reported that on 17 April he was sent off by bicycle to find the field cashier. The ten-mile ride proved abortive, for when he reached the cashier the latter had no money. What was more;

'the populace took the fact that (he) was riding a bike in a kilt very quietly, with the exception of the infants, who either laughed, expectorated, or threw bricks.'

Although there were obvious moments of mirth, by now the war had reached a level of savage impersonality. On 5 May Lieutenant Cyril Hose complained;

'Hot oppressive morning, expect thunder. There is a cemetery just behind the trenches here, about fifty graves, three more poor men were buried this morn, Scots Guards, two shot through the head and one in the body - it is very terrible how these poor chaps are buried; a hole, a few men from the dressing station and the clergyman, a few words from the priest, and the body is lowered by the means of two ropes looped round it, clothed just as he was hit, he is laid in this rude hole with hardly any ceremony - despite all he has done - later a rough wooden cross is erected over him and his name and number inscribed.'

The Official History reports that two attacks were launched on 9 May, the left towards Fromelles, the right over the old battleground of Neuve Chapelle. As a subultern later stated,

'for the last four or five days we have been preparing to attack; everyone knew about it, including civilians, so doubtless the Hun knew too!'

The Regimental Gazette noted that;

'the 8th was passed more or less peacefully and that evening we moved to our positions, this Brigade having to get back a little to allow others who had to do the attacking to come in.'

Immediately before the assault the following message was circulated, how it was received may only be imagined!

'Just as we were moving, and when one's thoughts were very much of the morrow and of the issue at stake, a notice doubtless of great importance, but hardly dealing with the matter in hand arrived. It dealt at length on the subject of "Flies". It told us that great efforts must be made to suppress these insects, that fly-papers would be found useful and could be procured locally, I never actually saw a fly-paper vendor the next day, but possibly there was one!'

The London Scottish were held in reserve, and thanks to the initiative of their officers suffered very few casualties. The 2nd and 3rd Brigades on the other hand attacked at dawn, and by mid afternoon had been annihilated on the enemy wire. The Scottish were due to advance, and indeed one platoon did assault in support of the Black Watch, but an order was given to abort the attack before the bulk of the battalion was uselessly committed. Between forty and fifty casualties were sustained, including Lieutenant Findlay killed and Captain Stebbing wounded. The Division as a whole faired less well. In the words of the recently promoted Corporal Moffat;

'Our losses that day were terrible and it was a sickening sight to see the constant and never ending steam of wounded, hobbling or crawling to the Dressing Station.'

Lieutenant Cyril Hose was more specific.

'The Munsters were wiped out almost before leaving our lines - Royal Sussex also badly hit - apparently the first attack was a failure - but the artillery continue their work. At half past two the Camerons go forward past us looking a fine lot of fellows - our artillery blow the German parapets to blazes, it is terrible to see the awful work, they lengthen their range and fire on the German second line. The Camerons and Black Watch climb over our parapets, bayonets fixed and charge!...the Germans receive them with machine guns from their redoubt - the Camerons lose more than half, the Black Watch 800. We have to sit, waiting for our turn, watching the poor devils come back - brave chaps - limping, crawling and being carried.'

Corporal Meake, a Harley Street doctor in civilian life, returning home on leave shortly after the battle gave a report to the press in which he stated that the Scottish were under fire for most of the time yet took few casualties. He also mentioned that the 4th Seaforth Highlanders, who suffered very considerably in the Neuve Chapelle action, were in large measure recruited indirectly from the London Scottish.

'They were', he said, *'composed chiefly of men who, being unable to join the London Scottish through there being no battalion immediately available, enlisted instead in the Seaforths.'*

Corporal Meake was, himself, typical of the almost unique make-up of the London Scottish at the time. While he was serving in the ranks of that Regiment his chauffeur held a commission in the Army Service Corps.

The Scottish were ordered back to the comparative safety of Bethune, and on 15 May took over the Vermelles sector from the French. The sector had seen savage fighting a few months earlier but was now relatively quiet, the Germans and French having agreed informally to 'live and let live' in the area. The town itself was destroyed, reported Private Inkster.

'Early in the war the Germans were driven out of here, and the damage to the town done by the Allies' guns is far worse than any I have seen done by the Germans. The church is in a terrible state.'

Notwithstanding this, the area provided excellent billeting, and with one company in the front line trench, a second in the reserve trench and the other two in reserve, life became tolerable. Despite the British propensity for aggressive reconnaissance the sector remained quiet, providing the Battalion with excellent facilities for both rest and training. They were destined to remain in the sector until the midsummer of 1915, suffering a few casualties to the enemy but an alarmingly large number to commissioning elsewhere.

Perhaps inevitably the London Scottish, which despite its losses still in the majority comprised professional men such as Corporal Meake, was seen as an ideal source of officer material for the large number of Territorial and Volunteer Battalions now flooding into France. Typical of those to be lost to the Battalion were Second Lieutenant Walter Mackenzie Wallace, a veteran of Messines, later commissioned into the 12th Battalion the Middlesex Regiment and killed in action in October 1915.

Not everyone saw the fate of the London Scottish as an honour. The *Aberdeen Journal*, in a stinging rebuke on 5 November 1915, complained that;

> *'It is a pity that recruiting was not handled in a more business-like way at the beginning, but that is not the fault of the London Scottish... .The battalion has provided no fewer than 1,200 officers of other units. The Idea that the Regiment should become merely an officers' training corps is not liked, and the appeal is made to Scotsmen to see that it is maintained as a distinctive nation unit.'*

Even the normally placid Lawrie Inkster complained shortly after Neuve Chapelle;

> *'Yes, the Lusitania business was abominable, but to us out here we hope things like this will bring the war home to the public at home. It seems to us that the general public will never realize the seriousness of the war, and the fact that we shall need every ounce of effort there is in the country. The fact that so many of the young men of the country have nothing else to do than attend to sport and pleasure is, at a time like this, wicked. And while some of our press continue their cheap nastiness I cannot imagine recruiting progressing as is should.'*

Chapter Four

With Green's Force at Loos

The summer of 1915 brought with it none of the successes so eagerly anticipated by the Allies. In the east the Germans were advancing into Poland and threatening Warsaw, the newly-established Italian front had failed to breach the Austrian defences, Gallipoli had disintegrated into a bloody and pointless farce, and on the Western Front stalemate prevailed. Notwithstanding every indication to the contrary, the General Staff was in optimistic mood. The British forces were growing daily with the arrival of new 'Kitchener' divisions while France had increased her fighting power by convincing the British to take over more of the front line.

The Allies decided to consolidate their resources and to assault the German defensive positions on a huge scale, the main attack from the French being centred in Champagne, with a subsidiary attack by the British in the north. For the first time the Allies were to use poison gas as a weapon, in the case of the British, as a partial offset against their critical lack of heavy artillery. The London Scottish spent the early part of July back at Vermelles, relieving the Black Watch on 12 July and being themselves relieved by the 5th Royal Sussex a week later. They returned to the line at Cambrin on 25 July, and on 5 August became the subject of a German barrage when their pipers played 'God Save the King' to celebrate the opening of the second year of the war.

The front line at Festubert, 7 March 1915.

Serjeants Bryden and Hetherington, India Village, Festubert, 1915.

Shortly thereafter rumours began to abound that there were to be changes in the Brigade. A new Guards Division was to be formed, with the two Guards Battalions taken away and replaced by two of the New Army Battalions. On 20 August, the 8th Berkshires and 10th Gloucestershires arrived to replace the Guards Battalions, and immediately a company from each was attached to the London Scottish in the trenches for instruction.

The London Scottish felt the loss of Brigadier Lowther, commanding 1st Guards Brigade, profoundly. He had always been magnanimous to the Scottish and they in turn had adored him. He had recognized that they were different from a Regular battalion and had never attempted to assimilate them. Instead he had played on their strengths and had helped to eradicate their weaknesses, and in so doing had turned them into one of the finest battalions in the line. For his part Lowther, unable to say goodbye on parade, bade farewell to the Scottish by letter, extracts from which demonstrate clearly his sentiments:

'I am very happy to have been associated with (the London Scottish) for nearly nine months, and I want to thank all ranks for the cheerful manner in which they have always performed the very varied work which has fallen to their lot.

'Numbers of you are more accustomed to working with your heads than your hands, yet you now carry out the heavy digging and disagreeable fatigues and work in billets with a thoroughness which

168 Brigade Trench Mortar Section.

many other troops would do well to imitate... .

'I know that you have wished to have a dash at the enemy and do a really big thing to avenge your comrades who fell at Messines and elsewhere... .

'The Army owes you a debt of gratitude for the numbers of officers you have sent out to it: the great number of others who, when they might have had commissions, preferred to remain in the ranks, is sufficient evidence of your fine Regimental spirit... .'

The sheer professionalism of the London Scottish was ably demonstrated on the night of 23 August when 1st Brigade was ordered to dig a trench system 300 yards into no man's land. Heavy casualties were anticipated, but in the event none was sustained. This was due almost exclusively to the excellent organization and careful reconnaissance of the Scottish, who had supplied all markers and guides for the three battalions that night. On 31 August the Battalion was ordered to Lespesses, near Lillers where it was to train for the forthcoming battle. Major Lindsay, who had assumed command when Lieutenant Colonel Green had been forced to return to England on sick leave, was summoned to Brigadier Reddie, now commanding 1st Brigade, and advised that the British main objective was to be the German positions around Loos. Initially it was planned that the Berkshires and Gloucestershires, newly arrived and up to strength, would form the first line of the attack, the Camerons and Black Watch the second, and the London Scottish the reserve.

The London Scottish passed the next few days honing their skills in open warfare, it being felt that they had little to learn about trench fighting. The battle had originally been fixed for 15 September but was postponed for ten days, allowing the Scottish to celebrate in concert the anniversary of their arrival in France.

Harry Hodskins stands at the left of the group. Shortly after the photograph was taken a mortar round hit the trench and all were buried. Hodskins was dug out. As he crawled out he saw the head of a captain who had entered the trench for a rest. He was to have recurrent nightmares for years.

The final British plan was to attack with six divisions along a seven-mile front between Loos and La Bassée. The 1st Division was allotted a sector from the northern outskirts of Loos to the Vermelles Road, an area in which the enemy fire trench was exposed on the forward ridge with the support trenches hidden from view on the reverse slope. The 1st Brigade was ordered to attack east along the Vermelles Road, the 2nd Brigade on its right was due to attack east-south-east across Hill 69. It was accepted that this divergence would cause the two brigades to split, creating the danger of an unprotected void between them. It was thus decided to create a detached force, under Divisional command, to plug this gap should it become critical. The detachment was to comprise the London Scottish from the 1st Brigade and 9th Kings Liverpools from the 2nd Brigade. It was to be commanded by Colonel Green of the Royal Sussex Regiment, and was to be known as 'Green's Force.'

Colonel Green received his orders on 16 September leaving him with scant time for preparation. To compound his difficulties the Artillery had been bombarding the German front line for a number of days, destroying all hopes of surprise. The move to the front line began on 21 September, the London Scottish marching to a bivouac at Le Marequet Wood, where they were visited by Sir Hubert Gough, under whom they had served so well at Messines. An NCO wrote home that,

'This morning reveille was at 5 o'clock and breakfast at 6. It was a

very cold night and very cold when we got up. After breakfast we packed up, got the billets cleaned, and paraded at 8.15. The Battalion moved off about half an hour later-all sorry to leave the place, I think, but all in good spirits; there was plenty of singing and whistling on the road along.'

The weather remained good for the next day, but before the battle changed, soaking the troops on the night before the attack.

The terrain around Loos was far from suited to an offensive, indeed until the last minute Sir John French did all in his power to have the attack cancelled. The area comprised undulating, open land virtually bereft of trees. No man's land was studded with high shale heaps from the local collieries and steel reinforced lifting gear and pit heads which the Germans had turned into strong points where possible.

George Ernest Walker, joined the London Scottish in August 1914, was sent to France in 1915 and commissioned into the Royal Scots in 1916. He was killed in action in 1917.

On Friday 24 September the Battalion was advised that the attack was scheduled for the next morning. That day a draft of thirty men arrived from England to replace those lost to commissioning during that week alone, and were distributed among the companies. Each man was issued with an additional 100 rounds of ammunition and at 8.30p.m. was given what for many would be a last hot meal. An hour later the men began their advance to the front line through a communication trench knee-deep in water.

'Well we marched, many with sad hearts, for some knew that it was to be their last march - some premonition warned them' reported Private Parker in a letter to his mother.

'On the whole we were a merry lot, singing sometimes hymns, sometimes songs.'

The trenches, when the Battalion reached them, were wholly inadequate, badly prepared and with room for no more than half the men.

'We arrived at our position at 2 a.m.' continued Private Parker,

'and found the trenches a foot deep in mud and water. We had no great coats - only ammunition and iron rations were carried. Even our water was to be kept in the water bottles until we should arrive in the German trenches. Sleep was impossible in the trench so we climbed out and lay down on top, just behind the parapet, with bullets singing overhead and sometimes striking the ground just ahead.'

59

France 1915.

Private Mabbs of C Company remembered the reserve trench in which he spent that night as *'ankle deep in mud and water.'*

> *'They were very narrow,'* he reported, *'so we got out on the top and slept in pairs, one water-proof under and one over us. Of course in the morning we were one mass of mud, and wet through with rain.'*

At 5.30 a.m. the artillery barrage opened along the line, deluging the German front with shells of all calibre. There was very little wind, with what there was blowing gently to the south-west. The conditions were far from ideal for the use of gas , but nonetheless the order was given for it to be released. The chlorine vapour hung low and drifted slowly into no man's land where it largely remained. A little drifted into the German lines, but not in sufficient quantities to produce much effect. Some even drifted back towards the British positions.

At 7.30a.m. the infantry began its advance. The battle on the right went well with 15th Division storming Loos and advancing to Hill 70. On the 1st Division front the 1st Brigade made steady progress, sweeping over the German front line and pressing on towards Hulluch. The 2nd Brigade, however, was soon in difficulties. The gas cloud in their sector had not dispersed and they found themselves having to negotiate not only the enemy artillery and machine-gun fire, but their own smoke and chlorine vapour. To compound their problems, when they reached the enemy line they found that the wire was largely uncut.

'Green's Force,' with the London Scottish on the left and the Liverpools on the right, remained in their trenches until the troops further forward had cleared their assembly positions. At 8.00 a.m. they were ordered to move forward to the recently vacated front line trenches, the Scottish advancing in two lines of companies with A and D Companies in the front line and B and C Companies in the second. The attack of the 2nd Brigade having failed, and the smoke having cleared away, the advance had to be made in full view of the enemy and under sustained fire. To compound the Battalion's misfortune,

The London Scottish manning a breastwork somewhere on the front line, 1915.

when they reached the forward trenches they found them full of gas, and were thus forced to seek what little protection they could from the parados behind.

> *'At the given time we jumped the parapet and started advancing'* remembered Private Mabbs.*'Our poor fellows dropped all round, as the rifle fire and machine-gun fire were pretty heavy. Being in reserve, we advanced from behind our front line, but I am sorry to say many of our boys went down before we reached our objective.'*

Early in the afternoon 'Green's Force' was ordered to attack 'with one battalion each side of Lone Tree.' Despite Major Lindsay's suggestion that the Scottish should advance in the rear of the 1st Brigade and then swing round to take the enemy in the flank, Colonel Green ordered a frontal assault. B and C Companies advanced by half company in short rushes to reduce casualties, but even so losses were heavy. To add to their misery, when the survivors reached the German front line they found the enemy wire intact and impenetrable. They were forced to lie down, answering the German fire with their rifles and suffering serious loss in the process. The carnage might have been greater had it not been for the bravery of the Scottish machine-gun teams. Private Bruce Hay later recalled how he and nineteen others were selected to take the machine guns into action.

> *'As we scrambled out of the trenches, with our guns, ammunition, etc, I immediately realized that we were running into a hell. It was raining bullets, and no sooner were we on top, than men began to drop all round....The battalion was just in front of us, and all the way up our poor fellows were lying, some dead, others wounded.'*

The machine gunners, by now reduced to ten in number, were ordered

Billets in France, 1915-16.

forward to the left flank where they were able to give desperately needed supporting fire.

The situation appeared hopeless, and when Division urged a further attempt, Major Lindsay was at last granted permission to attempt a flanking movement with D Company. They had hardly emerged into the open when the unexpected happened. Suddenly the Germans rose from their seemingly impregnable positions, hands above their heads, and surrendered in their hundreds. B and C Companies were able to rise and occupy the trenches without further immediate bloodshed.

> 'The Hun's defence broke down absolutely and they surrendered wholesale, putting their arms above their heads and shouting "Scottish, don't shoot"' reported Private Parker. 'From all over the place you could see small bodies of British troops escorting larger bodies of Germans. We captured more Huns than we had men to guard them. One platoon of nineteen brought in ninety odd.'

The prisoners, of whom there were eventually about 600, were mostly drawn from the 51st Regiment. They had seen the 15th Division on their left and the 1st Brigade on their right outflank them and felt themselves cut off. D Company had acted as a catalyst in convincing them of the hopelessness of their situation. Rather than face annihilation they had surrendered

14 Platoon, D Company, France July 1915.

By now 'Green's Force' had been reduced to no more than 400 men and was in need of reorganization. Crucially, the 2nd Brigade had yet to come into the line and could not be made ready for further action before nightfall. At about 6.00 p.m. the Scottish were ordered to attach themselves to 2nd Brigade which by then had reached a position near the Loos Chalk Pit. This proved a most uninviting bivouac.

'We then marched about a mile further on to a big chalk pit up a hill,' remembered Private Mabbs. *'We were here in the wet and mud, and consequently had to walk about all night to keep warm. Connell and I were huddled together, and snatched half an hour's sleep, but woke up with our teeth chattering, and wet to the skin.'*

At 3.00 a.m., as the leading elements of the 21st Division came into the line, the London Scottish were ordered to leave the chalk pit and return to the Lone Tree.

'The scene going back was appalling,' remembered Private Mabbs. *'The dead and wounded strewn about in the grey light of the dawn made a sight I shall never forget to the end of my days.'*

To compound their misery the last troops to leave the pit were heavily fired upon from the direction of Hill 70 and took a number of casualties. The attacking troops were, by now, exhausted. Their casualties had been enormous, yet all ranks were full of hope, believing that they had won a great victory. The situation demanded exploitation by fresh troops, yet the only two divisions available, the 21st and 24th, had already been put into the line after a long march. The Guards Division, hurrying to the area, would not be available for several hours.

The London Scottish were ordered to rejoin 'Green's Force' and move to the captured first and second line of German trenches south of the Vermelles-Hulluch Road. Confusion reigned when the Scottish arrived at their destination only to find it occupied by the 2nd Gloucestershires. They moved to a vacant position beyond where, true to the chaos of war, they received conflicting orders from the 1st Brigade, 3rd Brigade and 'Green's Force.' On the morning of 27 September orders were received that 'Green's Force' was to be broken up and the Scottish were to return to 1st Brigade. The Battalion spent a trying day under severe artillery fire.

'At seven that night we again moved to another very shallow trench forming our new support line,' reported Private Parker. *'This we held all next day (Monday). We then experienced the most severe shell fire we have ever been under. The earth shook with the vibration, and outside the trench the land was one mass of holes, torn up by the explosions. The regiment bore charmed lives, for though several men were buried temporarily by the trench falling in no one was actually wounded.'*

At noon the Guards Division was thrown into the fight on the right flank. It won some ground, but was forced to abandon most of it at a cost of 3,000 officers and men killed and wounded, including Lieutenant Jack Kipling, the

Taken just before the Battle of Loos, 1915.

only son of Rudyard Kipling, killed in his first action with the Irish Guards. On Monday evening the London Scottish were relieved and withdrew to the Fosse Way trench system near Le Rutoire. The next two days were spent in extreme discomfort, lashed by rain and under the barrels of a British heavy battery which was continually in action, and which frequently attracted long-range answering fire.

'*We were shelled and gassed out of these trenches several times that day,*' complained Private Mabbs, '*and in the evening it was raining so hard that we got out of the trench to save ourselves from swimming.*

'*Our cookers were good to us, and brought us hot tea and rum,*' remembered Private Parker, ' *but I think it was nerve-fatigue we were suffering from, for everyone looked wrecked. Muddy and covered with dirt, many had lost their bonnets, me included, and no shave since the 21st. We were wrecks.*'

That day, reported Private Hay, the Battalion was visited by the Prince of Wales.

'*In the midst of all this I look up and who should I see but the Prince of Wales. He did not appear at all nervous, and later in the day his chauffeur was killed.*'

64

On Wednesday afternoon the Battalion was relieved by the Guards and went into billets at Les Brebis where it was joined by a draft of forty-seven men. After one night it moved back to Noeux-les-Mines, where it was billeted with the remainder of the 1st Division. Reduced to a total strength of about 300 officers and men its losses during the battle had amounted to five officers and 260 other ranks.

Perhaps thankfully few, if any, of the Scottish were aware of the true severity of the situation.

'Things are progressing splendidly, and the French have done wonders,' wrote Private Mabbs. *'In our part of the line we know for a fact that the Huns are right out in the open, and we don't intend to let them dig in again in a hurry.'*

Little could have been further from the truth. Enormous losses, amounting to over 40,000 men, had been incurred in the main attack, yet the German main defensive line remained secure. A French attack at Vimy Ridge had failed, and in the south the main Champagne attack, after a few initial successes, had bogged down.

The luxury of rest was to last for no more than four days, and on 5 October the 1st Division was again ordered into the line. It was to hold the front from the Loos Chalk Pit to the Vermelles-Hulluch road, with the 2nd Brigade on the right, the 1st Brigade on the left and the 3rd in reserve. The London Scottish were on the right of the 1st Brigade near the junction of the roads from Lens and Loos to Hulluch. Their trenches had been hastily constructed during the battle and did not link up with those of the 2nd Brigade, nor were there any communication trenches on that flank. The position was under constant enemy fire, there was no fresh water, and rations had to be brought by hand under cover of darkness. On 7 October the Battalion was ordered to reconnoitre a ruined estaminet which had stood at the junction of the two roads. It was found to be occupied by the enemy.

On the next day, after another tremendous bombardment, the Germans launched their expected counter-attack. That afternoon, after heavy shelling, they attacked in the south but were repulsed with heavy losses. On 11 October 1st Brigade was ordered to attack the German line opposite the new position. Although the attack would be preceded by artillery fire it was

A street in Loos, September 1915. Tower Bridge can be clearly seen in the background.
Taylor Library

accepted that the guns would not cut the enemy wire which would have to be cut by the troops themselves under cover of a smoke cloud. All five battalions were brought into the line, there being no one left in reserve. One hour before the attack, smoke bombs were to be thrown out on the front, not only by the 1st Brigade but also by the 2nd, which was to take no further part in the battle. Gas was to be employed with the smoke, although not on the front of the London Scottish, who were warned to be prepared for a possible counter-attack. Immediately prior to the attack the battalion busied itself building a new fire-trench.

Realizing that even if the wire were cut, the gaps would be few and narrow, Colonel Lindsay ordered D Company to be given all the available wire-cutters and to make the initial assault. A Company was directed to follow in close support ready to go through the gaps when made, B Company was to remain in the firing line until this was done and then go through A Company and take the second trench. C Company was held in reserve in the support line to beat off any counter-attack. The attack was postponed until 13 October and the 2nd Brigade, which had suffered heavily in the earlier German counter-attack, was replaced by 3rd Brigade. Zero hour was set for 2.00 p.m. and punctually one hour earlier the troops began to throw out smoke bombs. The Germans responded with a tremendous bombardment which only served to emphasize the strength in which their trenches were held.

Unfortunately 3rd Brigade exhausted their supply of bombs prematurely. With the wind driving what smoke there was north-east, the screen to the front of the London Scottish had virtually disappeared by 2.00 p.m. D and A Companies advanced with the greatest gallantry, some even reaching the line where they found the wire quite unbroken. With most of the platoon and section commanders hit, the remainder could do nothing but form a firing line and await events elsewhere. The rest of the brigade fared no better. The Black Watch managed to infiltrate a few men into the enemy trenches where they were overwhelmed. No other battalion even reached the wire. B Company was committed to the battle when wholly inaccurate news reached Battalion Headquarters that A Company had penetrated the wire, but at 4.30 p.m. the awful truth became apparent when a message from Captain Sayer of A Company got through to Headquarters, advising that the attack had been a total failure. C Company was ordered to remain in its trenches while those already engaged were told to hang on until dark after which the survivors were withdrawn to the old firing line.

The next morning, under cover of a thick mist, the Battalion was withdrawn to the old pre-Loos lines. Of the twelve officers who took part in the attack five became casualties, including all who had joined since 25 September. Private G. C. Ford, a former officer of the Regiment who had resigned in 1905 to take Holy Orders, but who had returned at the outbreak of war to serve as a stretcher bearer, was among those killed.

After this engagement the Battle of Loos gradually petered out into normal trench warfare. After a few days the exhausted veterans of the London Scottish, now no more than 200 strong, were withdrawn to Lollers.

A Winter in the Trenches

The Battalion had not been up to strength since its first few days in France. True it had received regular replacement drafts, but these had hardly compensated for the battle casualties, let alone the loss to commissioning. It had become a regular occurrence for wounded soldiers to be evacuated back to Britain, and once there commissioned and transferred elsewhere. The position became no better when the 2nd Battalion, originally raised as a training centre to provide drafts for the 1st, was selected as a fighting unit, and a 3rd Battalion organized for depot purposes.

At Lillers the Battalion received a draft of sixty men, but these failed to compensate for those lost in battle let alone to commissioning. To compound the Unit's difficulties two experienced officers, Lieutenant Brown-Constable and Second Lieutenant McGregor Lowe, were seconded to Divisional duties. Tragically, the latter fell victim to a sniper's bullet a few days later. McGregor Lowe had been born in Berlin, where his father had worked for *The Times* for many years. In June 1915, while holding the rank of Serjeant and acting as Chief Battalion Scout, he had been awarded the DCM;

> 'For conspicuous gallantry and marked ability and resource consistently shown throughout the campaign, when he constantly acted as a scout in front of the entrenchment, often under a heavy fire from snipers and machine guns. He supplied sketches and much invaluable information in connection with the enemy's trenches and wire entanglements.'

Two months later he was commissioned, unusually into his own Battalion,

The Lone Tree at Loos, September 1915.

and was appointed First Brigade Scout, or Chief Intelligence Officer, in which capacity he was acting when killed.

On 28 October the 1st Brigade was inspected by the King. Hallowe'en, the anniversary of Messines, was celebrated by a concert in the Lollers theatre. The *Regimental Gazette* noted that;

> *'as Hallowe'en fell on a Sunday it had been decided to hold the concert on the Saturday evening with a dinner on the Sunday. The concert was postponed and reinstated on a number of occasions during the preceding hours but eventually took place to the satisfaction of all. As The Gazette noted, "Sergt-Major Milligan in his humorous recital of "The Village Blacksmith", and Sergt. Campbell in "The Old Dun Cow" provoked roars of applause. Private Lancaster's rendering of "Bonnie Wee Thing" and Private Hargreaves' singing were treats in themselves. A Reel and a Highland Fling were other contributions to a concert which was worthy of the Regiment and which will remain a pleasing memory to those present.'*

The arrangements for the winter were designed to ensure that the troops enjoyed maximum rest commensurate with the requirements for security in the front line. The 4th Corps had two divisions in the line and one in reserve at Villiers with each division taking two months in the line and one in reserve. The 1st Division front, which extended from Loos Chalk Pit to near

St Lie, was held by two brigades, with a third in reserve at Noeux-les-Mines. The brigades at the front alternated between right and left and remained in sector for twenty-four days, thereafter passing into reserve for a week. The 1st Brigade itself held its front with two battalions, with a third in close reserve in the old German front line, and a fourth in brigade reserve. The 10th Gloucestershires were temporarily converted into a Pioneer battalion and played no part in the relief.

The weather in the winter was bad, with cold night fogs and rain interspersed with sleet. The Loos battle had resulted in the formation of a sharp salient which exposed the 1st Division's position to artillery fire from three directions. The occasional bursts of artillery and rifle fire resulted in few casualties, but some that were caused were critical. In January 1916 the Reverend Guy Cecil Ford, the London Scottish chaplain, was shot by a sniper as he was attending to a wounded man.

'Yesterday our stretcher-bearer and chaplain were killed,'
were the words contained in a letter received by Thomas Holmes from his son fighting with the Battalion, and reprinted in the *Westminster Gazette.*

'It happened this way,' he wrote. *'A man was lying wounded in the open, and the chaplain went to attend to him in full sight of the German lines. They must have seen the Red Cross on his arm, nevertheless, he was sniped, shot through the heart, and died with a smile on his face. Our battalion mourns for him, for he was a splendid man and very popular. The Black Watch called him the "big meenister." The serjeant major said "he was the only man in the regiment fit to die".'*

There were other acts of courage that winter. Holmes went on to report that,

'Our dresser, Lander, went out to dress the wounds of a man in the open, and while attending to him was shot in the lower part of the body and legs. He had administered morphia to himself to deaden the pain, and continued his efforts for the other man. We knew that Lander was wounded, and stretcher-bearers went out to fetch him in. "Let me finish with this man, and then take him, he is worse than I am." They brought in the other man and then returned for Lander, but he was dead. Lander was a fine man, and was all through the previous Balkan wars with the Red Cross Ambulance.'

Trench warfare seemed to have become a settled state of existence by early 1916, with little hope of a speedy salvation and with scant belief in 'one final push' when the weather improved. An officer noted in his diary;

'I am anxious about the situation. The labour of keeping up the trenches is incessant and frightfully severe. The men have no dug outs or any kind of shelter, and they are in a constant state of being absolutely done. If the Huns attack they cannot help taking the first line, and, as we choose to pin our faith to the first line, it is quite doubtful if we can stop them afterwards. The proper way to defend

this sector, in my opinion, is to scrap the first line altogether, and to meet the attack with our main force in the old German line; but we have strict orders to hold on to every inch of ground whether it has any tactical value or not.'

Fortunately the Germans were in no mood for a fight. Indeed, their predicament, fighting as they were on two fronts, was, in many ways, worse.

On 4 January 1916 the whole of the 1st Division was withdrawn from the line and moved into billets at Lillers. Two weeks later the London Scottish took up their quarters in the village of Burbure for 'rest and training.' Rumour quickly began to spread that the battalion was to be transferred to the 56th Division, newly-formed and comprising London Territorial battalions. The news was greeted with mixed emotions. The Scottish felt a part of the 1st Brigade, and were particularly close to the Camerons and Black Watch, regular units with whom they had been closely associated since shortly after Messines.

On 6 February Brigadier General Reddie, commanding the 1st Brigade, bade farewell to the Scottish with the following words;

'Colonel Green, officers, NCO's, and men of the London Scottish, it is my unpleasant duty to come here this morning to say good bye to you on behalf of the 1st Brigade. Your Battalion has now been with the Brigade practically a year and a quarter, and during that time has always done whatever it was required to do in a praiseworthy manner. I came to the Brigade in August last, and it was one of the proudest moments of my life when I heard that the London Scottish was one of the Battalions under my command. Being a Scotsman myself, I was delighted to hear that I was to have three Scottish Battalions. During the time you have been with the Brigade it has sustained very heavy losses, a large number caused by casualties, but your loss will be nonetheless regretted by those old friends who still remain.'

Two days later, headed by the pipers of the Camerons and Black Watch, the London Scottish marched to the railhead and took a train for Pont Remy under the eyes of Sir Henry Wilson, commanding the Fourth Army, who had come to wish them well. The Battalion established its new Headquarters at Neuville and awaited the arrival of the other three battalions destined to form the new 168th Brigade, the 1/4th London (Royal Fusiliers), the 1/12th London (Rangers), and the 1/13th London (Kensingtons). The Brigade Commander was to be Brigadier General C.G. Loch of the Royal Scots.

Chapter Five

With the 56th Division on the Somme

During its stay at Neuville the Battalion was re-equipped and brought up to strength. The appalling weather conditions and unsuitability of the ground meant that little training could take place. Indeed, the *Regimental Gazette* reported that the most combative action of the period was comprised of snowball fights in which *'a number of the officers joined in spiritedly.'* The three weeks of comparative inactivity did however allow the Brigade to bond, and to begin to establish a new elan which would prove crucial in the months ahead.

On 14 March the Battalion undertook a twenty-mile route march to Bouchon, and the following day a march of fourteen miles to Doullen.

> *'Foot slogging was nothing new to us,'* remembered Private Donald Bliss, *'and soon some of the men were fast asleep as they marched, like automatons. A pot hole in the road caught a man off balance and there was a mad scramble as men following piled on top, to be pulled up by companions with much cursing and rattling of equipment. A bend in the road found the outside file of men going off in a straight line in the darkness, to be grabbed back by companions.'*

From Doullen they moved to Villers St Simon where they remained until 7 May. The *Gazette* reported that the Scottish *'arrived in the freshest possible condition'* but lamented that the area comprised perhaps the worst that the Scottish had ever occupied. The ground was agricultural with few facilities for training beyond twice-weekly route marches and the occasional company exercise.

> *'April was a month of intense training,'* noted Lance Serjeant Alex Richardson,
>
> *'physical jerks, bayonet thrusts, and much grousing.'*

Matters were further exacerbated when the scale of equipment carried by every infantryman was increased to include two gas masks and a steel helmet; the latter heavy, ill-balanced and exceedingly hot. As the months progressed many Scots returned to their old habit of wearing the bonnet when not in action, but for the first few weeks standing orders were adhered to rigidly and the helmet

Private Harry Spooner and Edward Laird taken at Gommecourt in June 1916. Both were wounded on 1 July.

The London Scottish marching along the Doullen-Amiens Road on their way to the Somme,
June 1916.

was worn during all aspects of training.

> 'A good deal of time was spent in clambering out of mud channels,
> crawling through barbed wire, and rushing at another line of trenches
> some hundred yards away,'

remembered Richardson. Almost prophetically, he noted that

> 'these trenches were duplicates of the actual trenches we would
> endeavour to capture in the near future. We had been practising the
> "Final Assault" for the opening of the Somme Battle.'

All was not work at Villers St Simon. Inter-company boxing competitions
were held and the Halley Claymore inter-company drill competition,
shunned before the war, was revived and won by C Company. A brigade
sports meeting was held and won easily by the Scottish.

One serious mishap befell the Regiment at this time. At Villeneuve St
Georges in 1914 the Scottish had 'acquired' a luxury motor car. It had
returned to the Battalion after Messines and had done invaluable service,
not only to the Scottish but to the entire 1st Brigade. It is even believed that
the Brigadier, although officially unaware of its existence, had gone on leave
in it. When the Battalion was transferred to 56th Division the car had been
entrained and disentrained without hostile comment. On one fateful
evening, however, it had been assigned to a party of Scottish due to appear
at a concert in St Pol. While in town a female impersonator had attracted
the attention of the Military Police who began to question the legality of

'her' transport. The Padre, in charge of the concert party, was unable to lie, higher authority was called, and the vehicle returned to its donor.

On 21 February the Germans began a massive assault against the wholly unsuspecting French at Verdun. The battle continued relentlessly, with the Germans gaining initial ground but sustaining enormous losses. The French, determined to hold the sector at all costs, called for help from their allies. In response the British Army took over more of the line, extending it southwards to the great bend in the Somme, increased the size of its Expeditionary Force to 600,000 and accelerated its plan for a summer offensive.

After considerable thought, and not a little compromise, it was agreed that the offensive would hinge on the Somme River, with the British to the north undertaking the bulk of the fighting. The front would extend from the area of Gommecourt in the north, across the bend of the Somme, to the Amiens-St Quentin Road to the south. Due to a lack of resources, particularly in artillery, the attack at Gommecourt would be a feint, designed to draw enemy firepower away from the major proposed axis of advance. Neither the 46th nor the 56th Divisions destined to attack at Gommecourt were advised of this crucial fact.

On 7 May the 56th Division was moved up to hold the line near Hebuterne, opposite the Gommecourt position. According to the notes of an unknown NCO, D Company's arrival was not uneventful.

'We arrived there after a jolly little stroll of some fifteen miles, feeling that we could drain the village pond with ease. Such an extreme measure was not, however, necessary, as our genial Quartermaster Serjeant having strolled up (with alas! a none too steady gait), informed us with mysterious twitchings and blinking of the eyes that he knew of a little place round the corner.'

The London Scottish were initially kept in reserve at St Amand, although parties of officers and non-commissioned officers were sent into the trenches to study the country in front. The trenches outside the village were about 400 yards from the German line, with the valley between the lines dominated by the strongly fortified Gommecourt Park which projected like

The London Scottish marching to the Somme; within days over half would be dead or wounded.

En route to the Somme.

a bastion towards the British line round Fonquevillers, on the left of the Scottish positions. On the first morning the D Company runners were called together, shown a map, and told to familiarize themselves with the trenches as they would eventually be wanted as guides.

It quickly proved one thing to study the trench lines on paper but quite another, when in the twisting trenches, to know their location.

Private Bliss noted,

> 'We had four lads set out, happy in the sunshine. We came on a shaft that was being dug at night time down from the side of one of the trenches. "Hullo! that's going to be a deep dugout!" "Yes! And here's another one and its got the tools in it!" "Going to have two entrances!" On we went until we came to a dugout that had received a direct hit. "I say!" one exclaimed, "that was a jolly good shot wasn't it?" "What's that sacking hanging up there?" We pulled the sacking aside to find two steps leading up to another curtain of sacking. Crowding in we slipped through the second curtain and found ourselves in a small observation post.'

Trench warfare was uncompromising, and tragedy nearly followed a moment of carelessness.

> 'I, who had had longer service out there than the others should have known better, but I had been away from the trenches too long and was careless,' admitted the contrite Bliss. ' "Have a smoke?" said one producing a packet of cigarettes. We lit up and puffed smoke through the green painted wire netting that covered the rectangular opening, overlooking the countryside. "What a fine view!" "Look at that chap digging behind the German lines!" There was a noise of a door slamming in the distance and a shell screamed over our heads. "Quick! Get out, they've seen us!"

'We rushed through the sacking covering the entrance and ran back up the trench with shells falling all round. "Get into the shaft round the next corner!" I called. "No, not that one!" "In here quick! This one has the tools in. If they hit the entrance we stand a chance of digging ourselves out!" For about twenty minutes the area was plastered with shells but fortunately with no casualties. "What a fool thing to do," I said "We were lucky to get away safely!"'

The immediate work undertaken by the British was the construction of new trenches nearer the German lines. These works were to be protected by an isolated position well in advance of the old trenches, as a forward defence. The positions had been marked out with tapes and pegs by the Royal Engineers and the work already commenced when the Scottish took over the sector.

'The next two months were devoted to making new communication trenches, rebuilding our front line and constructing machine-gun emplacements,' recalled Lance Serjeant Richardson. 'This interested me particularly,' he mused, 'for by this time I had reached the dizzy heights of being No. 1 on a gun, with a Vickers Machine Gun and five men under my control. I was made responsible for the construction of a Machine Gun emplacement, which had to fulfil the very important duty of enfilading the enemy front line of the 29 June, the opening of the offensive. With the help of two Edinburgh Engineers, who smoked all my cigarettes and made us do the work, we built a position twenty-five yards in front of our line. The gun

Private William Kelly Saunders. Joined the London Scottish in early 1915 and was posted to the 1st Battalion later that year. Killed in action 1 July 1916. His name is on the Thiepval Memorial to the missing.

emplacement was reached by two staircases; one from the trench down to the dugout, and the other from the dugout up to the position, each staircase being twenty-five feet deep. We worked in shifts of six hours, and after six weeks of extremely hard toil we were ready for the "Push." This work was difficult, as it was not easy to dispose of the earth dug up, and all the time Brother Boche had his suspicions and did not approve of our energy. The result was whizz-bangs by day and machine-gun fire by night.'

On 20 May the Scottish moved back to huts at Halloy for intensive training. A full scale model of the enemy trench systems constructed with the help of aerial photographs was attacked in company, and later battalion and eventually brigade formation. Nothing was left to chance, with orders issued for every contingency. These intensive rehearsals continued until the end of May, culminating in an attack on the model trenches under cover of a smoke screen.

On 1 June the Battalion marched to Souastre, and the next night took over a sector of trenches in front of Hebuterne from the 4th Londons. The French, who had until recently occupied the line, had concentrated their defences to the rear. However, true to their tradition, when they had taken over, the British had concentrated their strength in the forward lines and had begun to construct a new system of trenches some 300 yards into no man's land. The first task of 56th division was to complete these trenches and to supplement them with a series of assembly trenches fifty yards to the rear. This resulted in a period of heavy work by night and day and difficult conditions. It was impossible to conceal this work from the enemy whose guns and trench mortars caused serious casualties, unmolested as they were by the British artillery, which was ordered to remain silent so as not to reveal its positions.

On 8 June the Battalion was relieved in the trenches by the Rangers, but was ordered to remain at Hebuterne on digging duties until the Brigade was relieved two weeks later. By then, Private Bliss recalled;

> 'the trench system in front of Hebuterne was now almost complete and under cover of the orchards surrounding the village, extensive work had been done in building gun pits and ammunition stores underground. Under cover of the surrounding hedge, vicious looking muzzles of light artillery protruded from the bank, set to cover the forward area. There was no lack of support from behind the line and supplies of ammunition were abundant.'

On 21 June the Scottish were relieved by the 1st Londons and the 168th Brigade went into reserve. The next morning the Battalion marched to a hutted camp at Pas-en-Artois where the attack was again practised and battle equipment issued. Each man was detailed to carry, besides his own equipment, fifty extra rounds of ammunition, two sand bags and either a pick or shovel. Each bomber was issued with thirty-two bombs.

On 23 June the preparatory bombardment of the enemy positions began. Hundreds of guns of every calibre opened fire by day and night until it seemed impossible that anything could be left alive or intact in the German forward trenches. During their final period of rest and training at Pas-en-Artois the Scottish experienced their first air raid. Private Bliss remembered;

> 'In the early morning after our arrival we were awakened by the long low hum of aircraft and on emerging from the canvas huts in which we were quartered saw a swarm of German aircraft that looked like insects in the clear morning air. Quite unopposed, they slowly circled and dropped some bombs, fortunately missing the camp but hitting an estaminet, wounding the proprietor and his wife and killing a horse in the stable.'

Pathetically, Bliss went on to report that;

'here and there were French folk trudging beside the few personal belongings heaped on a cart drawn by horses and on top of the load a mattress on which sat the grandparents, while behind came the family cow, led by one of the youngsters. These poor folk were being evacuated from the forward areas and presented a pathetic sight as, deprived of their homes, they saw no future.'

The final practice took place on 26 June in the presence of the Army and Corps commanders and their staffs. Next evening, in the pouring rain, the Battalion moved off to its billets in Bayencourt village, which it shared with a battery of 9.2 inch howitzers which fired incessantly, making sleep all but impossible.

'It was almost a nightly occurrence,' complained Richardson, *'to waken with my bivouac on top of me having been brought down by the fire of our guns. It was no pleasure to crawl from under waterproof sheets and corrugated iron on a wet night, and flounder about in a frantic endeavour to replace the roof before the interior was in a state resembling cold porridge.'*

Bliss also remembered Bayencourt with distaste.

'In the village street the Battalion was halted and split up into sections for the various available billets. The section of which I was a member was shown to a stable from which horses had been moved at short notice. The place was ankle deep in wet manure. This was where we were to sleep. A wheelbarrow and a couple of forks were obtained from the farm to which it belonged. Soon we were clear to the earth floor and members were sent to scrounge for straw, while others hammered four inch nails, which we carried for the purpose, into the wooden supports of the stable, on which to hang our equipment.'

During the period immediately preceding the attack, disease compounded with enemy action to add to the casualty list. Lance Serjeant Richardson noted that four men from his section alone were hospitalized suffering from diphtheria during the eight days of the barrage. At 4.00p.m. news was received that the attack had been postponed for forty-eight hours due to adverse weather conditions. Next morning the bombardment ceased abruptly, but on 29 June it began again. The next morning, after Church Parade, the Scottish moved into the assembly trenches approximately twenty-five yards ahead of the front line to await the signal which ultimately would lead to the destruction of over three quarters of the Battalion.

That night Richardson found himself detailed as his section officer's runner in place of a man who had been wounded two days earlier. He was far from pleased; not only was his gun 'going over' in the initial assault but, injuries permitting, as a runner it would be his duty to pass through the enemy's counter-barrage many times on the coming day.

'I made my last round of the guns about midnight on the 30th,' he reported. *'While making these rounds I found it most interesting to see*

the different effects the coming ordeal had on the men. I saw some reading, others writing what might be their last letters home, some crying over photographs, others brewing tea, sleeping or playing cards. I envied the men who could sleep, and enjoyed the company of those playing cards. Human nature is, proverbially, a strange thing, and it showed itself in strange ways that night.'

Gommecourt

Haig found himself in a considerable dilemma when planning the Somme offensive. Unlike Joffre, in command of the far larger French Army, he had yet to accept that he was in a war of attrition. His aim was to achieve a breakthrough to the communications centres east of Bapaume, to exploit northwards with his cavalry and thereby bring relief to the French fighting for their very existence at Verdun. Acutely aware of the lack of experience of the New Army volunteer battalions which comprised the greater bulk of his available forces, Haig conceived an extremely simple plan comprising two phases, a protracted and massive artillery barrage followed by an infantry assault across the entire fifteen mile front. As has already been stated this included a deception plan involving the southernmost divisions of the Third Army at Gommecourt. The assault was in fact designed to be more of a walk across no man's land. Infantry would move in extended lines to the enemy's trenches from which little resistance was anticipated due to the devastating effects of the artillery. Indeed, success was considered such a foregone conclusion that the staff decided the troops would assault in full kit to avoid any loss of momentum when the enemy's trenches were breached in depth.

Tragically the British had not learnt the lessons of earlier battles. About two-thirds of the 1.5 million artillery shells fired in the barrage were 18-pounder shrapnel rounds which failed to cut the wire as effectively as predicted. The remaining third were high explosive, but they failed to penetrate the extensive overhead protection of the German trench systems. To compound this problem much of the ammunition was badly made, about one round in three proving defective. At the receiving end the effects of the barrage were extremely unpleasant, but nonetheless many of the enemy were able to sit it out in the comparative safety of their well-designed dug outs and deep shelters. Crucially little damage was done to the German artillery, which enjoyed reasonable cover on the reverse slopes behind the lines. Unlike the French and Germans who had both adopted simple forms of fire and manoeuvre the British advanced at walking pace, shoulder to shoulder. To add insult to injury the assault was postponed to 7.30a.m., in broad daylight, to allow the French gunners to the south to register on their targets.

The German trenches facing the Scottish ran along the margin of Gommecourt Park to the south of the village, forming a close network within the park. To the north the line ran outside the boundary of

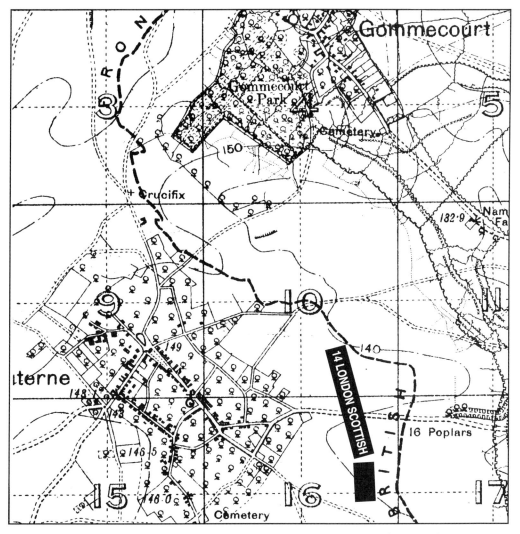

14 London Scottish position at Gommecourt on the morning of the attack.

Gommecourt Wood, and was supported by trenches in the wood. The two systems were linked together by entrenchments covering and running through the ruined village. The position was held by the 2nd Reserve Corps of the Prussian Guard, among the best troops then in the area. The German positions were covered by more than 120 machine guns, few of which had been damaged in the barrage. The material damage to the forward trenches however was considerable, causing them to look very unlike the model trenches against which the Scottish had practised their assault, and it was thus no easy matter for the attackers to carry out their elaborately detailed orders.

Little damage was done to the Germans by British artillery fire. Here we see German troops posing for a photograph after the British barrage at the wood of Gommecourt.

The plan of attack was simple. The salient was to be assaulted on both sides, by the 46th North Midland Division on the left and the 56th London Division on the right. In the 56th Division there were to be two brigades in the front line and one in reserve. In each brigade two battalions formed the front line of the attack, the remaining two being organized as carrying and mopping-up parties. In the 168th Brigade, the Rangers and London Scottish were detailed as the lead battalions, with the London Scottish forming the extreme right flank of the entire Gommecourt feint. The lead battalions were to attack in line of companies on the frontage of a platoon. The Commanding Officers were not allowed to retain reserves, and could thus exercise no immediate influence on the battle.

A Company occupied the right of the line, the line curving round slightly to the right rear. Thus the company would not be facing directly towards the enemy when they left their trenches and would have to swing about a quarter left in no man's land which, in the smoke would be far from easy. As a precaution a tape was laid during the night showing the line on which the company was to form. Crowded in their assembly trenches the Scottish got what rest they could, but for many it was a sleepless night. Private Bliss recalled that, during the night;

> *The Colonel with a grave face stood before his men. Some 850 men who, with rifles and bayonets, were due to go "over the top" the following morning to take their part in the Battle of the Somme.'*

In an attempt to steady frayed nerves the Colonel gave his final speech.

'I just want to tell you men, that tomorrow, we are to take part in one of the biggest battles our Country has ever undertaken. You are members of the biggest volunteer army that the Country has ever known. As far as we can ascertain, you will be opposed by members of the 2nd Prussian Guards' reserve and I am confident that you will give a good account of yourselves.'

Morale, raised momentarily by the Commanding Officer, was then in the eyes of many shattered when the Medical Officer advised that hot soup, and not the traditional tot of rum, would be served immediately before the assault. Not wishing to disabuse them of their probable fate he warned them that *'You can all expect to be wounded!'* and then went on to advise the chastened ranks that *'rum would increase the action of the blood stream and you stand a better chance of survival if you don't have it.'*

As had been the tradition since the Battle of Loos a cadre of approximately 100 officers and men was left in the trenches to provide a nucleus for recovery should the battalion be annihilated. Thus twenty-three officers and 811 combatants, the Medical Officer and twenty-one stretcher bearers were detailed to go 'over the top.' Lieutenant Hunter was detailed to lead the attack on D Company's front on the left flank. Lieutenant Brown-Constable had relieved Captain (Skinny) Anderson as Officer Commanding and was to go over in the second wave with No 14 Platoon. That night Brown-Constable accompanied by Bliss crawled out to the enemy wire which they found to have been fairly broken up by the shell fire. Finishing their tour of inspection without incident they returned to their own lines, causing Bliss to consider how at that time the entire battalion could have walked over, but how in the morning they were to herald their coming *'with a damn big bombardment before advancing.'*

'We found the waiting in the trenches a weird sensation,' recalled Bliss. *'To each man his own thoughts. We had up till now accepted danger as and when it came. Scared stiff at times but laughing and joking as soon as the danger was past. It was always the other fellow who got wounded or killed. This coming attack was however rather different. We were going into the unknown, further from home, with the possibility of not returning... .Thinking of this and that, till the mind got tired, we dozed often, saying little when awake.'*

When the hot soup arrived it proved little substitute for rum. Served in two gallon petrol cans it was so impregnated as to be virtually undrinkable.

'The day dawned hot and cloudless with a thin mist,'
noted Lance Serjeant Richardson.

'Our guns had been firing constantly for eight days, but at 6.30 on that morning every gun on our front opened fire and for one hour there was intense bombardment. At 7.30 the firing ceased for a few seconds, but again broke out, as it seemed to me more intense than before.'

Enemy heavy guns, untouched by the barrage, began to respond and quickly tore into the hastily dug assembly trenches causing heavy casualties among the waiting Scottish. Nonetheless, many in the British lines openly pitied the Germans, whom they assumed had largely been slaughtered in the preceding days. When, at 7.20a.m., the mine at La Boiselle was blown, few believed that anyone could be alive in the German positions. Nothing could have been further from the truth. Realizing that 1 July was the day destined for the attack, and warned of its imminence by the mine, they swarmed from the comparative safety of their underground burrows as soon as the barrage ceased, and within seconds of the advance beginning were ready.

The attack by 46th North Midlands Division to the left fared disastrously. As the Staffords and Sherwood Foresters moved out of their assembly trenches they were caught by a heavy barrage and the leading platoons annihilated. As the advance continued through the shower of shells the enemy managed to bring their heavy machine guns into action mowing down the survivors. A handful of men pressed on into Gommecourt village, only to be cut off and killed or captured, but everywhere else the attack was held from the outset. Its failure was soon apparent to the Germans who were then able to devote their entire attention to overwhelming the assault on the right.

The attack of the 56th Division thus became isolated. It received little help from the beleaguered 46th Division to the left, and as there was a gap of some five miles between itself and the left hand position of the 10th Division operating against the trenches at Serre, it received none from the right. The London Scottish were on the extreme right of the attack, with A Company almost on the line of the Hebuterne-Puisieux Road. As A and D Companies pushed forward into the smoke cloud they found it far denser than had been anticipated, and it became no easy matter to keep direction, particularly as the advance through the initial 300 yards of no man's land was made under the murderous umbrella of a heavy enemy artillery barrage.

A Company, under command of Captain Sparks, fared worst. No 2 Platoon leading, lost its direction in the smoke cloud and veered away to the right, only two or three men rejoining the Battalion in the German lines, the rest being either killed in no man's land or captured. Initially No 3 Platoon followed, and was eventually caught by a shell before running up against

A war torn landscape, where once stood the village of La Boiselle. Taylor Library

uncut wire. Only Lieutenant Petrie and a few men eventually reached the German trenches. The two platoons following were more successful, and although they found the wire to their front uncut, discovered a patrol path through and were thus able to enter the enemy front line without further molestation.

B Company, under Major Francis Lindsay, could see nothing as it advanced, so dense was the smoke. It found the wire to its front completely destroyed and the trenches beyond badly battered. It was able to push forward to its first objective, Fame Trench, which it found abandoned, and began to consolidate. On its right Sparks was by now blocking the enemy approaches on his flank, and was establishing fire positions in the communication trenches between them. Ominously, the German bombers and snipers were already beginning to probe the vulnerable flanks as a prelude to a counter attack.

Henry Smith, one of only two members of 8 Platoon, B Company, to survive unscathed recalled:

'Many killed and wounded before we "went over." Zero hour 7.30a.m. then "over the top and the best of luck." No. 8 Platoon leading the Company. Reached the German front line to find our bombardment had driven them back to their second line. Went on to their second line. Tremendous hand-to-hand fighting and here I killed my first German - shot him clean through the forehead and sent his hat spinning in the air. Just afterwards I killed two more. Bombs and bullets by the thousand and the ground blowing up under our feet. Awful sights and fearful casualties. Our Platoon Commander, Lieutenant Curror, killed, and all other NCOs of No. 8 either killed or wounded. I was the only NCO left. Went onto the third line, having driven the Huns back further. Started to consolidate the trench and hold it. I killed three more Germans here, making my total bag six. Realised that we were in for it as the Scottish were out there alone.'

Nos 11 and 12 Platoons, leading C Company under command of Major Claud Low, also found the wire cut and took the first German lines without opposition. Nos 9 and 10 Platoons following, found their way barred by a number of Germans who had left the protection of their dugouts only after the first wave of the assault had passed. These they dispatched with the bomb and bayonet before proceeding towards Farmyard and Farmer Trenches which were by then the subject of a heavy enemy barrage. Shortly thereafter Lowe was badly wounded and command passed to Lieutenant Lamb who later noted that,

'Our bombardment has been so severe that it was impossible to distinguish the Hun trenches, which were all linked up by shell holes outside. I asked Major Low if he knew what trench we were in. He was not certain, but thought it was Farm. As the smoke was still thick it was not possible to see many yards in front.'

He was actually in Fable Trench, which meant that C Company had borne to the right and was now in part forward and to the right of B Company. Sending his wounded commander back, Lamb took two platoons approximately 120 yards forward to reach Fable Trench, but as the smoke cleared he found that he had gone far too far forward and was now in the direct line of heavy machine-gun fire from higher ground. The remnants of the Company returned fire as best they could and withdrew in small parties to Fable Trench where they began to consolidate. At 7.55a.m., only twenty-five minutes after leaving the dubious protection of his own trenches, Lamb sent a runner to Headquarters advising that he was the only officer remaining, that he had no senior NCOs, and that the Company had been reduced to sixty other ranks.

D Company, under command of Lieutenant Brown-Constable and on the extreme left of the attack, fared worst. No 16 Platoon was almost completely destroyed by shell fire in the assembly trenches. Private Bliss, who had recently served in that Platoon, noted his good luck in having been ordered back to the new command trench which was out of immediate enemy range.

'The very ground rose and fell, jolted and bounced under the hail
of shell. Sandbags, limbs and debris flew into the air.'

No 13 Platoon, which led the advance, reached Farmyard Trench to find the wire ahead completely uncut and the trench itself held by bombers and snipers. When No 14 Platoon came up with Brown-Constable and his headquarters, a way was found round or through the wire and the Germans were driven back. Brief contact was made with the Rangers to the left but quickly lost. The Company, by now reinforced by No 15 Platoon, continued

These German soldiers of the 55th Regiment, rest in Gommecourt village on the night of 1 July, after the British offensive. Taylor Library

its advance along a communication trench and over two more trench lines. A third trench was taken but at considerable loss, particularly on the left flank which was exposed to enemy rifle fire. The remnants of the Company made an attempt to push on to the fourth trench but were met by a counter attack of enemy bombers forcing the survivors to withdraw to the third trench which they held with great difficulty, harassed by snipers and bombers from the front and exposed left flank. The Officer Commanding was killed, it is believed on the initial assault on the third trench.

'The order was passed along,' reported Bliss. *'Fix bayonets and wait for the whistle to advance. The hiss of the bayonets being withdrawn from their scabbards, followed by the metallic clip-clack as they were secured on the rifles, brought a sense of relief after the waiting. Thinking of the possibilities of things to come, I released the safety catch of my rifle, pulled back the well-oiled bolt to test the spring of the magazine with the thumb on the cartridges, closed the bolt home with a snap to guide a cartridge into the barrel, muttering "One up the spout for the big fellow."'*

A Company, by now reduced to half strength, was meanwhile busy securing the right flank. Only one officer and a few men of No 3 Platoon, and an NCO and two or three men of No 2 Platoon had reached their assigned position and losses had been sustained by the platoons in support. The communication trench between Fair and Fancy Trenches was consolidated as a fire-trench facing to the south and east, while the Royal Engineers succeeded in blowing in and trimming off four traverses to establish two barricades. Lance Corporal Aitken led a bombing party into Fair Trench, clearing it of the enemy. As the Official History records,

'All this was undertaken under continual bombing attacks from the flank, harassing fire of snipers, and a rain of high-explosive shells, which were bursting over the whole of the ground into which the attack had penetrated. The position was thus not only systematically bombarded, but also a heavy barrage was maintained on No Man's Land in rear of the attack, rendering it difficult to send even a runner, and still more to get supplies through to the Scottish in the German lines.'

Lance Corporal Richardson and his machine guns did not go forward until the first positions were taken.

'From my position' he noted, *'I could see the battalion advancing, with the brown kilts swinging across the broken ground, and they went forward, as they did in Richmond Park, with a perfect line.'*

Richardson did not have long to wait before the first positions were reported carried and he was ordered forward.

'The trench ladders had all been smashed, and it was no easy matter to climb over the parapet carrying a machine gun and ammunition.'

Losses were sustained at once.

'We lost our first man while clearing the parapet. The open was

crossed by a series of short rushes, and we reached the enemy first line with our strength reduced to eight. This was serious, as we now had only two men to a gun.'

On his way back to the trenches to report the position Richardson saw that two of his guns were out of action, their crews having been killed or wounded.

'The number of wounded lying all about was appalling. Most of them had crawled into shell holes and were smoking. One man had lost his left arm, and I helped him back. The peculiar thing was that he felt no pain, but was concerned about his sound arm, as he said he could not get it into a comfortable position.'

By 8.00a.m. the position was critical. The enemy had completely neutralized the 46th Division on the British left and was thus able to concentrate his entire resources against the 56th Division. On the immediate left of the Scottish only portions of other battalions had occasionally managed to penetrate the German lines, and these had quickly been neutralized. A mere remnant of D Company was holding on to the left flank in Fall Trench; Major Lindsay, with B and C Companies, was holding a line well to the front in Fame Trench and in the west end of Fable, while to the right A Company held the trenches running back to the junction of Fair and Farmyard. The Germans were attacking everywhere with bombing parties, snipers and machine-gunners and, despite the efforts of the Royal Artillery to suppress hostile fire there was no slackening of the bombardment by enemy howitzers and field guns. The hopelessness of the position was further compounded by the isolation caused by the barrage in no man's land and by the fact that the Scottish positions were in many places overlooked by the enemy on higher ground. Having made his report Richardson made a further perilous crossing of no man's land in an attempt to locate his two remaining guns. He remembered that efforts were made to send up supplies and ammunition but for the most part these failed, leaving the beleaguered troops in the front positions with nothing but their resources to keep them alive.

In B Company, Henry Smith remembered that;

'Our supports could not come up owing to the terrific curtain of fire the Germans were putting up in no man's land. We had Germans in the same trench as us on both sides and they started to bomb us from both sides, gradually hemming us in closer and closer. We hung on until all our bombs and ammunition was exhausted. We then retired to the German second line and had a bit of fun sniping at the devils, but could do no good, so the order passed along to get back to our own lines as best we could. Many of our wounded pals had to be left behind.'

Some of the Scottish wounded came in through the barrage, and twenty-five German prisoners, some of them wounded, were sent in. Among the wounded was Private Bliss.

'*A blow from a giant sledge hammer hit me on the left side which sent me staggering. A machine-gun bullet had pierced my left upper arm just missing the bone but severing a nerve and tearing another. As the useless hand released the rifle, the reflex muscular reaction slung the arm around the back of my neck. The body, unconscious from shock, folded up in a ball to squat on its feet and remained there, anchored by the death-like grip of the right hand on the heavy rifle on the ground in front.*'

Bliss lost consciousness, but when he recovered was able to pick his way through the torn ground to the comparative safety of his old front line.

'*I got to the top of the trench and looked around. I hadn't the strength to climb down into the trench. I hadn't the strength to jump across. I looked to see if there was anyone who could help me.*'

Smith was more lucky.

'*We rushed along what was left of a German communication trench to the old German front line, having to clamber over a shell crater on the way on which the Germans had trained a machine-gun. As each man went over he was either killed or wounded. When my turn came I flung myself over and fell on to a heap of bodies, but they had not hit me. The worst part of all followed, getting back to our own lines, a distance of 300 yards across no man's land. Shells dropping every square yard of ground and machine-gun bullets whistling everywhere. The din was deafening and literally Hell let loose. Made wild dashes from shell hole to shell hole and crawling along on my tummy. Stopped to bandage up two of our boys lying in a shell hole wounded. Took me three-quarters of an hour to cross that Hell-on-earth. Don't know how I escaped death.*'

Towards 9.00a.m. the Rangers' right was driven back towards the German front trenches leaving the Scottish left dangerously exposed. Fame Trench quickly became untenable forcing Major Lindsay to withdraw what was left of his two companies to the line of Farm and Fall Trenches. Fire positions were found for the men, the Lewis guns were brought into action and blocks were organized in the flank. Three trench parties were made up from those still in the British lines and sent forward carrying bombs, small arms ammunition and three Lewis guns, but so intense was the enemy barrage on no man's land that only three of the fifty-nine men involved got through. At 10.30a.m. Lieutenant F.S. Thomson, attached to the 168th Brigade Machine Gun Company, went forward through the barrage and successfully positioned one of his guns in the A Company front line.

As the day progressed the position on the left became more serious. The Rangers were being forced to fall back allowing the enemy to attack Fall Trench with enhanced determination. A party of snipers on the flank maintained a deadly fire into the Scottish trenches while enemy bombers attempted to get round to the rear. Reinforcements from the Kensingtons did their best to help but very few got through the barrage. At about

2.00p.m. the Scottish were reinforced by a mixed party of Kensingtons, Victorias and Rangers driven in from the left, and were later joined by more of the Kensingtons who brought with them five boxes of bombs, a welcome if scanty supply.

At 2.15p.m. Major Lindsay, who for nearly seven hours had so valiantly organized and directed the defence of the captured ground, was shot through the head by a sniper and died instantly. Captain Sparks then took command of the rapidly deteriorating position. The Scottish were now in a salient with both flanks under severe pressure. They were virtually out of ammunition, the enemy was working round to the rear and they were cut off from all help by the barrage. There was an eager search for ammunition on the dead and wounded, and captured German rifles were brought into action against their former owners but even so the volume of fire decreased.

The Regimental History notes that at 4.00p.m. there was little ammunition left, the Battalion had been reduced by losses to a mere handful of tired men, the left was in the air and there were unceasing attacks on both flanks. Realizing that the position had become untenable, Captain Sparks decided to withdraw. Before doing so he sent back the following message:

'I am faced with this position.

I have collected all bombs and S.A.A. from casualties. Every one has been used.

I am faced with three alternatives:

(a) To stay here with such of my men as are alive and be killed.

(b) To surrender to the enemy.

(c) To withdraw such of my men as I can.

Either of these first two alternatives is distasteful to me. I propose to adopt the latter.'

Orders were given for the methodical evacuation of the captured trenches. Arrangements were made for the recovery of such of the wounded as could move. A final stand covering the exit from the trenches was made by a party of five; Captain Sparks, Serjeants Latham and Leggatt, and Corporals Fairman and Weston. Richardson was serving the machine gun when Lieutenant Thomson order its evacuation from the A Company position.

'The passage was decidedly rough, as we had literally to slide into and clamber out of shell holes, hugging a machine gun. The man who was with me received a slight wound in his arm at this point. About twenty-five yards from our trench a very small piece of shrapnel lodged itself in my thumb joint. I could find no assistance to get the gun back to our lines, and with my damaged thumb I could not carry it myself, so I had to leave it in no man's land. I removed the vital parts, the lock and feeding block, and then placed a Mill's Bomb in the breach, released the pin and got away as quickly as possible.'

Thomson, about fifty yards after leaving the front line turned to fire a last shot at the enemy with a captured German rifle, and was himself hit and killed. Serjeants Latham and Leggatt were killed in the same shell hole.

Many of the survivors, including Captain Sparks and Lieutenant White who remained in the cover of a shell hole, did not get back until after dark.

The Battalion reformed in the old British front line, some way behind the forming up point, on the road to Puisieux. Of the 856 all ranks who had gone into action that morning a mere 9 officers and 257 other ranks survived. Richardson, writing some years later, caught well the mood of the moment.

> 'Our original front line was by this time levelled and an absolute shambles. I saw a number of my friends lying there whose names appeared later in The Times among the costs of the conflict; wounded waiting to be removed, and all kinds of equipment which had been discarded by the wounded. Everything was now comparatively quiet, and as I could not find my Headquarters I assisted in removing the wounded. We were relieved by the reserve battalion about 7.00p.m., and I spent the greater part of the next two hours looking for my Company. At 9.30p.m., the Boche treated us to a most unhealthy bombardment of gas shells, and an old brewery was set on fire. The building had been converted to the mere Christian use of a Dressing Station, and it was a heart-breaking sight to see the wounded coming out. I eventually crept into a battered cellar about midnight and slept during the next fourteen hours. I did not find my section for three days, and as a result was posted on the "missing" list.'

The British attack on 1 July had been universally a disaster. From Gommecourt for eight miles until the Ancre there had been a failure to capture strong natural positions, elaborately prepared for defence, and the losses everywhere had been heavy. Further south a few British divisions, and beyond them the French, had taken considerable ground against weaker German defences. No one could have done more that day than the London Scottish, a fact recognized by the General Officer Commanding in his Divisional Order published the next morning.

> 'I cannot congratulate you on making a name for yourselves on 1 July - that had been already done - but I want to express to all ranks of the London Scottish my sincere thanks for the glorious example of dash and heroism which they set to all arms of the service who were in action with you yesterday.'

The Commanding Officer, in prefacing this Order, wrote,

> 'I wish to express to all ranks my supreme admiration of the conduct of the battalion in the action of the 1st inst. The great traditions of which we are all so proud were maintained and added to, while the individual feats of heroism will be handed down to history. Though I deplore the loss of so many brave men I feel that those who remain will carry on and will add to the splendid history of the Regiment.'

Richardson summed up his and his colleagues feelings in a few words.

> 'Every man who was in the assault of the Somme knows that

heroism and sacrifice were not the monopoly of one battalion in action. All did great things that day, and every man was as proud of his battalion as I was of mine.'

The true losses of the first day of the Somme, nearly 20,000 killed and a further 40,000 wounded, were not published at once for fear of the effect that they would have on civilian morale. Instead, the casualty lists were released in stages, leaving some to learn over a period the true extent of their bereavement. Two weeks later, on 14 July, *The Times* published the following article:

'The part played by the London Territorial battalions in the great attack of July 1 is gradually becoming known in London. The Division, which included the Rangers, the London Scottish, the Queen's Westminster Rifles, and other battalions of the London Regiment, were in the line where the battle was violent, and we were unable to retain portions of the ground gained in our first attacks.

'We understand that when the order for the advance was given the London Territorials attacked with an irresistible fury and penetrated to the third German line. The enemy, it is stated, had amassed piles of ammunition and many guns in this sector in preparation for the attack, and our men suffered heavily in the advance. Later, owing to the barrage put behind them by the enemy, supplies were unable to get up, and the troops underwent the mortification of having to retire from the ground they had won, again losing many men and officers as they fell back.'

The Battle Continued

Survivors, most of them wounded, continued to make their way to the lines over the next three nights, the last of them, CSM Bell of A Company, reaching the British lines on the 3rd. He had been wounded in the leg before the advance from the assembly trenches, but after medical treatment had gone over with B Company. He had been separated from his comrades during the withdrawal, and for two nights and a day had lain in a shell hole feigning death to avoid capture. Those who were taken prisoner were universally well treated by the Prussians.

On the evening of the battle the remnants of the Battalion moved to Sailly where they were rejoined by the officers and NCOs who had been kept out of the fight to form a reserve. When the next afternoon it formed up to march back to Souastre, it was about 300 strong. They were shelled as they marched off and the Medical Officer, Captain Glover, who had striven so valiantly to save the lives of the many wounded, was himself hit, though not seriously.

'Felt a bit better after a good sleep,' remembered Henry Smith. *'Remnants of the Battalion lined up at 1.45p.m. Pitiful roll-call. Marched off to Souastre - our pipers met us along the route and played us the rest of the way. Many of our boys (me too) on verge of tears*

through the reaction. Arrived at Souastre about 4.00p.m. and got a wonderful and overwhelming reception from the other "Tommies" there. They lined the road and cheered us like mad. We learned afterwards that news of our attack had gone right down the line.'

Such were the number of casualties that many of the wounded had to move from clearing station to clearing station before being treated. When Bliss was at last seen it was discovered that a bullet had passed through his arm, tearing the flesh but not shattering the bone. Others were less fortunate. As he waited for his details to be taken prior to evacuation home, Bliss and a colleague were confronted by an appalling sight.

'Rows of bodies, some rolled in blankets, some slightly moving. Cases that couldn't be helped, already half dead and suffering with gangrene. Cases that had been brought all the distance from the line before the attack. That had been the anxiety of their comrades, the care of the stretcher-bearers. All the sweat and toil of the men and the care of the Doctors brought to naught. Virile bodies brought to nothing but a slug on the ground.'

The Scottish remained for only a few hours at Souastre before marching to Foncquevillers en route for the trenches facing Gommecourt. The line was far from secure and on the 3 July the weather broke, but at least the enemy was quiet and the Battalion gradually grew in strength as it was rejoined by the slightly wounded and by those on detached duties. After living in liquid mud for three days the survivors were relieved by the Queen Victoria's Rifles and went back to Souastre for four days' rest.

'The village was a mere shell of its former self,' Richardson remembered, *'and I am sure that there was not a wall which escaped the enemy fire. The Church which, before the 1st, was untouched, now resembled a gigantic heap of stones. The Crucifix alone stood as before. The only Cross I saw brought down by gun fire was at Neuve Chappelle, but the figure of the Christ was intact.'*

On 10 July the Battalion was again brought into the line, relieving the 7th Middlesex in the old trenches in front of Hebuterne, facing the southern part of the Gommecourt position. Heavy rain following on the bombardment had reduced the trenches to a very bad condition forcing the men to stand up to their knees in mud and water in places.

On 7 August 1916 the *Daily Graphic* reported;

'A landmark in the history of the London Scottish is the announcement that by Royal warrant, dated July 12th, the regiment is affiliated to the Gordon Highlanders. In the old incongruous days the Scottish were affiliated to the Rifle Brigade, an English regiment. Now they are affiliated to a regiment with which they have complete affinity.'

The sector now held by the Scottish was vastly different to that adopted before the battle. The new advanced trenches were now largely abandoned, the main force occupying the old French positions to the rear. At night sentry groups and patrols went forward to cover the dangerous and gruesome work of reconstruction. A raid was organized for 16 July to be carried out by B Company under command of Captain MacGregor. However, the artillery announced it with a burst of fire which put the enemy on alert. No man's land was swept with tremendous machine-gun fire making it impossible for the raid to be pressed home, causing it to end with the blowing of some enemy wire and a brief bombing exchange. Gradually the position was consolidated, although the front line was still only held by sentry groups when the Battalion left the sector.

On 17 July the Battalion was relieved by the 4th Londons and went into Divisional reserve at Bayencourt where it was joined by a draft of 200, many from the Argyll and Sutherland Highlanders. Six days later the Scottish returned to the Hebuterne trenches and for a week continued to consolidate them until again relieved by the 4th Londons. From there they were sent as Brigade reserve to Sailly until 4 August when they were again in the Hebuterne trenches.

> 'We passed through many places the names of which I have forgotten,' recalled Richardson. 'At Cobie where we detrained, I saw a large Red Cross Train and no optimist could call the remarks of the wounded encouraging. The first night we were billeted in this town, and the following three nights at the "Citadel", which was, I think, officially known as Camp 13. This was literally a mud camp. The Somme! ... Our first night in the camp there, when packed eighteen to a bell tent, we were washed out by a thunder storm. How we slept, I cannot remember - probably in layers or relays. On the fourth night our passage towards the line through our own artillery blazing away at and blasting the Hun, I shall never forget; the thunder of the guns wheel to wheel in the open, and the crash and rip of exploding shells, the squadrons of aeroplanes, divisions of cavalry, then the wounded, the unburied dead, the disinterred bodies of those who had been suddenly engulfed and of those whom kindly hands had laid to rest, the nerve shattering scenes of the debris of life and property - one comes down from the glory and sacrifice of it all to the senseless folly of war.'

On 16 August it was at last announced that the remnants of 56th Division would be relieved by 17th Division. The 10th West Yorkshires took over the line, allowing the Scottish to march back to Bayencourt en route for the rail head at Doullens and from thence to Drucat. The Division now ceased to form part of the Seventh Corps, and went into a period of training for the main offensive which for the last seven weeks had succeeded at massive loss to push the enemy back, in places less than a mile, towards the Bapaume Ridge.

Prior to handing over command, the General Officer Commanding 7th Corps sent the following farewell message:

> 'The Lieutenant General Commanding the Seventh Corps, in saying

goodbye to the 56th Division on their leaving the Corps, desires to record his appreciation of the manner in which the Division has fought and worked while it has been with the Seventh Corps. The gallant manner in which the Division fought at Gommecourt will be appreciated in history, but the Corps Commander wishes the Division to know that the less spectacular but more irksome work which the Division has put into the line which they have been holding, has not escaped notice. It is invidious to make distinctions where all have worked so well, but he particularly congratulates those units who have so far repaired that part of the line knocked about in the fighting of the 1st of July.'

The Last Phase of the Somme Battle

Major James Lindsay, who had recently assumed command from Colonel Green who had had to go into hospital, was given a fairly free hand in planning his training programme, save that a minimum period of six hours thirty minutes work per day was stipulated. The ground was far from ideal, the training ground was two miles from the billets and sown with crops which had to be paid for if damaged. As part of a general reorganization Captain Paterson MC, who had acted as Adjutant since May 1915, was promoted second-in-command and his place taken by Lieutenant Douglas. The Chaplain, the Reverend J. S. Stewart, who had been with the Battalion since March 1915, was relieved by the Reverend D. C. Lusk. While at Drucat the Battalion was taken to see a squadron of 'tanks'. These were extremely slow, going at the rate of only twenty yards per minute, making it virtually impossible to combine their movements with an infantry advance. Nevertheless the Scottish tried, but by the time of their departure on 31 August, had failed to resolve the problem.

When the London Scottish received orders to move at 5.00a.m. it was to

Robert Alexander, seated centre, late 1916 or early 1917. He was badly wounded in the right shoulder at Gommecourt and evacuated to the United Kingdom.

Private G.S. Plant. Joined the 3rd Battalion in 1915 and was posted to the 1st Battalion on 12 June 1916. Wounded in December 1916, he transferred to the Royal Flying Corps on 11 March 1918.

an unnamed destination. This proved to be Ville-sur-Corbie, from where the Battalion marched to Sailly-au-Bois, arriving at about 4.00p.m. 'Rotten march from Corbie,' remembered Henry Smith, 'took wrong road.' On Sunday 3 September a Church Parade was interrupted by sudden orders to move, on this occasion via a long route march to Fricourt. The Scottish were now on the old battlefield of the first days of the Somme. Northwards the German front was still intact from Gommecourt to Thiepval, but to the south considerable ground had been taken in continuous fighting, albeit at heavy cost. From Thiepval the British line ran along the crest of the ridge beyond Pozieres, and then followed the line of heights to Guillemont. Beyond this the Germans held the high ground about Morval and around Combles. Here the German line extended into a strong salient, the front curving round the entrenched farm of Falfemont, with a spur crowned by the woods at Leuze and Bouleaux to the west. Beyond this salient the French held the line, running south across the Somme by Cléry to the high ground opposite Péronne. In this sector the immediate Allied objective was the capture of Falfemont Farm and the woods and thereafter to envelop Combles. This would straighten out the line as a prelude to a major assault from Pozieres to the Bapaume-Péronne Road.

On 3 September the British took Guillemont and pushed on towards Falfemont Farm while the French took Le Forest and advanced towards the southern outskirts of Combles. The next day the Germans counter-attacked without success, and that night in torrents of rain were pushed out of Falfemont Farm.

Considerable ground was taken from Gommecourt to Thiepval but at heavy cost. Here stretcher bearers carry wounded in Thiepval village. Taylor Library

The shattered remains of Main Street in the village of Combles. Taylor Library

The stage was set for an attack on Leuze Wood.

On the morning of 5 September the London Scottish were temporarily attached to the 5th Division and told that they would remain where they were for the day. But shortly after midday they were ordered to move at once, and in the pouring rain were directed to march on to Chimpanzee Trench near Maricourt, and there report to the 95th Brigade. Movement was never easy and as they approached the trenches at about 7.00p.m. they came under long-range shell fire. New orders were now received. Packs were dumped and battle stores issued before the Battalion moved forward to relieve the 2nd East Surreys in Leuze Wood, where they had been fighting all day. The relief proved to be fraught and was not completed until daylight. The Brigade provided two officers to take the Battalion to a point where they would meet the East Surrey's guides. It quickly became obvious that they did not know the way and all were quickly lost. It was only when one of the officers reconnoitred forward that the location was found. It was

The remains of a captured German gun emplacement at Combles. Taylor Library

far from uncommon for men to lose their way in a part of the line where there were no natural features to guide them, where for hundreds of square miles the country had been swept bare. As the *Official History* of the 56th Division reported, '*The Somme field of battle was the most hideous place and absolutely bewildering. A guide was a treacherous person to trust, or perhaps we should say he was a broken reed to lean on; for the poor fellow had no treacherous intent in his heart, he was anxious enough to lead troops in the right direction, but nine times out of ten was completely lost a few minutes after he started. And there were, perhaps, more mistakes made in attempting to trace the front line in that great battle than in any other.*' Henry Smith was less charitable.

> '*Sudden pack up and moved up the line. Raining and cold. Messing about all over the place. Our ration party blown up - Dodd, Hutchins, Fyffe, Andrews and others killed. Wandering about communication trenches all night - what a guide.*'

Richardson wrily remembered an incident a few days later when,

> '*I was stopped in the early morning by a Brigade General and a Staff Captain, both very excited. The former asked me if I knew where his brigade was. Think of it! A Brigadier losing about 3,000 men! A Tommy might well be excused for losing his way! However, we gained that day, as this Officer in looking for his Brigade was captured by the Germans!*'

The Scottish were to relieve the Surreys in the support line in the wood, some companies of the Royal Irish Rifles being further forward in contact with the enemy. There were however no formal trenches as the Surreys were simply occupying the positions which they had reached in the battle. During the day the wood was heavily shelled. As dusk descended C and D Companies were ordered to relieve the Irish in the front line. As they did so the Germans put a heavy barrage down on the British right and put in a counter-attack against the French who had been attacking south of Combles during the afternoon. The Irish Rifles suffered heavy casualties but held on, A Company of the Scottish coming to their rescue. The Germans pressed in between them and the support line causing a report to reach Battalion headquarters that the wood was lost. Soon, however, it became clear that this was not the case and that the Germans had been held. C Company was thereafter ordered to move directly on the wood; D Company round its western flank. They had hardly started when the enemy's barrage suddenly lifted as they broke off their attack. A and B Companies had held, but at considerable loss including Captain Ellis, commanding B Company, who was badly wounded. An attempt was made to dig a trench on the edge of Bouleaux Wood, and that morning a platoon was sent forward to complete the work. It was successfully carried out, and the covering party managed to inflict a good many casualties on the enemy, Serjeant Smith of B Company killing eight and capturing a further three.

> '*Nasty place this,*' noted Henry Smith (by now promoted to

Serjeant). '*Continuous bombardment. More of our boys killed and wounded. Kensingtons joined us in the line. Advanced under cover of darkness to what we thought was an abandoned trench - when we got there we found it full of Germans. Very hot time till we got back.*'

The 56th Division now took over the sector from the 5th Division and the London Scottish again came under the orders of its parent 168th Brigade. On 8 September the Battalion was relieved by the Queen Victoria's Rifles and went into Brigade reserve at Maltzhorn Farm. On arrival at the Farm Colonel Lindsay was advised that the 16th (Irish) Division was to attack Guinchy with 56th Division assaulting to its right. The 168th Brigade was to occupy a strong point known as the Quadrilateral on the left of 56th Division in support of the Irish. They attacked with the 4th Londons on the right and the Rangers on the left. The Londons, pivoting on the north of Leuze Wood, gained their first objective under the close cover of the British barrage. The Rangers, however, came under heavy machine-gun fire from their left and were driven back to their point of departure. The London Scottish were in reserve, but about 8.00p.m. were ordered to send one company forward in support of the Kensingtons who were in Brigade support. C Company, under Captain Syer, was dispatched, and some two hours later information was received, erroneously, that the Irish had taken Guinchy and that the 168th Brigade had occupied its objective. However, a party of Germans was holding out in a trench between the Quadrilateral and Guinchy, and the Scottish were ordered to move to the left to link with

British soldiers await treatment for wounds received on the battlefield near Guinchy.
Taylor Library.

The awful aftermath of trench warfare. German soldiers lay where they were killed in a trench between Guinchy and Guillemont. Taylor Library

the Irish to cut off the enemy.

This operation proved extremely difficult as the ground had not been reconnoitred, the night was pitch dark and there was a thick fog. The companies moved off in succession led by Captain MacGregor of A Company. They advanced about 600 yards and then, failing to see any landmark, or recognize where they were, they halted and sent out patrols. The rear companies, by now completely disorientated, lost direction and joined the 4th Londons and Rangers on the right. The lead companies, before they reached their objective were attacked in the open. A fierce hand-to-hand fight ensued in which the enemy were driven off, but Captain MacGregor was killed and in the confusion they lost direction and returned to their starting point.

'*Moved up into the front line in the evening. Over the top again,*' reported Serjeant Smith.

'*Advanced in extended order. Tore both my legs on the German barbed wire - very painful, but carried on. Hellish shelling. Reached our objective but the Germans had bunked. Hellish time.*'

The Scottish made a second attempt to extend the line and eventually took up a position to the left of the Rangers. However, it became clear that the entire Quadrilateral had not been captured and that there was, therefore, no question of linking with the 16th Division. The Scottish carried on a bombing fight with the Germans throughout the next day and were hard-pressed to maintain their position, losing two other officers killed and 100 casualties from the other ranks.

'*Waiting for five hours to go over the top again,*' complained Smith. '*No go after all. Our position such that we had Germans in front and behind us. Posted sentries facing both ways. Three of them killed within an hour, so called for volunteers and stood up with them.*

Bombing raid on our left. We and the Germans bombing each other all day and plenty of shelling too.'

The Brigade was relieved in the evening, the London Scottish returning to Billon Farm as Divisional reserve. Richardson and his gun crew were cut off and forced to remain in their position overnight. Only later, when he successfully returned to his own lines, did he learn that he had been posted missing and that for over a day he had been holding a position officially in the German lines. Many of the wounded were forced to lay out in the open, seeking such protection as they could until stretcher parties were able to recover them four days later.

On 14 September the Scottish marched up to Angle Wood in preparation for a large-scale attack scheduled for the next day. The attack was to be launched by nine divisions along a front of more than seven miles, from near Pozieres on the left to beyond Leuze Wood on the right. Its objective was to be the enemy third line running along the reverse slope of the heights by Courcelette, through Flers to Morval. The attack had been preceeded by three days of intense bombardment and was to include an appearance for the first time of a squadron of tanks. On the left and centre the assault met with complete success, the line being carried forward for more than a mile on a front of over five miles, but on the right things were less successful.

Three divisions attacked on the right; the Guards from Guinchy towards Lesboeufs, the 6th against the Quadrilateral and the 56th on the extreme right against Bouleaux Wood with orders to form a defensive flank facing Combles. The 167th and 169th Brigades were to lead with the 168th Brigade in reserve. Two tanks were employed by the Brigade, but with little success. The Scottish remained in reserve throughout the day taking no part in the battle. They remained in their position for two days. Fighting was in progress to their front and in the direction of the Quadrilateral, and the artillery was active on both sides, but the only casualties sustained by the Scottish were caused by a premature burst of one of their own shells, which killed two men.

The after effects of an intense bombardment on Flers village. Taylor Library

'We moved to a position opposite Bouleaux Wood for the advance of September 15th,' remembered Richardson. *'Our duty was to carry this Wood, and we did enter and take it, but owing to a Division on our left being hung up our advance was checked. This was the first day the tanks came into action. It was a wonderful sight to see them crawling on like giant beetles and spitting fire from their sides. Had they been German tanks advancing on us I would not have been enjoying myself.'*

Late on the evening of 16 September Colonel Lindsay was informed that the Scottish, together with the 4th Londons, were to be lent to the 167th Brigade to carry out an attack the next morning on the northern edge of Bouleaux Wood. The weather broke that night making movement in the chalky terrain very difficult, so much so that by 4.00a.m., the time appointed for the two battalions to be in position, only the lead companies of the Scottish had arrived. The remaining companies were strung out en route with the Londons, who were following the same course, hardly out of their original trenches. Colonel Lindsay suggested that the Scottish attack alone, but by the time that agreement was attained it was too late and the attack was cancelled. Dispirited, and in many cases not a little confused, the Scottish returned to Angle Wood.

To the men, all was confusion.

'Turned out at 3.00a.m. and moved up to the front line,' remembered Serjeant Smith. *'Told we were going to attack at once. All waiting for the order to go over the top. Didn't come off. Came down again very wet and muddy. Raining hard. Everybody fed-up to the eyes. Back to our shell-holes again. Moved up to the front line again at 8.00p.m. What a business. B Company suffered heavy losses by German shelling from Leuze Wood.'*

Three days later he succumbed to his leg wounds, reported sick and was invalided back to England.

That night the Scottish relieved the London Rifle Brigade in the trenches north-east of Leuze Wood. The position, enfiladed as it was on the right by Bouleaux Wood and open on the left, there being no connection with the 5th Division on the flank, was far from satisfactory. Steps were taken to consolidate the area by digging a trench further forward, through Middle Copse, approximately 150 yards ahead of the existing, rather dilapidated trenches. While engaged in this duty Captain Syer, in command of D Company, was seriously wounded by a sniper, and two months later died of his injuries in England. He had been seconded to regimental duties in January, but after Gommecourt had voluntarily returned to the Battalion upon hearing that officers of experience were badly needed. His calm and reassuring presence was to be sorely missed. Shortly thereafter the Battalion was bolstered by some 200 transferees from the Glasgow Highlanders which had been broken up to provide casualty replacements elsewhere. It was felt unwise to try and incorporate the newcomers during the battle and they were therefore kept in reserve. During the next few days, however, the Battalion became so weak that fifty of the draft were brought in, the remainder undertaking excellent work as carrying parties.

As dawn approached on the morning of 24 September Richardson remembered being woken and advised that a man had been seen in the open, about thirty yards into no man's land.

'The sentry challenged him three times, but was not answered. My advice was to shoot the man. Anyone walking between the lines at dawn and not answering a challenge deserved to be shot. Our Section Officer, who was with us at the time, over ruled my suggestion, and countered it by ordering me out to see who it was. I did not at all relish the idea, but with my hand in my coat pocket grasping a revolver I left the trench. I got to within ten yards of the man before he saw me, and when he did he bolted like a frightened rabbit. I could not distinguish his uniform, but as he was carrying a pack I soon overtook him. To our mutual horror we found we were enemies. The quickest thing I ever did was to get that revolver out of my pocket. He immediately put his hands up and said something which sounded like "No, No!" He asked me if I was French, and when I replied that I was not, he enquired if I was English, and I also said "No" to this. My prisoner was now at a loss to know who or what I was. I informed him that I was Scottish, and to illustrate this I pulled up the feet of my greatcoat and exhibited bare knees. I believe the man's hair stood up on end at this information. The Germans were in mortal terror of the kilties, and this one was so frightened that he could not speak.'

The prisoner turned out to be a medical orderly who had lost his bearings. He was mightily relieved when he was returned unscathed to the Scottish trenches and thereafter packed-off, unmolested to the rear.

Later that day orders were received for a further attack the next day. This was to follow the pattern of the failed attack ten days earlier. The Guards, 5th, 6th and 21st Divisions were to capture Grandcourt, Lesboeufs and Morval while the 56th Division established a defensive flank facing Combles. That night the Scottish and 4th Londons returned to the new trenches which they had so labouriously dug a few days earlier. The move through the night was far from easy.

Richardson recalled,

'On the 25th we were on the programme for another "stunt". We left "Happy Valley" to take up our old position, our orders being to fire on Bouleaux Wood and so keep down the fire of enemy snipers. The distance from "Happy Valley" to our position was probably five miles, and I shall never forget that journey. We had to go, as it seemed to me, miles through communication trenches with liquid mud up to the thighs. Whatever you may think, this is no exaggeration. When I stood to rest, my kilt was floating in the slimy mess. As I had not experienced the joys of a bath or a clean change for nearly four

A general view of Morval, which was captured on 25 September.
Taylor Library

> *months, I was not too particular about the mud, but the physical energy necessary to move was abnormal. To cover this distance we were struggling for fifteen minutes short of twelve hours. Fortunately the enemy's shells were few and far between. I find it difficult to describe this journey, but it can be imagined; travelling in darkness, sometimes over the open and sometimes through trenches which not many days before, the Germans had used as burial grounds. They were pushed back so quickly that they had no time to bury their dead, and they had simply put them into the trenches, and in many cases had no time to cover them. It was ghastly, offensive to the senses and trying to the nerves.'*

The attack, which was scheduled for 12.35p.m., was to be led by C and A Companies, the latter bolstered by many of the Glasgow Highlanders. In support of the attack the 168th Brigade Trench Mortar Battery War Diary noted,

> *'25 Sep 1916 12.44p.m. 20 rds per gun were fired onto objective of LONDON SCOTTISH and ROYAL FUSILIERS immediately prior to infantry assault. 10 rds per gun were then fired ahead of the objective.'*

C Company, attacking a trench to the north of Bouleaux Wood, was successful. A Company, under Lieutenant Speak, fared less well and was quickly involved in a savage bombing duel. At one stage it is reported that the Bavarians manning the trenches before A Company resorted to subterfuge. A number of them stood up on the parapets, their hands in the air as if to surrender. As the Scottish approached with their guard down the enemy threw egg bombs secreted in their palms of their hands. Richardson, who while manning his machine gun had witnessed this, later retaliated, shooting dead a large number of Germans attempting to surrender. He was stopped by an officer from the Royal Fusiliers, placed under open arrest, subsequently court-martialled, reduced to the ranks and given six days Number One Field Punishment.

The Support Company lost its Officer Commanding, Captain McClellan, and second-in-command, Captain Wilson, and was thus unable to render immediate assistance to A Company. The reserve companies were ordered forward, but before they could come into action the Bavarians surrendered, three officers and forty-nine men being made prisoner. That night the enemy evacuated Bouleaux Wood and a day later abandoned Combles. The Scottish were thus completely successful in their endeavours, but at a loss of four officers and fifty other ranks killed or wounded. On the evening of 26 September the Scottish were relieved by the Kensingtons and went back to Falfemont Farm. The French took over the sector from 56th Division two days later, but this was not to lead to rest for the exhausted British. The London Scottish were moved back into the line at Le Transloy and ordered to dig a seven foot deep cable trench, a hard task made all the worse by atrocious weather.

On 4 October the Battalion was ordered to take over from the London Rifle Brigade in a new position close to Lesboeufs. The trenches were badly sighted, shallow, without communications and the subject of constant enemy shelling. On 5 October, while reconnoitring, Colonel Lindsay was hit by a sniper and seriously wounded. Major Paterson MC then assumed command and two days later led an attack on the German positions covering Le Transloy. The London Scottish were placed on the right flank of the attack in liaison with a French battalion from their 56th Division, also attacking because so many of the Scottish were able to speak French. The attack was made without the benefit of a preliminary barrage so as not to forfeit the benefit of surprise. B and C Companies assaulted in the first line with D in support and A in reserve. The Scottish took their objectives after fierce hand-to-hand fighting, but were left with both flanks in the air when neither the 4th Londons to their left nor the French to their right were able to take theirs. Losses were severe, with B Company reduced to an officer and eighteen men, before the entire Battalion was forced to retire.

On the night of 8 October 56th Division was withdrawn from the line and took no further part in the battle. After a long march it reached Fremont, near Amiens, where it was awarded ten days' rest to refit, reorganize and train. Between 6 September and 7 October the Battalion had suffered 531 casualties. If one added to these the losses of 1 July the total exceeded 1,000 including over fifty officers. The Brigade Commander wrote after the battle the following 'Lessons to be deducted from the Operations on the Somme.'

> *'The results of the operation carried out by this brigade bear out more than ever the necessity for an assault being made direct at the objective. Failures, or partial failures, are attributable to present-day troops being asked to perform complicated manoeuvres such as a wheel or change of direction during an assault.*

'The objectives allocated should be as far as possible definite, and should be chosen on the ground so that well defined landmarks may be included. With the heavy casualties which occur among officers, and considering the partially trained state of NCOs and men, it is seldom any use leaving the site of the objective to the judgement of the assaulting troops.

'In order to comply with this suggestion, it is essential that a proper scheme of assembly trenches should be thought out, and proper time given for their construction even in the rapid advances which have been taking place.

'As usual there was a complete lack of touch throughout the operations with the heavy artillery. It is thought that the artillery group system should be extended so as to include some heavy artillery.'

In the months ahead a few, but far from all, of his words would be heeded. One year later the *Regimental Gazette* recorded that, 'On the farthest point reached by the 1st Battalion in the Battle of the Somme, September 5 to October 8 1916, there was erected on the first anniversary of "Ours" entering the battle, a large memorial cross. For miles behind it and around it is a rolling moorland, pitted with the myriad shell holes of a year ago, and covered now with soft knee-deep green undergrowth. The cross is a plain one of two great beams and stands about eight feet high. At its base is a cairn in which is embedded a strong block of oak bearing a metal plate with the inscription:

"Sacred to the memory of the Officers, NCOs, and Men of the London Scottish, who fell in action in the Battle of the Somme, September 5 to October 8 1916.

"This cross is erected by the Battalion on the farthest point they reached. - September 5 1917."'

Chapter Six

The Battles of Cambrai and Arras

The Battle of the Somme, in effect a series of desperate attacks interspersed by periods of intensive bombardment, hard digging and vicious trench raids, petered out in the winter of 1916. By late October the Allies had broken through the third German trench system leaving the enemy secure on the Bapaume Ridge. Ground had been won, initially by the French and later by the British, but at a tremendous cost in lives. In one final attack the Highland Division and Naval Division stormed the stronghold of Beaumont Hamel, but otherwise the sector fell silent. Further south, around the Verdun salient, the French were gradually regaining the initiative. To the east matters were less secure. The enemy had overrun the Balkans and were probing deep into Russia. The Allies were advancing towards the frontiers of Palestine, but at Salonika there was deadlock compounded by sickness and disease.

Sir Douglas Haig wrote of the winter months:

'Certain outstanding features of the past five months' fighting call for brief comment before I close this Report. In spite of a season of unusual severity, a winter campaign has been conducted to a successful issue under most trying and arduous conditions. Activity on our battle-front has been maintained almost without a break from the conclusion of last year's offensive to the commencement of the present operations. The successful accomplishment of this part of our general plan has already enabled us to realize no inconsiderable instalment of the fruits of the Somme Battle, and has gone far to open the road to their full achievement. The courage and endurance of our troops have carried them triumphantly through a period of fighting of a particularly trying nature, in which

Lance Corporal Gordon William Davey; born 11 February 1898, severely wounded at Inchy November 1917, died (aged 19) in 3rd casualty Clearing Station at Grevillers on 3 December.

they have been subjected to the maximum of personal hardship and physical strain. I cannot speak too highly of the qualities displayed by all ranks of the Army.'

For their part the London Scottish spent the winter months in continuous and strenuous training away from the fighting. After its ten days rest and recreation at Fremont, the Battalion moved north with the rest of the 56th Division to take over the Laventie sector near the Belgian border. After an initial heavy bombardment the enemy left the sector in relative peace interrupted by frequent raids into no man's land so beloved of the British High Command. The usual routing comprised six days in the Farquissart sector, followed by six days in support at Laventie with an occasional break of twelve days out of the line in Divisional reserve. When in reserve the Battalion underwent steady training in company and battalion drill, physical drill, musketry, gas drill, bombing, bayonet fighting and route marches. A steady stream of replacements joined the Battalion and were quickly inculcated into its ways.

On 28 October tragedy struck when Corporal C. H. Anderson with five men was preparing for a patrol. Each had been supplied with two bombs and Anderson was showing the newcomers how to prime them. When he discovered that by some mischance the fuse in one had been set in action he quickly moved to the door with a view to throwing the bomb away. When the door jammed he pressed the bomb to his chest and his chest to the door. It exploded, mortally wounding him. But he had saved the lives of the others, none of whom was seriously injured.

In February 1917 Captain E. D. Jackson of the King's Own Scottish Borderers assumed command of the Battalion. He had links with the London Scottish, his father having served in its ranks in the 1860s. The early months of 1917 led the most optimistic to anticipate success. At Verdun the Germans, 'bled as white' as the French, called off their attack. In the north the high ground around Serre was taken and the flank of the Bapaume Ridge exposed. Virtually everywhere the Germans appeared to retire, surrendering ground over which for years they had fought tenaciously. What the Allies did not realize was that the Germans were withdrawing to pre-prepared positions on the Hindenburg Line, a tightly interlinked complex of fortified positions with only lightly-held trenches to the front. Unaware of its strength, the Allies planned to attack the Hindenburg Line, the British around Arras to the north and the French around the Aisne to the south.

The Battle of Arras

During the second week of March the 56th Division began to move southwards to take up its position for the new offensive. On 9 March the London Scottish were relieved in the line and moved into billets at Vieille Chapelle. The next day they marched to Merville and entrained for Doullens, from there marching into billets at Brevillers. On 12 March the

106

Battalion marched into Ivergny, where it was reinforced by a strong draft of officers. There followed a fortnight of strenuous training, designed to rid the men of their winter trench-routine complacency and prepare them for the combat ahead. While at Ivergny the officers were sent forward to reconnoitre for an attack on Beaurains, a strongly fortified village some two miles to the east, but before the attack could be mounted the enemy withdrew to the Hindenburg Line, allowing the 169th Brigade to occupy Beaurains unchallenged.

> 'Our stay at Ivergny was of a pleasant nature, and we had a spell of easy training,' recorded the D Company journal. 'While there we were joined by a draft of well known officers from the third (Third Battalion), viz., Captain Young, Captain W. Mackinnon, Second Lieutenants Crawford, McAskell, Fraser, and several others.'

On 23 March the Scottish moved to Gouy-en-Artois for three days training before moving to the ruined village of Agny, where they were attached to 169th Brigade for the purpose of digging assembly trenches opposite the village of Neuville Vitasse, one of the objectives in the forthcoming attack.

> 'The march from Ivergny to Agny was long and heavy, but accomplished in good style,' reported D Company. 'En route we passed the line Fritz had just a fortnight previously evacuated, and marched along roads which a few days previously had been only useable during the hours of darkness. Already in the villages French workmen were repairing the houses. Agny was the usual cumulation of ruins, and D Company was quartered in dug outs in a sunken road.'

Movement was restricted as far as possible by day to avoid the constant attention of German reconnaissance aircraft. However the nights were spent in strenuous labour. The trenches were two-and-a-half miles from the billets, requiring a march in darkness over slippery, narrow tracks, often harassed by enemy artillery. Casualties were nonetheless light for a number of days, until 28 May when A Company, while leaving Agny for the trenches, was hit by two shells. Ten men were killed outright and thirty-nine wounded, five of them fatally. Among the seriously wounded was Captain Worlock, the Officer Commanding, yet it is recorded that the rest of the Company pulled itself together and continued its journey to the trenches.

A young Second Lieutenant, new to the trenches, remembered the experience well.

> 'The night following, two companies (mine included) were ordered forward to dig a line of trenches in no man's land, and so get nearer the Hun. (Windy job for a new Sub.) We started at dark far up the line, crossed the British front line, spaced out our men, and then they began to dig. The enemy did not worry us so digging was good, and a new trench was dug about 2.5 feet deep. Next night we did the same, and by this time we were down four to five feet with good head cover. After our work we went down to reserve, and during the day watched the Hun 'planes come over and look at our new trench.

'One of our planes engaged three Huns and brought down one, much to our delight. The following night we went up to the front line, my platoon on the left flank nearest valley and river, and in consequence had to keep very strict watch. Everything O.K. British delivered gas attack on Huns on our left - great success. Next night I was ordered to take out a listening patrol, myself and three men. Went out at dark in front of our outposts about 200 yards. Returned O.K.'

On 1 April the Scottish went into reserve at Achicourt, and two days later relieved the Kensingtons in Brigade reserve in the old British front line. That night the British guns began their preparatory bombardment along a front of fourteen miles, from the western slopes of the Vimy Ridge southwards by Arras to the Cojeul valley.

'After about six days we moved to Achicourt,'
records the D Company journal;

'where we took up our abode in billets in the village, and subsequently in a shallow trench across the railway line. Nightly working parties were again our lot here. Gradually things began to assume a ship-shape look, and our artillery friends opened out a four-days' bombardment on April 4, and for the rest of our stay there we were living in a constant roar of guns of every calibre up to 12-inch Howitzers. On Easter Sunday afternoon Captain Lusk held a most impressive open air service, which was interrupted by some of Fritz's shrapnel occasionally bursting nearby, though such was the last thing one would have thought to judge from the Padre's absolute indifference to falling pieces. His conduct was the admiration of everyone.'

On 8 April, Easter Sunday, the barrage reached a crescendo, the prelude to the next day's attack. Nor were the German guns inactive. During the afternoon the village of Achicourt was heavily bombarded for several hours, causing severe damage to the British ammunition columns and stores. The London Scottish took up their position after darkness fell.

'Dusk that evening saw us on our way, each with his usual complement of impedimenta, the thought of which gives such point to Captain Bairnsfather's cartoon, showing Private Golightly arriving at the conclusion that this will be a war of exhaustion. After spending the night in the assembly trenches previously dug by us, we moved up the communication trench to our taking-off place. Our last experience in the line having been at Laventie sector, where there were good duck boards, it was a bit of a trial to suddenly land into the awful mud and

Canadians digging in on Vimy Ridge. Taylor Library

wet of these trenches. The suction power when one is loaded with buckets of Lewis gun ammunition, a spade, bombs, etc. is really past believing. At length we arrived at our destination, and within a few minutes of this our troubles began. We had three hours to wait our "curtain." It began to snow huge, soft flakes of wet snow, then Fritz began to put his barrage too near the parapet to be altogether pleasant, and, to crown all, we were gradually sinking into the all-pervading mud.'

Along most of the line the attack began at 5.30a.m. on Easter Monday, 9 April. On the left the Canadian Corps stormed the Vimy Ridge. In front of Arras the British had to attack the strong German lines two to three miles east of the city, the chief objective of the 56th Division being the village of Neuville Vitasse, some four miles south-east of Arras. The 168th Brigade was tasked with clearing the village itself, the 167th Brigade on the right was to attack the line to the south with 169th Brigade held in reserve. Haig planned that the attack be carried out by a succession of comparatively short advances, the separate stages of which were arranged to correspond approximately with the enemy's successive systems of defence. A short pause was scheduled for each stage to enable the troops continuing the assault to form up.

The advance of the 56th Division was scheduled for 7.30a.m. when the Rangers and Kensingtons, with the London Scottish in support and the 4th Londons in reserve, attacked towards the village. According to Haig's dispatches the earlier attack had taken all its objectives save for Observation Ridge and Railway Triangle from which the enemy were able to direct fire against the now advancing troops.

It was not until 11.30a.m. that the Scottish received the order to prepare to attack. Their objective, about 1,400 yards in front of the assembly trenches, was a part of the German line known as the Cojeul Switch, itself comprising three trenches; 'Telegraph Hill' in front, 'Card' in support and 'Back' in reserve. The Battalion advanced with three companies in the front line, each on the frontage of a platoon. The initial stage, across broken and muddy ground, was made in artillery formation under a steady shell fire.

'At last the order came along for overcoats to be dumped, and under the command of Captain Filchill... .16 Platoon "went over the top." For the first few hundred yards the going was pretty good, but soon we reached the zone which had received the brunt of our four days' bombardment, and then it was heavy going; this ground was also receiving the Hun 5.9 and machine-gun barrage. However, noon saw us in Neuville Vitasse, well up to schedule time and with few casualties. While resting there Captain Bishop caught a "Blighty" in the shoulder, and was with difficulty induced to remain behind.'

After a pause for regrouping in the village the three lead companies pushed on into open country. However, they quickly discovered that the barrage had lifted too quickly to be of much help and that Telegraph Hill, their immediate objective, was well defended. A Company experienced a tough but successful fight for Telegraph Hill before moving on to Card, and in the case of one platoon Back. D Company on the right completely overran its objectives and became separated from the rest of the advance, three of its platoons disappearing for a while into the Cojeul valley towards Wancourt. The 167th Brigade to the Company's right had been checked and it soon found itself in a dangerous position, all but cut off, and fired into by machine guns from the flank and right rear.

'Fritz was pounding salvoes of 5.9s into our position as well as sweeping it with machine-guns, and it was here that 16 Platoon "copt out," being so much decimated that the following day the few survivors were distributed amongst 13, 14 and 15 Platoons. A few of

*us who had managed to seek safety in some deep Hun trenches after
several hours wandering, fell in with the remainder of D Company,
who had established themselves in a portion of the famous
Hindenburg Line.'*

That afternoon the leading troops were forced out of Back Trench. C
Company was brought up to clear the position but, by the time they were
in position night was falling and they were unable to secure Back, their final
objective, until the next morning. Despite strong enemy resistance losses
among the Scottish were relatively light; three officers wounded, seventeen
soldiers killed, a further sixty-six wounded and four missing. A total of 290
German prisoners were taken together with two machine guns, a trench
mortar and a large quantity of ammunition.

*'After a period of digging and the usual consolidating work, some
of the deep German dug outs were explored, and many souvenirs of
their recent inhabitants secured. Equipment in great quantities,
together with a lot of great coats were found. Practically everyone
obtained a greatcoat and a "Hun wetter sheet", which was most
acceptable, as we had a heavy fall of snow that night which had to be
spent in the open trench.'*

The battle so far had gone well, particularly along the Vimy sector where
the Canadians had taken the ridge. Cavalry was brought up in the hopes of
exploiting a breakthrough but the wire ahead of the remaining enemy
positions proved too strong and they were withdrawn.

Early in the afternoon of 11 April the Scottish were relieved by the
Queen's Westminsters, and marched back through a driving snowstorm to
their assembly trenches, where they spent an uncomfortable night in
miserable wintery weather. The next morning they were ordered to re-
occupy the trenches vacated the day before to allow the Queen's
Westminsters to move forward to the ridge above Heninel. That day, with
the help of tanks, the villages of Wancourt and Heninel were taken in the
midst of a heavy snowstorm. Two days later the Scottish were moved to Hill
90 to assist the 167th Brigade in repelling an anticipated German counter
attack which did not materialize, and on 14 April were again ordered to
relieve the Queen's Westminsters in the front line. This was far from easy as
darkness was falling and there had been no time for a daylight recce.
Nonetheless the take over was completed by daybreak, and for the next
forty-eight hours the Battalion was set the task of improving the narrow
trenches by day and patrolling by night.

*'Fritz was shelling this spot in a desultory way when we arrived, but
at midnight he commenced in real earnest, and systematically shelled
the support line. Our casualties were exceedingly heavy during this
"strafe." It was then that Serjeants Hudson and Lock were buried. At
daybreak we moved into another portion of the sunken road, where
we spent the day. The afternoon proved a strenuous one for our nerves
again, for Fritz gave us a two-hour "dusting-up," during which*

Serjeant Reynolds was wounded, Serjeant Howse going down with shell shock, Corporal Nicholson being also wounded, Privates McClew and Starling being killed, as well as many others wounded.'

The Scottish were advised that they were to be relieved by the Kensingtons on 16 April, but the threat of a counter-attack compounded by a series of conflicting orders delayed the move for a day. The Battalion went back to the Cojeul Switch for two days, but a combination of atrocious weather made rest all but impossible. The Scottish were ordered back to Arras on 17 April by which time they had sustained one officer, Captain Crawford, killed and five wounded, twenty-six other ranks killed, 109 wounded and five missing, of whom two were later reported prisoners of war.

'The march down to Arras was a very trying one, owing to everyone being so thoroughly tired out, but when we found the Company piper waiting for us at Beaurains to "pipe" us the remainder of the way, it was remarkable to see the effort everyone made to "buck up," and D Company arrived at our billets in good spirits, though very tired and dirty, shaving and washing having been quite impossible during the whole period. The Company mustered about fifty-six after this entire episode.'

The first and main stage of the Battle of Arras was now over. The attack had been intended to draw the German reserves away from the French positions to the south, to enable General Nivelle to attack against the Aisne heights. The French offensive proved a disaster with few gains and enormous losses. Their advance came to a standstill, Nivelle was sacked, and his command given to Petain. When the French advance halted, the Battle of Arras ceased to have any meaning. Furthermore the British advance had reached a point at which communications and artillery support had become difficult. Moreover the German reserves from the south had enabled the enemy to recover from the temporary disorganization caused by the first British attacks. Haig accepted that further success without a return to more deliberate methods could not be anticipated without excessive loss.

On 25 April the London Scottish were sent by bus to Couin, from where they marched to billets at Coineux where they were rejoined by Major Claude Lowe as Second-in-Command. The Scottish were in dire need of a rest. They had been for more than ten days in the open without shelter from the weather, and with the exception of a few who had salvaged German coats from the enemy trenches had not even their greatcoats. These had been 'rescued' by a salvage party shortly after they had been discarded on 9 April, but unfortunately the carrying party sent back to meet them failed to do so. After only three days rest the Battalion was ordered to Gouy and from there to Simencourt. On 28 April they found themselves back again at Arras in Divisional reserve.

On 3 May another attack was launched along a sixteen mile front to make a diversion in favour of the French who were scheduled to renew their attack in the south two days later. Ground was gained initially, but after a series of spirited German counter-attacks largely lost. The 56th Division attacked on a front east of Arras, north of the Arras-Cambrai road. The 167th and 169th Brigades were sent forward, with the 168th Brigade in reserve. The London Scottish spent the day near Tilloy-lez-Mofflaines. During the night the 168th relieved the two forward brigades, the Scottish taking over the line just north of the Arras-Cambrai road, about six miles from Arras. The next few days were spent in consolidating the line, the chalk trenches of which made distinct aiming marks for the enemy artillery, which throughout the period was both active and accurate. The pipe band, then acting as stretcher bearers, suffered severe losses when their aid post received a direct hit from a high-explosive shell.

On 8 May the Battalion was relieved and moved back to the old German trenches near Wancourt. Two days later it returned to the front line, and on 11 May played its final part in the battle when it attacked an enemy position known as 'Tool Trench' immediately north of the Arras-Cambrai road. Three companies took part in the attack, which to maintain surprise was made in the dusk at 8.30p.m. without an artillery barrage. The ruse worked, and by the time the startled Germans were able to call for artillery support the Scottish had cleared their lines and were upon them. Most Germans fled without putting up serious resistance allowing the Scottish to take their objective with minimum initial losses. D Company, however, over ran its objective, which consisted of a line of shell-holes and was difficult to recognize in the dusk, and was caught by heavy machine-gun fire. Severe losses were sustained including two officers killed while the survivors withdrew to the correct position. A counter-attack that night and another the next day were both repulsed and on 13 May the Battalion was relieved. Six days later the 56th Division was replaced by the 37th Division and moved to the Berneville-Simencourt area.

British losses at Arras had been heavy while the French attack of 5 May against the Chemin des Dames proved disastrous. Yet Haig, in his dispatches, made it clear that he regarded the entire battle as a success:

> 'On the British front alone, in less than one month's fighting, we had captured over 19,500 prisoners, including over 400 officers, and had also taken 257 guns, including 98 heavy guns, with 464 machine-guns, 227 trench mortars, and immense quantities of other war material. Our line had been advanced to a greatest depth exceeding five miles on a total front of over twenty miles, representing a gain of some sixty square miles of territory. A great improvement had been effected in the general situation of our troops on the front attacked, and the capture of the Vimy Ridge had removed a constant menace to the security of the line.'

Haig now felt able to turn his full attention and to divert the bulk of his resources to the development of a new, vastly larger campaign further north across the Belgian border.

Messines and Passchendaele

On 8 June 1917 *The Daily Telegraph* reported, '*On Monday last there was published a flamboyant telegram from Kaiser Wilhelm to his Consort, in which the "War Lord" said:*

"According to the report of Field Marshal von Hindenburg the great British and French spring offensive has come to a definite end."

'*Once more his Majesty has proved both a perverter of the truth and a singularly unhappy prophet.*

'*At dawn yesterday morning there was launched on a front of nine miles a great British attack against the German positions on the famous ridge which begins about three and a half miles south of Ypres and runs southward past Wytschaete Village for about a mile and a half to Messines, where the London Scottish achieved immortal fame in the early stages of the war.*'

When it had become clear that Nivelle had not won through on the Chemin des Dames, plans were made for a British offensive in the north. General Herbert Plumer with the Second Army was tasked with clearing the Messines Ridge as a prelude to Haig launching an assault from the Ypres salient. The Fifth Army under Gough was gradually moved north in support. Rawlinson, with the Fourth Army, moved to the Belgian coast behind Nieuport, the Belgians themselves concentrated in the same area while the French held the line between them and Ypres. On 7 June, after a seven-day barrage, nearly a million pounds of Amothol was ignited in nineteen mines under the German positions. The front line simply disintegrated, allowing the British to take the enemy's forward positions with minimal loss. The village of Messines offered initial resistance but was captured by the New Zealanders in a vigorous attack. Wytschaete fell to the 36th (Ulster) Division. By 6.30a.m. the scene of the London Scottish's first great battle was back in Allied hands.

The Scottish played no part in the Battle of Messines. They spent the period from 19-24 May in rest billets at Berneville, before moving to Simencourt where they remained until the 56th Division returned to the line on 10 June. The weather during this period was fine, allowing excellent opportunities for training and sport, including a Halley Claymore competition won by C Company. On 20 June the Scottish, having spent the previous ten days in Divisional reserve at Achicourt, moved with the rest of the Brigade into the line east of Arras. With the bulk of the fighting elsewhere the line was quiet, although the Scottish did suffer a minor setback when one of its outposts was overrun at the cost of ten casualties. A counter-attack was almost immediately organized, but by then the enemy had escaped, taking with them a wounded man as prisoner.

On 22 July the London Scottish marched to Berneville, and early the next morning entrained for St Omer from where they marched to Moulle. Thereafter training continued until 6 August when the Battalion moved to Steenvoorde, just inside the French frontier and close to the Ypres sector.

The devastating result of the British seven-day barrage 7 June. Taylor Library

Haig's third great offensive along the salient, known universally as the Battle of Passchendaele, began on 31 July along a front of twelve miles from Bixschoote to the Lys. The 56th Division entered the fray on the extreme right of the British line, close to the Menin Road, on 16 August. They moved into the line four days early with the 168th Brigade in reserve near Dickebusch. The Battalion was brought up to strength, sixty-six officers and 1,095 men, and the number of pipers was increased to thirteen to allow all but three of the platoons a dedicated piper. While at Dickebusch the Division made the acquaintance of its new Commander, Major General F. A. Dudgeon CB. Fortuitously for the Scottish, before entering the Regular Army Dudgeon had served in its ranks.

The attack on 16 August was not a success. Minor advances were made on the left, but in the centre and right the attack was held up. Short of manpower, the Germans had adopted new tactics. Their front line was now only lightly defended, enabling the real fight to take place in the second, which was studded with well-placed and mutually supporting pillboxes, armed with machine guns and strengthened with belts of barbed wire. The 167th and 169th Brigades suffered so severely in their attempts to take these pillboxes that it was felt inexpedient to commit the 168th Brigade in their wake. Instead the 14th Division was brought in to relieve the 56th. During the night the Battalion was relieved and marched back to Chateau Segard. Four days later it moved back to New Dickebusch Camp, and on 24 August to Moulle. Six days later the Division was transferred from Gough's Fifth Army to Byng's Third Army and returned to the Somme region in front of the Hindenburg Line.

115

Private McLellan remembered joining the Battalion as a casualty replacement at about this time. He recalled that as he passed soldiers from another unit en route to the Battalion they reversed arms as an indication of the losses recently sustained by the Scottish. Nonetheless he remained optimistic, happy at last at the prospect of seeing action.

'I recollect that the rain threat had gone. It was harvest country; the cornfields, unfenced, surged against the roads.'

When McLellan and the other over 100 members of Nos 79, 80 and 81 drafts reached the Battalion, they were stood in a field and addressed by RSM Wilkinson before being invited to choose companies. Having elected for C Company, McLellan and three others were alloted to No 9 Platoon whom they got to know that evening in the comfort of a dry barn.

It was not always easy for a new member of a Company to integrate.

'In those first days we came to know our fellow privates in the platoons and the more immediate officers and NCOs,' reported McLellan. *'As days and weeks went by our knowledge spread. But since we spent so much time in the line, where companies, and even platoons, were normally sealed off from contact; and when out of the line we did not get much beyond our own circle for either training or recreation, I think that most of us knew the greater number of officers only by sight, not by name; and the other ranks in even lesser degree.'*

The London Scottish were destined to spend a few idyllic days in a hutted camp by the Bapaume-Peronne road before, on 4 September, the Scottish moved into Divisional reserve when the 56th relieved the 3rd Division in the line. There followed the usual routine of trench warfare combined with the digging of a new support trench and communication system. As no man's land in this sector was wide, the Battalion had to carry out extensive patrolling which led to the occasional skirmish.

The only raid attempted by the enemy occurred on the morning of 25 September when a raiding party made a spirited attack on C Company's positions in the frontline. The assault had, however, been heralded by a very specific localized barrage and had been anticipated. A fire bay was overrun and its two occupants captured, but otherwise the raid was unsuccessful, leaving a large number of Germans dead and wounded in its stead. On 8 October a retaliatory raid by No 11 Platoon under Lieutenant Gibson met with no greater success when it found itself incapable of penetrating the enemy wire.

The Battalion enjoyed an otherwise uneventful stay of more than two months in this sector. It would, however, be wrong to regard the period as something of a 'jolly.' As Haig mentioned when writing his dispatches shortly after the cessation of hostilities around Ypres:

'Before passing from the subject of the operations of the past eight months, tribute must be paid to the work accomplished on the defensive portions of our line.

'In order to meet the urgent demands of battle , the number of

divisions in line on other fronts has necessarily been reduced to the minimum consistent with safety. In consequence, constant vigilance and heavy and unremitting labour have been required at all times of the troops holding these fronts.

'The numerous feint attacks which have been organized from time to time have called for great care, forethought and ingenuity on the part of Commanders and Staffs concerned, and have demanded much courageous, skilful and arduous work from the troops entrusted with the task of carrying them out. In addition, raids and local operations have continued to form a prominent feature of our general policy on our defensive front, and have been effectively combined with our feint attacks and with gas discharges. In the course of the 270 successful raids carried out during the period covered by this dispatch, the greatest enterprise and skill have been displayed by our troops, and many hundreds of prisoners, together with much invaluable information, have been obtained at comparatively light cost.'

The Battle of Cambrai

After more than two years of unremitting trench warfare the British now decided to adopt fresh tactics. Repeated British attacks in Flanders, and French attacks along the Chemin des Dames had caused the enemy to concentrate his forces in these areas, with a consequent reduction in his garrisons elsewhere. Of these weakened sectors the Cambrai front was selected as the most suitable for a surprise operation. The ground there was favourable for the employment of tanks, which were to play an important part in the anticipated battle. There would be no prolonged bombardment heralding the forthcoming attack. The might of 400 tanks, not heavy artillery, would smash a way through the wire of the Hindenburg Line, lead the infantry across its trenches and parapets and allow the cavalry to deploy into the open.

Cavalry deploying over open ground. This was only made possible by the use of tanks not artillery to break the Hindenburg Line. Taylor Library

British tank speeding into action at Cambrai. This was a successful fresh approach to trench warfare employed by the British. Taylor Library

In order to maintain the element of surprise the tanks were ordered to move only by night, their tracks being obliterated before daybreak. The Royal Flying Corps increased its number of sorties, partly to deter enemy aerial reconnaissance and partly to mask the considerable noise of the tanks as they manoeuvred. The infantry assembled for the attack were hidden away, with strict orders to remain concealed during the hours of daylight. Major R. M. Hamilton MC, the Deputy Assistant Director General of Transport of Third Army and a London Scot, remembered,

> *The next major operation in which I was concerned was the Tank attack on Cambrai in 1917, which much depended upon the delivery of about 400 Tanks by rail, as near as possible to the Front Line on three successive nights, with as much secrecy as possible. This was achieved and hardly any of the troops in the front line knew of the support behind them when the attack was launched.'*

The 56th Division was advised that it would not be required for the preliminary stages of the attack, but would be kept in reserve. The attack itself was launched suddenly on 20 November over a front of nearly ten miles stretching from La Vacquerie to the Bapaume-Cambrai road. Simultaneously, feint attacks were made elsewhere, in some cases made more realistic by the use of dummy figures and smoke-screens. The London Scottish remained at Beugny at this time, cheered with reports that the surprise had been complete.

> *'We were billeted at Beugny, a few miles north-east of Bapaume, when the news of the successful opening of the attack reached us,'*

reported the *Regimental Gazette.*

'We heard several barrages, varying in intensity, and the most marvellous rumours were persistent everywhere. Our hopes ran high. The Boche had been taken by surprise and a complete break-through had resulted. Cavalry were reported in Cambrai and everywhere things were going well.'

The attack had indeed been a success, but not all of its objectives had been won. A large number of attacks had either bogged down or had fallen victim to German artillery. Many hits were registered by an unknown German artillery officer who, remaining alone at his battery, served a field gun single handed until killed. Nonetheless a bridgehead had been forced across the Scheldt Canal and a salient formed seven or eight miles across and four or five miles deep. Over 100 guns and more than 10,000 prisoners had been taken.

But the position was far from secure. The left flank of the newly created salient was completely commanded by the Bourlon Ridge, so much so that unless this were taken it would be necessary to withdraw. To the right the canal had indeed been crossed and a bridgehead established by Canadian cavalry, but only in one place and the entire position now looked tenuous. To compound matters the attacking troops were exhausted and would require rest and reorganization before undertaking a large-scale attack, while German reinforcements were arriving and enemy numbers would soon be as great as before the battle. Haig had little option but to attack Bourlon Ridge and to this end brought the 56th Division into the fighting line on the extreme left.

'We received orders to be ready to move at any moment, and battle order was arranged in each company,' reported the London Scottish *Regimental Gazette. 'After several false alarms we actually left Beugny one morning about nine o' clock, and marching eastwards reached the old British front line in front of Louveral about midday. We succeeded in taking over the line in daylight owing to disorganization in the enemy's camp, but had to suffer for it later on. The remainder of the day was spent in keeping ready for action and yet playing "possum" so to speak, in order to deceive the Hun as much as possible.'*

The position facing the Scottish was thus: the extreme left troops of attacking infantry had worked their way up the Hindenburg Line and Hindenburg Support to a line between Moeuvres and the Canal du Nord. The 56th Division was tasked with continuing the advance on the Hindenburg Line system while continuing to hold the British front line opposite Inchy and Pronville. The former task was allotted to the 169th Brigade, the latter to the 167th while the 168th was held in readiness to support the 169th. On 22 November the 169th Brigade began its attack, and early in the same day the London Scottish moved forward into trenches at Louveral.

'About midnight we were ordered to move up, and proceed to the Hindenburg line via "The Willows" (where we were heavily 'whizz

banged'), "The Crater," "Houndsditch," and "Piccadilly." The latter was a particularly ghastly neighbourhood, certainly not living up to the traditions of its name. A heavy barrage of field guns and "emma gees" greeted our arrival in "Fritzdom". Everybody was thoroughly tired out after our all night tramp, but we had to forget that - a strenuous day lay before us.'

At about 7.00p.m. information was received that the 169th Brigade had done well and reached its objective, a communication trench known as Tadpole Lane. Rumours abounded that the British had been successful in their attack on the Support System, and that they had taken Moeuvres, but this proved to be unfounded. At about 2.00a.m. the Scottish received orders to move into the Hindenburg front line before daybreak. They were then to attack forward from Tadpole Lane at 8.00a.m. under cover of a preparatory bombardment due to begin at 6.30a.m.

'We got out of the trench and moved on into no man's land in single file,' recounted Private McLellan. 'This sounds simple, but it was pitch dark, the natural slight unevenness of the ground had been torn up during over a year at least by shelling, and for a much longer time lack of any village had let nature run wild. We had to twist this way and that, and every burdened man had to keep all his wits alert so as not to lose sight of the barely seen figure of the man in front.'

Due to the darkness, heavy enemy artillery and the lateness of the orders, the Scottish did not reach their assembly positions until zero hour, and only then found that the information as to the situation was incorrect. The 169th Brigade had not reached Tadpole Lane as reported, but had mistaken it for another communication trench about 200 yards short of it, separated from Tadpole Lane by a deep valley known as Tadpole Copse.

The Scottish had, therefore, to begin by attacking the very line from which they were supposed to advance from the outset. This involved an advance over the machine gun swept valley of Tadpole Copse over which a nest of machine guns positioned in Inchy Mill had a magnificent field of fire. It was not until 2.30p.m. that D Company on the right flank was able to infiltrate behind the enemy positions to facilitate a successful frontal assault by the rest of the Battalion into Tadpole Lane. A total of seventy prisoners, six machine guns and a trench mortar were captured, but at heavy loss. It was now possible for the Scottish to proceed with the attack as originally planned, and at 4.30p.m. they assaulted and took Adelaide Street, their original objective.

One of the many guns captured in the Cambrai offensive. Here a German 5.9 naval gun is being towed away under camouflage. Taylor Library

Inevitably, the Scottish soon found themselves short of bombs and ammunition. B Company, forward on the left, received a supply just in time to beat off an enemy counter-attack, but A and D Companies, in a support trench, were forced back to a point just east of the Inchy Road. The German counter-attack then gradually died away as darkness fell, allowing both sides to pass a quiet night in consolidation in the snow and rain that was by then falling.

'Our first spell in the Hindenburg line lasted, I think, two days, but it seemed like two very long weeks,' reported the *Regimental Gazette*. *'Everywhere the Boche offered stiff resistance, and we soon realised that we were in a hot corner. "Bombing up" became the order of the day and night, and much heavy work was done in the communications trenches. "Asgard," "Beowolf," "Frigga" and "Odin" were the scenes of particular liveliness. These names seemed most appropriate and had Thor only been present he might have found many fitting inmates for Valhalla.'*

At dawn on 24 November the enemy began a persistent bombardment, followed in the early afternoon by a counter-attack from Inchy Mill executed with such ferocity that the Scottish were forced to evacuate the support trench. Those who could, made their way to safety through the communication trenches, but many could not and were forced to withdraw over the open, suffering serious loss. The Germans continued their attack, but now with less success, until nightfall ended the fighting.

'It was about three o' clock in the afternoon before the attack matured and then once more the sun was shining. Gunfire on both sides had somewhat abated and we could see the green fields behind Inchy beckoning to us with an alluring finger. "All in the garden's lovely," they seemed to say... .Suddenly a violent outburst of bombing from our advanced positions brought everyone to the firestep. A cloud of smoke hung low in front, but as this cleared away a terrible spectacle was revealed - our own men rushing across the open with bayonets fixed and bombs in their hands... a deafening din smote the ear - the earth seemed to crackle up, and then like ripe corn beneath the reaper, they fell never to rise again. The enemy's machine-gun barrage had mown them down, breaking up the attack in front of a cunningly-concealed strong point. A few survivors reached us headed by an officer with a smoking revolver in his hand.

'The events of that day left their mark upon us all. Memory of it will linger for the rest of our earthly stay. The official communique, in tones cold and precise, announced our earlier victory to the world, but of the aftermath nothing was said.'

Private McLellan, who with C Company went to the aid of their colleagues in B Company, remembered encountering the British dead.

'We stepped carefully over and by them; already their faces, their hands, their knees were of a grey pallor, smooth worry-like. I do not remember any German dead, but there may have been.'

McLellan later recalled being put on guard that night, with an unknown young soldier who kept falling asleep. McLellan felt no bitterness towards him. Guards were rarely relieved, and must find themselves lying in dangerously exposed positions for hours on end. The pair were eventually relieved by an advance party of the Rangers.

The Scottish were relieved by the Rangers in the early hours of the following morning, and left the scene of their tragedy just before dawn. The Official History indicates that the Battalion now spent three days in reserve, but in reality much of this was spent in transit severely limiting the time for rest.

'*Back we trudged to the old British front line, and then on to dug outs at Louveral for twenty-four hours' rest, feeling more dead than alive. Hopes of final relief were running high, but our luck was out, and at dusk the same evening we were once more trudging eastwards. The ground was more familiar this time, but we knew better what was in store for us! The prospect was black enough in all conscience without the mud, but, with it - oh Heavens! - conventionality will not allow me to express our feelings!*'

On 27 November the Scottish relieved the Rangers. At that time they comprised the extreme left Battalion of the whole British attacking force, wedged into the Hindenburg Front Line system with the Germans on their left and forward in the communication trenches of the support system. The 1/8th Middlesex Regiment, part of the 167th Brigade which had now joined in the fighting, were on their right and beyond them the troops of other divisions. To the Scottish and Middlesex rear was open country, the nearest British supporting troops being 1,500 yards away in the old British front line. At first it appeared as if the battle were dying down, but by 29 November aerial reconnaissance made it clear that the Germans had yet to accept defeat. On 30 November, St Andrew's Day, they launched a surprise attack.

The day was warm, with mist rising from the ground. Between 7.00a.m. and 8.00a.m. the German artillery began a bombardment of the British right. As Hague later noted the nature of the bombardment, which seemed to have been heavy enough to keep the British under cover without at first seriously alarming them, contributed to the success of the subsequent attack. In complete secrecy, using the ground to its best advantage, aided by the extensive use of smoke and by the barrage itself, the Germans brought four divisions forward and without warning assaulted the three exhausted British divisions to their front. Surprise was complete, and despite valiant localized resistance six miles of the front were driven in, allowing the enemy in places to penetrate the old British line. Only when all available British reserves, including three battalions of tanks preparing to move away from the battlefield to refit, were committed were the enemy halted.

In the northern area the German attack was not launched until two hours later. This was the enemy's main attack, and was carried out with large forces in great resolution. After a heavy preliminary bombardment, and covered by an artillery barrage, the enemy advanced shortly after 9.00a.m. in dense blocks, reverting to the human-wave attacks of 1915. In the course of that day no less than five principal attacks were made in this area, and on one portion of the line as many as eleven waves of infantry advanced successfully to the assault. As Haig noted,

'On the whole of this front a resolute endeavour was made to break down by sheer weight of numbers the defence of the London Territorials and other English battalions holding the sector.'

The London Scottish, with C Company holding the extreme left flank, were engaged from the outset. As the *Regimental Gazette* rather graphically reported,

'At first a singular quiet seemed to reign supreme like a lull before the storm...at 9 o'clock in the morning the storm burst - a devilish barrage, a perfect storm of shot and shell poured upon us with all the intensity of Hunnish hate. Smoke and fire everywhere, the air foully polluted with the ghastly smell of H.E. - blood and iron - the trail of the Beast! A few minutes later a shower of stick bombs on the block in the extreme left company's area announced an attack by the Boche, but this manoeuvre proved merely a feint to cover the main push on the right. The latter developed with great ferocity, Prussians forcing the communications trenches round Battalion Headquarters and cutting us off from our right supports.'

At one stage the Germans forced their way through the lines of the 1/8th Middlesex leaving the Scottish right flank, containing its Battalion Headquarters, exposed. Things looked serious, until a brilliant counter attack by a small party of the Scottish recaptured the line enabling contact to be regained with what was left of the 1/8th Middlesex. Throughout the day pockets of resistance fought on heroically, often to the last man. Near Bourlon Wood to the right of the Scottish position, a platoon of the 17th Battalion, Royal Fusiliers acting as company rearguard died fighting to the end, while nearby a company of the 13th Battalion, The Essex Regiment held their ground for over twelve hours until annihilated in an attempt to buy their comrades time. Gradually German losses began to take their toll, and as their victory became pyrrhic the momentum of their attack waned. Haig reported that one battery of eight British machine guns fired 70,000 rounds of ammunition into ten successive waves of Germans.

'Long lines of attacking infantry were caught by our machine-guns in enfilade, and were shot down in line as they advanced. Great execution was also done by our artillery, and in the course of the battle, guns were brought up to the crest line and fired direct upon the enemy at short range.'

In the Scottish positions,

'Several SOS signals were sent up and gunfire on both sides was deafening. A wonderful machine-gun barrage directed from our Brigade machine-guns descended upon the left trench block, and for an hour we were treated to a magnificent crescendo of "heavenly music," the "angelic whispers" being audible between the shell-bursts.'

The *News of the World*, in its edition of 24 February 1918, reported;

'some thrilling details of the great fight on the Bourlon-Moeuvres

front on Nov 30, when four German divisions, with three other divisions in support, were utterly crushed by the unconquerable resistance of three British divisions in line.'

The account continued,

'Though much reduced in strength by the fighting of the preceding days, and hard pressed by superior forces, the troops of the 168th and 169th Brigades beat off all attacks. Queen's Westminsters, London Scottish, and men of the 1/2nd Batt. London Regiment and 1/8th Batt. Middlesex Regiment vied with one another in the valour of their resistance. At the end of this day of high courage and glorious achievement, except for a few advanced positions, some of which were afterwards regained, our line had been maintained intact. The men who had come triumphantly through this mighty contest felt that they had won a great victory, in which the enemy had come against them in his full strength, and had been defeated with losses at which even the victors stood aghast.'

That night the battle died down and the enemy, fearing a counter-attack, put down a defensive barrage. A few hours later the Scottish were again relieved by the Rangers and withdrew, exhausted to Beugny.

'The remnants of a somewhat straggling Battalion found Beugny once again, exhausted, famished, caked in mud, grim and silent. We could not believe the ordeal was over, relief had so often seemed a forlorn hope that now the reality was almost too good to be true.'

Fighting continued until 4 December, when the British withdrew after dark to a shortened line, abandoning most of the ground gained in the early days of the battle. The action, known to the Scottish as 'The Cambrai Stunt,' became a turning point to those who survived. It was a period of tremendous strain, weariness, horror and thrill. The Battalion losses were high: 61 killed, 282 wounded and 20 missing, 363 in all. The Adjutant, Captain Douglas MC, was killed, Captain Lamb, Officer Commanding A Company, wounded and Captain Walker, Officer Commanding D Company, taken prisoner.

November, 1917

There's a red-eyed pack stands back to back
In the depths of Bourlon Wood;
And they know no sleep, for their watch they keep,
And their hunger can know no food

There's a red-eyed pack stands back to back,
In the mud and the sleet and the rain,
And the blood-soaked ground lies all around,
And their ramparts are heaps of slain.

There's a red-eyed pack stands back to back,
As the hours drag slowly by;
But they'll ne'er give in, so they sit and grin,
And they curse and they pray, and - die.

There's a red-eyed pack stands back to back,
'Mid the battle's hellish din;
Through the shell-torn night they sternly fight,
And the ranks draw closer in.

There's a red-eyed pack comes straggling back,

And they growl as they wolf their food;
But their proud eyes shine, for they've held the line
In the depths of the Bourlon Wood.

W.J. Campbell

Chapter Seven

The Last Battles

When the 56th Division was withdrawn from the Battle of Cambrai it moved northwards to the Vimy sector where it remained for seven months. On 1 December the London Scottish marched to Bertincourt, and from there to Beaulencourt and on to Fremicourt where it entrained for Beaumetz les Loges. The 168th Brigade was then taking over the line at Arleux and Gavrelle, east of the heights of the Vimy Ridge where it remained for the winter. The position was comparatively quiet, but in other respects was less than satisfactory. The enemy were only 200 yards away, while the British communication trenches were in parts up to three miles in length. Most were in a dilapidated state, the product of earlier savage fighting for the ridge. Derelict trenches were blocked and those remaining reconstructed, much time being spent in rewiring.

The Scottish spent Christmas in the line, but found itself in reserve for the New Year. The 56th Division was relieved by the 62nd early in 1918, allowing the Scottish to spend the first weeks of the year training in the St Pol area. Life, however, was far from restful. Wiring parties were constantly required by the units defending Vimy and Arras while 300 men were attached to a Tunnelling Company engaged in the construction of dugouts. On 6 February the Division began to move back to the line, and on the 10th the Scottish took over the support position in the front facing Oppy.

Officers of the 1st Battalion at Mont St Eloi, March 1918.

Onto the Defensive

Uncharacteristically Haig was forced into a defensive mode in early 1918. The victories dearly bought in France and Flanders in 1917 had only in part relieved the pressure of the Atlantic blockade. Although the United States had entered the war, her troops were only coming very slowly to Europe; indeed, it was considered that they would not be in a position to take the offensive until the middle of the summer. On the other hand the capitulation of Russia had set free the great bulk of the German and Austrian divisions on the eastern front. By late 1917 the transfer of German divisions from the Russian to the Western Front had begun. It was to be expected, moreover, that large numbers of guns and munitions formerly in the possession of the Russian armies, would fall into the hands of the Germans, on some future date to be turned on the Allies. In January the British took over a further 28 miles of the line from the French, bringing their active front to a total of 125 miles. In Venetia the Italians had been driven from the Alpine frontiers, and had only managed to hold the enemy at the Paive with the help of British and French divisions badly needed elsewhere.

Given that the Germans had attacked at Verdun in February it was widely anticipated that they would launch their 1918 offensive in the same month. It was all important, therefore, to be ready by the third week of February for the forthcoming campaign. In order to consolidate its limited

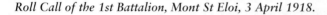

Roll Call of the 1st Battalion, Mont St Eloi, 3 April 1918.

128

1st Battalion coming back for a rest near Arras, lead by Piper Stewart, 1 April 1918.

forces the British reorganized, amalgamating several battalions in the process. As a consequence it was forced to reduce the size of each brigade from four battalions and a pioneer battalion to three battalions and a pioneer battalion, a reduction from thirteen to ten battalions. As Haig noted in his dispatches of 20 July 1918:

> *'Apart from the reduction in fighting strength involved by this reorganisation, the fighting efficiency of units was to some extent affected. An unfamiliar grouping of units was introduced thereby, necessitating new methods of tactical handling of the troops, and the discarding of old methods to which subordinate commanders had become accustomed.'*

To compound the British problem, although patrolling remained active on both sides Haig was forced to order a marked reduction in raiding activities, an excellent method of introducing new troops to the realities of trench warfare. From 8 December 1917 to the opening of the German offensive three and a half months later, 225 raids were attempted by the Germans of which 62 breached the British lines. The British launched 125 raids against the enemy, of which 77 were successful.

Towards the middle of February 1918, it became clear that Germany was preparing for a big offensive on the Western Front. Haig had learned from his Intelligence sources that the enemy had been steadily increasing his forces in that theatre since the beginning of November 1917. As these reinforcements were far more than was required for defence, and as they took place at the very time that Germany desperately required its scarce rolling-stock for the distribution of food and fuel, it was clear that an offensive was due at an early date. Constant air reconnaissance showed that rail and road communications were being improved and stores and

Trench Mortar Battery in 1918. Note the London Scottish officer in the centre.

ammunition, particularly for the artillery, stock-piled. However, such was the success of Germany's deception plan, combining as it did a prohibition on daylight movement and the introduction of excellent camouflage, that what Haig did not realize was that a vast army of twenty-eight infantry divisions had been transferred from the Eastern and six from the Italian theatres. By 21 March, the anticipated date of the attack, the number of German infantry divisions in the Western theatre had risen to 192, an increase of 46 since 1 November 1917.

In front of Arras, where the London Scottish held the line towards Oppy, the defences were well organized by dint of persistent hard work. Lectures had been given in the tactics of defence, interspersed by warnings of the new, and highly successful, German methods. At Cambrai and later at Caparetto specially trained bodies of hand-picked *Stosstruppen*, or shock-troops, had been employed to drive wedges into the defence, to exploit individual successes and to cut deep into the defenders' rear echelons. Losses were generally light, although gas attacks became more common. This was particularly annoying, as victims of phosgene gas invariably had to spend up to two months in hospital recovering at the very time that every man was needed at the front. Matters worsened in early March when the unsuspecting Scottish sustained their first mustard gas attack, suffering over a hundred casualties. In early March the German artillery began to fire sudden barrages onto the front-line and support trenches, ceasing fire as quickly as they had started, as if to confuse their operational pattern and lull the British into a false sense of security. The British were, however, on the alert. On 19 March British Intelligence reported the final stages of the enemy's preparation, with its centre on the Arras-St Quentin front, were approaching completion, and that the probable date of attack was either 20 or 21 March.

On the night of 20 March, in anticipation of an attack, Wood Post, the second post on the left of the London Scottish, was evacuated. It was badly sited, and might easily have proved a death-trap had its garrison been attacked. Towards morning a heavy bombardment was opened on the Post, allowing its former occupants to look on from a position of safety, as it was torn apart by tons of trench mortar explosives. The bombardment became general with the coming of the dawn but no attack followed. After about an hour the bombardment ceased, to be replaced by a tremendous attack to the south along the Monchy sector, east of Arras. This represented the extreme right of the great German attack, which extended for fifty miles.

In all, at least sixty-four German divisions took part in the operations of the first day of the battle, a number considerably exceeding the total forces comprising the entire British Army in France. The majority of these divisions had spent many weeks and even months in concentrated training in offensive operations, and had reached a high pitch of technical excellence in the attack. During the course of the next day, the London Scottish learned the awful reality of the extent of the German success. General Gough's Fifth Army front had all but disintegrated. A few bridgeheads had held along the Somme, but everywhere else the front had largely ceased to exist. Prisoners, guns and materials had been captured in large quantities. Soon thereafter it was reported that the Somme had been lost and that the Germans were pushing for Amiens.

German planning had been excellent. Shortly before 5.00p.m. on 21 March a massive gas and high explosive bombardment of artillery and trench mortars was opened along virtually the entire Fifth and Third Army front, while their heavy guns were ranged against the British lines of communication. Equally violent bombardments were opened against the French to the north and east of Rheims, and against the British on and to the north of the Ypres salient. Dunkirk was bombarded from the sea. The effect was to cause panic, insecurity and an initial unwillingness to release reinforcements from any sector. However, as soon as it became evident that the enemy had thrown practically the whole of his striking force against a single front, it became both possible and necessary to collect additional reserves from the remainder of the front and hurry them to the battlefield. Leave was cancelled and reinforcements rushed across the Channel. American troops were brought into the line. French troops from Champagne and the Vosges were brought north to help bolster Byng's Third Army, the right of which was under threat from the northern extremes of the new German salient.

The London Scottish were not immediately involved in the great battle. However, on 28 March, the offensive was extended to their front when Otto von Bellow, commanding the German right, attacked in force with a view to securing Arras and the Vimy Ridge. After a bombardment, three fresh divisions were committed to an assault against the 4th and 56th Divisions, and were supported in their endeavours by two divisions already in the line.

Private John F. W. Pell, 1st Battalion, killed in action on 31 August 1918 at Bullecourt and buried in the H.A.C. British Cemetery, Ecoust-St Mein.

During the initial attack six days earlier, the Germans had enjoyed the advantage of thick fog which had helped to mask their activities. In this instance the weather was clear, giving the British artillery and machine guns every opportunity to engage the German infantry when assembling and while advancing to the attack. Byng had partially reorganized his front the night before. The 169th Brigade had taken over the trenches before Oppy, with the 168th Brigade to its left. The London Scottish were placed in the 'Red Line,' a line of strong posts linked by a trench, and were in support of the 4th Londons in front. The move necessarily took place at night, giving the Scottish scant opportunity to reconnoitre their new positions.

The anticipated barrage of gas and high explosive shells of all calibres began at 3.00a.m., and four hours later the enemy infantry advanced, silhouetted against the clear morning sky. They advanced in dense masses and sustained heavy losses, yet the weight and momentum of their assault coupled with the courage of their infantry sufficed to carry the enemy through a number of gaps in the British line. The London Scottish in the 'Red Line' could see little of the initial battle as the advanced trenches were enveloped in dense clouds of smoke. At about 7.30a.m. they were engaged by an enemy vanguard of bombing parties. The Scottish counter-attacked, drove the enemy back and re-took two British machine guns which had been captured from a detachment of the Machine Gun Corps.

Shortly after 8.00a.m. the 4th Londons had both flanks turned and were forced back to the 'Red Line' which now became the front. The enemy made

Locrehof Farm, September 1918.

1st Brigade Signals, 1918.

a series of determined attacks on Bailleul East Post, but these were successfully beaten off. That night attempts were made by the 416th (Edinburgh) Field Company, RE to construct two new posts close by, but their activities were spotted by the Germans who brought down such heavy fire on the positions that the Engineers were forced to abandon them. Dawn came, but did not bring with it the anticipated attacks. German infantry were spotted in large numbers in their forward trenches, but were so actively and accurately bombarded by Allied artillery that they made no attempt to advance. During that night the London Scottish were relieved by the 54th Canadians, and moved back to Mont St Eloi, north-west of Arras.

The casualties sustained by the Battalion during the battle numbered fifty-four. The Scottish had inflicted much heavier losses on the enemy, as was confirmed by the Canadian patrols in the following days. Colonel Jackson later wrote,

> 'Some months after, I met a Canadian General, who commanded the brigade which relieved the 168th on this occasion. He said, "Are you the Colonel of the London Scottish?" I said, "Yes." He then jumped off his seat, held out his hand, and said, "By Gawd, shake!" After I had shaken hands with him he went on to tell how impressed he had been at seeing the number of German dead in the neighbourhood of Bailleul East Post, and how he had appreciated the fine fight put up there by D Company of the London Scottish.'

The stand before Arras had, indeed, proved crucial. Otto von Bellow's attack had ended in disastrous failure, and by 5 April was completely spent. The 56th Division enjoyed a week of 'rest and recreation' in the Mont St Eloi area, the Scottish being at Durham Camp. During this time the Battalion received a mixed draft of over 300 men; many of them Gordon

133

Highlanders, but others from the Royal Fusiliers, East Kents, East Surreys and other English regiments. There was initial disillusionment and not a little resentment when it was discovered that at the same time 300 London Scottish had been sent to the Highland Division close by. However, the new arrivals were quickly integrated, the senior non-commissioned officers from the Gordons proving particularly welcome.

On 7 April the 56th Division relieved the 2nd Canadian Division over the Tilloy-Beaurains sector south-east of Arras. Many of the troops were quartered in the town itself, in vast underground excavations dating from the Spanish occupation and adapted for habitation before the first Battle of Arras. The London Scottish relieved the 5th Canadians in 'Blenheim Cave', moving on the following night to 'Christchurch Cave', where they were kept in constant readiness to move to the old front line.

They returned to the line on the night of 10 April, relieving the 1st Londons. There followed several days of hard work consolidating the battered and shallow trenches by day and patrolling by night. The immediate objective was the recapture of a group of trenches which the enemy had taken in the first days of the March offensive. Unusually they had not wired them, and it was felt that a short dash across no man's land would secure them. The Scottish and the 4th Londons, holding the 168th Brigade frontage, were directed to carry out the projected attack on the night of 19 April. The Scottish were to lead with C Company under Captain White, a company of the 4th Londons attacking from their front trench eight minutes later. The companies were in position at 3.10a.m., but the precise timing of the advance was left to White. The weather was broken with occasional showers of hail, during which observation was obscured, and there was noise enough to conceal the movement of the men, making surprise a distinct possibility. The attack was launched at 4.20a.m. during one of the showers. The Germans, who had been relieved only thirty minutes earlier, were taken completely by surprise. Most fled, a few allowed themselves to be taken prisoner and those who did not were disposed of with the bomb and bayonet. German artillery was quick to retaliate and a few half-hearted counter-attacks were made in the morning. These were easily driven off.

The position itself was uncomfortable with a limited field of fire. It was dominated by a pillbox immediately to its front while the shallowness of the trenches left the defenders vulnerable to sniper and machine-gun fire. Battalion Headquarters ordered Captain White to attack the pillbox, once again leaving the time and manner of the assault to his discretion. White decided that the attack could not be made until dusk, and spent the intervening hours of daylight in consolidation. In the interim a reconnaissance by Colonel Jackson convinced him that an attack by a diminished company alone would be unfeasible. It would be necessary either to withdraw to the original British front line or to commit the entire battalion to the assault.

Pending further directions from Brigade Headquarters, arrangements were made for a withdrawal to be carried out at dusk. At 6.00p.m. enemy artillery fire increased as if to herald a counter-attack. The British guns retaliated with a slow protective barrage, and when no attack followed Captain White decided to attempt the capture of the pill box. At 7.20p.m. Second Lieutenant Bennett with eight bombers led a diversionary attack to draw the enemy artillery. Meanwhile a second bombing party left its trench and pushed close up to the pillbox, which was found to be protected by a belt of wire. They came under heavy machine-gun fire from both flanks and were forced to retire with a number of casualties. Lieutenant Bennett's party, attacked by superior numbers, was also forced to retire. Captain White, now expecting a general attack on his position called for an SOS barrage which was actioned at 7.50p.m. The German artillery retaliated, and by 8.00p.m. the area was subject to a heavy barrage on both sides.

Lieutenant Frank A. Baker, killed in action by a gas shell near Oisy le Verger, Canal du Nord, October 1918.

At 7.40p.m., not long after the engagement had opened, the order to withdraw reached Battalion Headquarters. As soon as all was quiet B Company began its withdrawal, which was completed in perfect order by 10.30p.m., covered by a bombing demonstration. All ammunition and stores were recovered, as were four captured machine guns and a German trench mortar of a new design. The total casualties in the operation were five killed, thirty-one wounded and one wounded and missing. On the following evening the 168th Brigade was relieved by the 169th, the London Scottish being relieved by the Queen's Westminsters. The German offensive now moved north, where after an initial success it was again halted.

Haig, in his dispatches summed up the role of the infantry in this last great German offensive thus:

'The British infantryman has always had the reputation of fighting his best in an uphill battle, and time and again in the history of our country, by sheer tenacity and determination of purpose, has won victory from a numerically superior foe. Thrown once more upon the defensive by circumstances over which he had no control, but which will not persist, he has shown himself to possess in full measure the traditional qualities of his race.'

No truer words could have been written of the London Scottish in the spring of 1918.

Taking the Initiative

By the end of April 1918 the German onrush had been stemmed. Yet the position for the British on the Western Front remained critical. Her reserves, both in men and materials, were virtually exhausted. Reinforcements had been called from England and numerous divisions were being diverted from elsewhere, but these would take time to arrive. A further period of training was required to allow troops brought from abroad to become acclimatized, and to enable the new drafts to become assimilated within their various units. Such was the crisis in manpower that it became necessary to reduce eight divisions to cadres, temporarily removing them from the order of battle. Two other divisions were so weak as to be virtually non-effective. No more than forty-five operational divisions remained in the British sector; three-quarters of these had been heavily engaged in countering the German offensive, all were urgently in need of rest, and all contained large numbers of young, only partially-trained and inexperienced recruits. Equally worrying, there was a massive dearth of young officers with sufficient experience to command in battle.

The state of the 56th Division was no better. For their part, after leaving the trenches the London Scottish spent the night of 19-20 April and the following day in Christchurch Cave at Arras. The next night they marched back to the Berneville area, about five miles south-west of the city. For the next four months they remained in this area; on occasions in the trenches in the front line or in support, at other times in reserve or 'resting and training.' Although there followed a distinct lull in the fighting, and it was

Arras, November 1918, shortly after the Armistice.

Officers of C Company, 1st Battalion London Scottish, Arras November 1918. Back row: 2nd Lieutenant Mancell, Lieutenant Thompson, 2nd Lieutentant Harper. Front row: Captain Bennett MC, 2nd Lieutenant Macherson.

Hearty Greetings from the 1st Battalion, Christmas 1918.

clear that the German Army had undoubtedly paid heavily for its earlier successes, it was felt that it still possessed a sufficient superiority in numbers to return to the offensive in the summer. The area around Arras remained critical, its defence imperative to the Allied cause.

Arriving at Berneville on 21 April, the London Scottish spent the following days consolidating and reorganizing, a task which was hindered by the requirement to supply large working parties to help construct the line of entrenchments then being dug around Beaumetz, to form another defensive position in case the lines at Arras should be forced. The period of partial rest came to a halt on 23 April when the 56th Division was ordered to take over and extend their front. The 167th Brigade, then in reserve at Arras, was brought into the line and the 168th Brigade moved forward to Christchurch Cave to take its place. For the next week the Scottish alternated between the trenches and the cave, but again their 'rest' periods were plagued throughout by the need to send working and carrying parties forward in support of the front line battalions. At the end of April General Dudgeon was invalided back to Britain, and General Hull resumed command of the 56th Division.

Private McLellan rejoined the Battalion from sick leave on the evening of 30 April. The sight which met him was far from a happy one, with many new faces from the 3rd Battalion and elsewhere replacing those of his friends killed in action. From within 9 Platoon alone Willimott had been killed at Vimy, Pitt was lost, presumed dead, Lance Corporal Clegg had been gassed and at least four others killed.

On the night of 2-3 May the Scottish relieved the Kensingtons in the front line. There followed a period of ten days hard and continuous work during which the defences were strengthened, wiring and blocks put in place, fire-bays constructed and the area generally cleared of mud. On one occasion there was a warning of impending enemy attack in response to which the Battalion stood to, but nothing came of it. As Private McLellan pointed out with great perception,

'The trenches and their vicinity became a hive of activity during the first hours of darkness. Sentry posts continued to be manned, of course, that was the essential duty. Most of the other men - not always all perhaps - were engaged on their various jobs. As a rule by midnight

or not long after the night tasks had been performed, and the men, back in their bivvies, dug outs, or other sleeping places, rested and slept, subject only to the sentry rota, until stand-to brought every man from Alps to North Sea out to watch the oncoming day.'

On the night of 12-13 May the Brigade went into divisional reserve, the Scottish being relieved by the 1/7th Middlesex before marching back to Daineville. During the next six days of 'rest and training' special attention was paid to work with the Lewis guns. On 18 May the Battalion moved into billets in Arras where it spent the days in rest and nights in the provision of working parties at the front. On the night of 21-22 May they moved into support in the Blangy system, still continuing to supply working parties at night for the front line.

On 24 May the enemy's artillery became more intense and for the next two days the trenches were shelled. It was assumed that this was a prelude to a German offensive but, although the enemy made an extensive raid on the trenches to the Scottish right, nothing materialized. This renewed activity by the enemy was a feint, like other similar feints at various places along the front, intended to divert attention from the real point of danger. This was the line of the Chemin des Dames and the positions covering Rheims, held at the time by tired divisions withdrawn from Flanders to recuperate. On 27 May the Germans suddenly attacked and carried the ridge of the Chemin des Dames, which they had been contesting for three years, in a single rush. Rheims was taken and for a while it appeared as if the enemy would take Paris. Further progress was, however, stopped by the Americans at Chateau Thierry.

Lieutenant Colonel Jackson DSO with the Reverend J.C. Lusk MC just before going to Germany, January 1919.

During the night of 27-28 May the London Scottish relieved the 4th Londons in the front line where they remained for more than a week. It was a quiet time, chiefly employed in the inevitability of wiring and consolidation. On the night of 8-9 June the Battalion was relieved by the 7th Middlesex and again moved back to Dainville, where there was a rest of eleven days. The 168th Brigade was brought back into the line on the night of 17-18 June, the London Scottish relieving the London Rifle Brigade in the Tilloy area, south of the Arras-Cambrai road. Considerable wiring and ancillary work was undertaken in the front and support trenches to counter the anticipated German attack.

New tactics were introduced; the front and support line trenches and the forward system of communications were evacuated except for sentries, and filled with barbed wire, the defence being concentrated in strong posts in the third line; all these posts containing ample dugout accommodation. In the event of an attack the enemy would have been badly surprised and held up by

Padre and Adjutant: The Reverend Lusk and Captain Valentine.

this scheme while the garrison of the third line would be allowed to remain safely in its shelters while a counter-bombardment was brought down upon its positions.

During the night of 23 November the Battalion was relieved by the 4th Londons, and moved back into support in the Blangy system, supplying the inevitable nocturnal working parties. On the night of 5-6 July the 168th Brigade was once more withdrawn from the line, the 1st Londons taking over from the London Scottish, who moved back to billets in Dainville. On 12 July the Canadian Corps began the relief of the 17th Corps in and around Arras, the 56th Division being relieved by the 1st and portions of the 2nd Canadian Divisions. On that day the London Scottish left Arras for Berneveille Camp in anticipation of once again taking the offensive.

Two months of quiet change had completely altered the condition of the British Armies on the Western Front. The drafts sent out from England had largely been absorbed. Many of the reinforcements from other theatres had already arrived and were now acclimatized, and the number of effective infantry divisions had risen from forty-five to fifty-two. In artillery the British were stronger than they had ever been; indeed, there were more gunners in France in 1918 than there had been members of the original British Expeditionary Force in August 1914. The London Scottish began their training for the forthcoming battle with a three-day route march. On

13 July they moved westward to Fosseux, and thence via Lignereuil to Chelers, where company training began. On 15 July they moved to St Lawrence Camp in the Chateau de la Haie training district. That day Rheims fell to the Germans still advancing in the south. Three days later the French began the long-awaited counter-offensive.

The training at Chateau de la Haie was intensive and successful. By the end of July the Scottish were in the best fighting trim they had known for several months, and when orders came for the 17th Corps to relieve the Canadians at Arras an air of optimism prevailed. The 168th Brigade was to take over the sector on the front astride the Arras-Cambrai road, and on the morning of 31 July the London Scottish moved by light railway to Anzin in the north-west suburbs of Arras, from where they marched through the city and out to the line on the following night. On the night of 3-4 August the Scottish were relieved by the Kensingtons, and moved into reserve in Arras where they spent the next four days in continued training. Movements in artillery formation were practised in the open ground near the old citadel, and musketry training undertaken on the Baudimont ranges. On the night of 8-9 August the Scottish returned to the line, relieving the 4th Londons. Earlier that day, which Ludendorff later described as *'the blackest day in the history of the German army,'* the British joined in the great counter-offensive. The Fourth Army struck with deadly effect at the German lines before Amiens, driving them back for miles. By the end of that day the British had completed an advance of between six and seven miles. Behind his lines the enemy was blowing up dumps in all directions while his transports and limbers were streaming eastwards, affording excellent targets for the Allied airmen. Over 13,000 prisoners, between 300 and 400 guns and vast quantities of ammunition were taken on the first day.

Although the London Scottish took no part in this battle they did send out two combat patrols per night. These found that the enemy was indeed

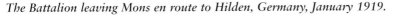

The Battalion leaving Mons en route to Hilden, Germany, January 1919.

1st Battalion London Scottish officers, Hilden, Germany, March 1919.

in disarray, and was very prompt in withdrawing behind his front line rather than give battle. On the night of 12-13 August the Battalion was relieved by the Kensingtons, and went into support for four more days, sending three companies per day to work on dugouts in the front line.

The time was approaching for the offensive to be carried to the Arras front. The enemy had been driven back from before Amiens, and the British were about to launch an offensive across the Ancre and over the old battlefields of the Somme. These were to be followed by an advance from Arras. In order to give the 56th Division a final opportunity for battle training, it was relieved by the 15th Division and taken out of the line on the night of 17 August. The London Scottish was relieved by the 10th Scottish Rifles and marched to Berneville, from where they were conveyed by light railway to River Junction, where they detrained and marched to Maizieres. On the evening of 20 August the 168th Brigade moved into Liencourt training area, the Scottish being billeted at Lignereuil village. Such time as was available was dedicated to teaching the Battalion the new method of attack known as 'the Blob system'. Instead of advancing slowly in widely extended lines, sections were kept together in small groups known as 'blobs.' These gave the officers and senior NCOs far better control and far greater freedom of movement. Ironically the system was far from new; the Germans had used a variant at Verdun, the French on the first day of the Somme.

Little enough time was given to rest. Late in the evening of 21 August the Scottish were ordered to make a ten-mile route march to La Cauchee, which they completed early the next morning. At 10.00a.m. Colonel Jackson was summoned to Divisional Headquarters and given his orders for the impending battle at dawn the next day. There was to be an advance east of

Arras on a front of sixteen miles. The 56th Division was to be placed in the line south-east of the city and to advance across the Cojeul river. The 168th Brigade was to be in the lead, the London Scottish being assigned the village of Boiry Becquerelle and the surrounding trenches as its objective. There was little time to waste, there being just enough time to get the Battalion into the assembly area and have a distant view of the objective before darkness closed in.

At Blaireville battle stores were issued and an Orders Group held. The first objective was to be Boiry Trench, on the eastern edge of Boiry Becquerelle. The final objectives were Boiry Reserve Trench and Boiry Work, further east of the village, towards Croisilles. The Cojeul river was to mark the left flank, the front was to extend some 800 yards with the 4th Londons on the right. A Company under Captain Brown was to lead on the right, C Company under Captain Bishop on the left. D Company under Lieutenant Newbigging was to be in support and D Company under Lieutenant Smart in reserve in the British front line.

The Battalion moved out of Blaireville at 11.30p.m. en route to the assembly position which was to be the British front line just east of the village of Boisleux St Marc. It was a bright moonlit night, making the advancing soldiers clearly visible to the enemy aircraft patrolling overhead. Artillery on both sides was extremely active. Notwithstanding this the assembly was completed by 4.00a.m. It proved to be difficult work, due to the complete ignorance of the ground and the accuracy of the German gas-shell barrage which forced the attackers to wear respirators for two hours and precluded them from eating their rations before going into action.

After a preliminary bombardment of only twelve minutes the Scottish advanced, preceded by a creeping barrage, at 4.55a.m. on the morning of 23 August. C Company gained its objective quickly, and was followed into the village by B Company. The area was cleared of a nest of machine guns with the help of a tank and yielded 100 prisoners and 8 machine guns. Having gained Boiry Trench contact was made with the 4th Londons on the right and the 4th Royal Scots on the left. Each of the forward companies then pushed out a platoon towards Boiry Reserve Trench, but these were met by heavy machine-gun fire and suffered considerable casualties before forcing a tenuous entry into the workings. The German artillery countered with a high explosive and gas-shell barrage at 8.00a.m. which continued until about 3.00p.m. Despite this the forward troops were able to consolidate, and when the enemy's fire slackened in the afternoon and it became clear that his resistance was shaky it was decided to exploit the success further.

Accordingly, at 5.00p.m. each of the front line companies sent two platoons forward to Boiry Reserve Trench and against Boiry Work. About 100 Germans in the latter position were still stubbornly resisting, but after a flanking movement executed by A and C Companies at approximately 6.00p.m. the eighty-six survivors surrendered. The ground beyond was clear of the enemy, and as darkness fell the Scottish were able to push out sentry

The London Scottish at Hilden, Germany in March 1919. The photograph shows the only members of the Regiment remaining who served with the 1st Battalion in 1914. Back row: (No3) RQMS J.C. Low (No4) Serjeant C.S. McNah. Sitting: Major W.E. Webb DSO, Captain R.V.A .Valentine MC, Captain W.B. Liebert MC, RSM R.M. Walkinshaw MM, MC.

posts some 400 yards east of the Boiry Reserve Trench. Every objective had been taken at a cost of twenty-five men killed, one officer and fifty-five other ranks wounded, and two officers and forty-four other ranks gassed. Some 250 prisoners had been taken, as had sixteen machine guns and five trench mortars. During the night sporadic shelling against the old British front line caused a number of casualties to D Company. The next morning the 168th Brigade was relieved in its captured positions by the 167th Brigade, which was to continue the advance towards Croisilles and Bullecourt.

The 168th Brigade went back into Divisional reserve in the old British line, the London Scottish returning to the trenches near Boiry Becquerelle from which they had assaulted on the previous morning. Due to the steady

British advance the area quickly became quiet and, but for the occasional long-ranging shell, safe.

Bullecourt

During the last days of August the fighting east of Arras spilled into the old Hindenburg Line. On the evening of 27 August the 168th Brigade was moved up in support of the 169th, the 167th Brigade coming back into reserve. The London Scottish marched out at 5.00p.m. to a position in the rear of 169th Brigade, which was then holding the high ground north-west of Croisilles. During the day the 169th Brigade, in conjunction with the Guards Division, had made several unsuccessful attempts to capture Croisilles village, which was strongly entrenched and bristled with machine guns. Orders were received that the 168th Brigade should make a frontal assault on the village during the course of the next morning, supported by the 169th Brigade which would move left along the Hindenburg Line and attempt to outflank the position. Preparations for the forthcoming battle were well underway when the orders were countermanded. Instead of making a frontal assault, the 168th Brigade was now directed to follow in support of the 169th as it flanked through the Hindenburg entrenchment.

Orders did not reach the Scottish until 10.00p.m., and thereafter were only disseminated with difficulty due to the fact that the Battalion was now deployed by platoons in a series of shell-holes to obviate possible dangers of long range shelling or aeroplane bombing. The Battalion learned that the objective assigned to the 169th Brigade was now the village of Bullecourt, east of Croisilles. The starting point of the advance was to be the Sensee river, north-east of Croisilles. From here the 169th Brigade was to fight its way forward towards Bullecourt through the trenches of the Hindenburg Line, followed by the 168th Brigade in support. For the Scottish, their move at midnight to the assembly position was fraught. They had never seen the ground before, there were no guides and it was pitch dark and raining. Notwithstanding, the move was completed by 2.30a.m. on the morning of 28 August. When the attack began, shortly after noon, the Scottish pushed forward in two lines with D and B Companies in the lead. Despite every endeavour they found it difficult to keep in touch with the 169th Brigade ahead, which by now was taking heavy casualties from well-placed enemy machine guns. These had taken refuge in tunnels and dugouts while the British barrage had passed over them and had now come out to the rear of the 169th, between it and the following brigade. The Kensingtons were dispatched to clear the area to the right and the 4th Londons to the left. There followed much bitter fighting before, late in the afternoon, the two

Return of the 1st Battalion Cadre from Germany, 18 May 1919.

battalions were able to establish themselves in a line of communication trenches about 1,200 yards north-west of Bullecourt.

Throughout this period the Scottish remained halted in support at River Road in the Hindenburg Line. There was considerable congestion in the area; five battalions of the 56th Division and elements of the 57th Division were operating in close proximity while the wounded from the contact battalions were being stretchered back along the Hindenburg trenches. There being no way forward, Colonel Jackson sought and was granted permission to stand fast. The situation remained unchanged during the night of 28-29 August. Although the 169th Brigade had got no nearer than 1,000 yards to Bullecourt and had suffered heavily in so doing, it had succeeded in advancing through the Hindenburg Line and had forced the enemy to abandon Croisilles which, with its nests of machine guns would have been stormed only at heavy cost. The next morning the London Scottish, supported by the 1st Londons, were ordered to attack Bullecourt village. On their right the Kensingtons, supported by the 4th Londons, were to assist by outflanking from the south. What was left of the 169th Brigade was to advance on the left, north of Bullecourt. Each of the leading battalions was to have sections of heavy machine guns and trench mortars attached.

Zero hour was set for 1.00p.m. The London Scottish moved from River Road at 8.00a.m. and were in their assembly position in Pelican Lane by noon. Although the movement was carried out in broad daylight there was no retaliation by the enemy, although snipers were occasionally busy. The barrage which was to cover the attack commenced at 12.55p.m., lifting and moving forward at the rate of 100 yards per six minutes. Its accuracy made up for its lack of intensity, although a few guns fired short into the leading British positions. As the barrage lifted at one o'clock the D and B Companies moved forward, with A Company 150 yards to the rear and C Company in reserve. The leading companies suffered immediate and heavy casualties from snipers and machine-gunners dug in to the ruins of the village. Matters might have been worse had the enemy artillery been heavier, but most had been withdrawn. A few shells were fired by long-range batteries, but most were directed into the support trenches. However, as the Germans realized the extent of the attack their artillery fire became heavier, but was still mostly directed on the communications.

The Scottish reached the north side of the village which they gradually cleared at the point of the bayonet, and by 2.30p.m. the survivors of the lead companies had reached Gordon Reserve Trench to the east. The initiative thus gained was quickly lost when it was discovered that the London Rifle Brigade assaulting to the north and the Kensingtons to the south had both been held up by machine-gun fire. Colonel Jackson committed A Company to the village to complete the mopping up and thereafter was compelled to send C Company to the left flank, where it was heavily engaged by German machine guns still holding out in the trenches to the north-east and east of the village. By 4.45p.m. the Scottish losses had proved so heavy that a decision was made to withdraw the leading survivors to a position within 150 yards of Gordon Reserve.

At 5.00p.m. B Company was east of Bullecourt, in two lines of platoons 100 yards in front of Gordon Reserve and 100 yards apart. D Company was to the rear in Gordon Reserve itself, A Company on the right of the eastern part of Tower Reserve, and C Company on the left of A, holding a line extending to the north of the village. Although the 169th Brigade was still held up, C Company was in touch with the advance parties of the London Rifle Brigade and consolidation was in progress. West of Bullecourt the 4th Londons in reserve put forward a company to Pelican Lane, while to the south the Kensingtons cleared Station Redoubt, but were unable to make any progress beyond it or along Railway Reserve. During the evening, the 4th Londons brought up a company to reinforce the left of the Scottish C Company positions, and at about the same time the enemy artillery fire slackened.

During the course of the next night the 168th Brigade was relieved by the

167th, the 1st Londons taking over Bullecourt from the Scottish who went into a reserve position on the Hindenburg Line. As far as the Scottish had been concerned their attack had been completely successful. Bullecourt had been captured, but the check to the advance north and south had made it a dangerous salient. The Scottish spent 30 August organizing and rearming and, although reduced in numbers, were by that afternoon ready to return to the fighting. In the afternoon the news came that the Germans had counter-attacked and retaken Bullecourt, and that in all likelihood the Scottish would be called upon to take it a second time. At 7.00p.m. this rumour was confirmed by a warning order, and at 9.00p.m. detailed orders were received for the 168th Brigade to assist in the recapture of the village.

The Battalion assembled at 3.00a.m. in preparation for zero hour at 5.15a.m. The attack was to be part of a general advance extending north and south for miles. The 168th Brigade, reinforced by the 7th Middlesex, was to take Bullecourt. The London Scottish on the right, the 4th Londons in the centre and the 7th Middlesex on the left were to assemble by the line of Pelican Avenue and lead the assault. The objective was to be a line north-east of Bullecourt along Saddlers Lane, Joyride Support, Fox Support, Tank Support and Tank Avenue. An artillery barrage would cover the advance, moving forward at the rate of 100 yards per four minutes. When the objective was taken the barrage would be advanced to the ground beyond for thirty minutes so as to protect the consolidating troops from counter-attack. The London Scottish were due to assemble in Pelican Avenue and Stray Reserve Trench and were to attack over the ground south of Bullecourt, retaking the Station Redoubt and pushing on along Railway Reserve to Tank Avenue. The Redoubt was to be bombarded by heavy artillery during the night, and two tanks, two machine guns and two Stokes Mortars were assigned to assist the assault. At 12.45a.m. on 31 August the Battalion moved along the Stray Reserve Trench to its assembly position which it finally reached at 3.30a.m. B and C Companies were forward on the left and right respectively, D Company was in support in Stray Reserve, and A Company in reserve behind the trench with orders not to move until so directed by Battalion Headquarters.

The assembly was made more difficult by German artillery which kept up harassing fire on the communication trenches throughout the night. The Germans, whom it was later learned were expecting the attack, put down a heavy counter-barrage of gas and high explosive on the assembly positions as soon as the British barrage began. Initially the attack went well, although Captain Bishop, commanding C Company, was wounded by his own creeping barrage. Station Redoubt, which had been the main target of the British barrage throughout the night, was recaptured with minimal loss, and thereafter the attack made good progress along Railway Reserve. When subsequent attempts to advance were held up by heavy machine-gun and rifle fire B, C and D Companies were deployed along the line of Bullecourt Avenue with orders to consolidate.

At 7.30a.m. contact was made with the King's Liverpool Regiment to the right, but the left flank remained in the air and the tanks had yet to appear. Inexplicably, at 8.00a.m. the German artillery fire died away. Taking advantage of this Colonel Jackson moved A Company from the reserve, placed the two attached machine guns with it, and ordered it into the Railway Redoubt. To the left the 4th Londons were meeting severe resistance as they attempted to move through the ruins of the village. Concerted efforts were made by the Scottish to assist them, but it was not until late in the evening that the enemy were driven out of Bullecourt and the gap between the Scottish and Londons' lines plugged.

At about 2.30p.m. aerial reconnaissance indicated that the enemy were massing in Tank Avenue and Tank Support and that a counter-attack was anticipated. British artillery at once registered on these positions and for a short period the Germans retaliated, but at 4.00p.m. their hostile fire ceased. The fighting died down as darkness came on. Although many of the objectives had not been taken the village of Bullecourt was again in British hands and a strong line secured and consolidated to the east. During the night the 52nd Division relieved the 56th in the line, the London Scottish being relieved by the 4th King's Own Scottish Borderers before returning to the neighbourhood of Boiry Becquerelle.

On 31 August Private Mclellan returned to France after seven days' leave. The next day he moved from Calais to Etaples and from there to the 56th Division reserve camp beyond Arras. Here he received news that the Division had been in action and that the Scottish had suffered badly. He and about ten others set off for Divisional lines the next day. *'It was a splendid sunny day, and the broken land laid no shadow on our souls.'* None of them had any idea of the news awaiting them. When McLellan, a veteran of a year in the trenches, discovered the extent of the carnage within his platoon, he cried himself to sleep.

The Last Battles

During the night of 2-3 September the enemy fell back rapidly along the whole front of the Third Army and the right of the First Army. On the following day he continued his withdrawal along the east bank of the Somme, south of Peronne and onward into the French sector. Throughout, the British followed closely, in many cases cutting off the rearguards, their forward guns and aircraft creating bloodshed among the retreating columns. For their part the London Scottish rested at Boiry Becquerelle, until on 6 September they were again brought into the line, moving up to the neighbourhood of Vis-en-Artois on the Arras-Cambrai road. The 56th Division replaced the 4th Division, the Scottish relieving the 2nd Northamptons in support between Lecluse and Etaing on the Sensee river. The enemy's artillery remained active despite his predicament, and any movement in the trenches provoked a heavy bombardment. On 13 September the 168th Brigade was relieved by the 167th, the Scottish marching to a point on the Cambrai-Arras road where motor buses conveyed them to Blagny in the suburbs of Arras, where dugouts and bivouacs were taken over from the 1st Londons.

After a spell of reorganization and company training the 168th Brigade received orders on 18 September to relieve the 8th Canadian Infantry Brigade in the Oisy-le-Verger sector of the front, the London Scottish and the 4th Londons relieving the 5th Canadian Mounted Rifles. The next day the Battalion moved by lorry to Vis-en-Artois, and at night relieved the Canadians; A and B Companies going into the front line, D Company in support and C Company in reserve in Rumancourt village. That day Fourth and Third Armies attacked in heavy rain on a front of some seventeen miles from Holnon to Gouzeaucourt, the First French Army co-operating to the south. The Allies penetrated to a depth of three miles through the much-battered old British and German frontlines. Over 12,000 prisoners and 100 guns were taken, and the stage set for a further advance along the St Quentin-Cambrai front through the Hindenburg system and on to Maubeuge. The 56th Division was brought into the line on the extreme left. On its left the Sensee river flowed through a hollow, its marshy banks forming a natural flank. To its right stood the Canadians and beyond them massed Allied forces prepared to advance on a front of some thirty miles. The Division was tasked with clearing the ground between the Sensee river and the Canal du Nord to its front, and thereafter to cross the line of the canal and cover the left flank of the general advance.

During the period of preparation the enemy were generally quiet by day but active during the hours of darkness. During the night of 23-24 September the Germans attempted a trench raid on a C Company outpost, but were dispersed by its garrison of sixteen men and two Lewis guns. A little later a second attempt was similarly repulsed, but thereafter a patrol sent out by the Scottish was forced to fall back before a very strong party of the enemy. The outpost was withdrawn and a five-minute artillery barrage brought down on its position. A strong patrol was then pushed forward and was able to report that the enemy had given up the attempt, after which the post was re-established.

On the night of 26-27 September the Battalion was relieved by the Kensingtons. During that night the artillery opened fire all along the thirty mile front and at 5.20a.m. the next morning the great advance began. Thirteen divisions swept forward across the Canal du Nord and the northern works of the Siegfried Line, and by evening were close to Cambrai. On the extreme left the 168th Brigade cleared the enemy from the west bank of the canal and from the Sensee hollow while the 169th Brigade crossed the canal and cleared its east bank. At 3.23p.m., by which time the Canadians to the right were safely across the canal, the Kensingtons attacked northwards towards the Sensee. As soon as they had advanced, the London Scottish in support moved into their assembly positions and from there sent patrols across the canal.

The advance continued throughout the next day, the 167th and 169th Brigades executing a successful pincer movement against the village of Palleul. The subsequent days were quiet on the left flank, the enemy having concentrated his forces in an effort to hold onto Cambrai and St Quentin. On 1 October the London Scottish took over from the 5th Dorsets opposite Aubencheul-au-Bac. The night was dark, dismal and unpleasant, made the more so by a constant drizzle. On such a night *'a man may feel himself to be a poor lost homeless unit in a hostile universe,'* mused McLellan. The weather cleared before dawn after which McLellan assumed that his platoon was in support rather than reserve, but due to the rather fluid state of the line was uncertain. The Battalion suffered continuous gas shelling throughout the next day and on 4 October sustained a bombing raid by enemy aircraft. The Battalion was relieved on 5 October by the 4th Londons and immediately prepared for an attack on Aubencheul. However, the enemy withdrew during the night, enabling the Scottish to occupy the position unhindered. On 9 October, the day that Cambrai fell to the Allies, the Scottish relieved the Lincolns in the outpost line. Two days later the Kensingtons drove the Germans out of Fessies, and on the following night the Scottish were relieved by the Queen's Westminsters and went into reserve at Rumancourt.

On 13 October the 56th Division was withdrawn from the line into Army reserve, the 168th Brigade being relieved by the 11th Canadian Infantry Brigade. The London Scottish marched from Rumancourt to Marquion, where the next morning they entrained for Arras which they reached at noon, thereafter marching to billets in the city. A fortnight was spent in rest and training. Arras, which for so long had stood on the front line was now secure and, although it bore the marks of war, hospitable. As a London Scot later related,

> *'Considering its four years' experience of war, Arras was, when I saw it last, remarkably well preserved in comparison with many other French towns similarly placed. The general destruction is comparatively slight, but those buildings which were specially marked for manifestations of hate have been wiped out in the approved Boche fashion. The cathedral figures among these, but in spite of everything it still boasts many upright columns and a figure of "Hope" practically intact! The latter strikes one almost forcibly, seeming to say, "The City is not dead but sleepeth." It awaits the triumphant call of "La France Glorieuse!"'*

The first phase of the great British offensive which was destined to bring about the end of the war, was now over. The Hindenburg Line, Germany's last and strongest prepared position, had been shattered. The threat to his lines of communication was now critical, some thirty-nine divisions had ceased to operate with any cohesion and 36,000 prisoners and 380 guns had been taken. The epicentre of the British effort now moved northwards to Flanders.

On 4 October Berlin contacted President Wilson seeking an armistice and peace. This information was kept strictly secret from the troops at the front. Orders were given that there should be no talk of the war being over as negotiations might be aborted at any time and it might yet prove necessary to fight all the way to the Rhine. Battalion training at Arras was therefore carried out with the same thoroughness as ever and by 30 October, when the 168th Brigade received orders to move again into the fighting, the London Scottish was in every respect capable of returning to the fray. Early on the morning of 31 October the Battalion, under command of Major Bishop MC, marched out of Arras via the Cambrai road where it was met by a convoy of buses which conveyed it to Noyelles-sur-Selle, from when it marched to Douchy on the Belgian border. Although Hallowe'en, the fourth of the war, was enjoyed in peace, the sound of the guns close-by were an ever present reminder that the war was far from over. At that time the Battalion was approximately 350 strong. C Company, which immediately before Cambrai could boast four platoons each fifty men strong, could now muster no more than ninety all ranks.

On the next morning Haig began his final attack on the German front between the Scheldt and the Sambre, moving on Maubeuge and Mons. On 1 November the British attacked south of Valenciennes, taking the town the next day. They then pushed the line east, extending the right south-eastward along the Valenciennes-Preseau road. The 4th Canadian Division, which had taken the town of Valenciennes held the extreme left, east and north of the position, allowing the 11th Division to take Preseau. The 49th Division was between these two formations, beyond the Rhonelle, near the road. The advance was to be resumed on 4 November with the Canadians on the left, the 56th Division, which was to relieve the 49th, in the centre with the 11th Division in the area of Preseau. The front of what was destined to be the final battle of the war extended for a distance of about thirty miles, from Valenciennes south to the Sambre. The nature of the country across which the advance was to be made was most difficult. In the south the river had to be crossed almost at the outset, in the centre the Forest of Mormal presented a formidable obstacle, and in the north the fortified town of Le Quesnoy and several streams which ran parallel to the advance offered frequent opportunities for successful defence. Conversely morale had never been higher, the troops revelling in the new-found opportunity to operate on ground not pitted by three years of trench warfare.

On 2 November the 168th Brigade moved from Douchy to Maing, near the bend of the Scheldt south of Valenciennes, and on the following night went into the line, relieving a brigade of the 49th Division. The 4th Londons and Kensingtons were in front, the London Scottish in reserve near Famars. Soon after dawn the Canadians discovered that the enemy had fallen back some distance in the night. Patrols were pushed out and found the village of Saultain, to the front of the 56th Division positions, unoccupied. It was then decided to advance, the 56th Division going forward in concert with the

Canadians on their left and the 11th Division on their right. They met with little opposition, the enemy having no stomach for a fight. The line was thus pushed forward beyond the railway, and the Headquarters of the 168th Brigade was established near Saultain village. Orders were issued on the evening of 3 November for the attack the next day. The attack would take place at dawn and would be preceded by an intense bombardment along the entire front. In the north the Corps cavalry would seize the crossings of the Honelle river and the village of Sebourgquiaux and advance to contact against the enemy. The 56th Division would advance with two brigades forward, the 169th on the right and the 168th on the left, the final objective of the latter being a line running through Angre village, on the Honelle, to a point north of Angreau. The 4th Londons were to be in the lead with the London Scottish in support and the Kensingtons in reserve. The 4th Londons were to gain all ground occupied by the cavalry, and to secure as their objective the line of high ground east of the Aunelle beyond the village of Sebourgquiaux. The Scottish were then to advance through them and take the final objective. After dark the London Scottish in reserve relieved the 4th Londons on the east bank of the Aunelle and in Sebourgquiaux village and prepared to carry forward the advance at dawn the next morning. B Company under Captain White was placed on the right, C Company under Captain Bennett in the centre and A Company under Captain Liebert on the left; D Company under Captain Newbigging was held in reserve.

The cavalry moved out at 5.30a.m. to seize the river crossings, and the infantry began its advance half an hour later. The crossings were secured without serious opposition as the enemy had decided to concentrate his limited resources in defence of the higher ground beyond. The Scottish moved forward at 7.30a.m. to occupy the ground west of Sebourgquiaux in readiness for their advance through the lines of the 4th Londons. However, no further progress was made that day. The steady advances which Haig enjoyed in the south could not be matched in the north, and although the Canadians reached the outskirts of Rombies, the 56th Division was hard-pressed to hold the ground captured against a counter-attack launched from the higher ground east of the Aunelle. By 8.45a.m. the 4th Londons had crossed the Aunelle river and had established themselves in the outskirts of Sebourgquiaux, but thereafter had been pinned down by heavy machine-gun fire. On their right the 169th Brigade seized Sebourg and reached the banks of the river, but was unable to establish a bridgehead across.

Unknown to the Scottish the events of the previous day had finally broken the enemy's resistance. That night, in almost continuous rain, the Germans began to fall back on practically the whole front. Throughout the day the roads packed with enemy troops and transport provided excellent targets for the British heavy artillery and aircraft. Only in the north did the advance meet serious resistance. At 6.00a.m. the Scottish advanced and quickly took the high ground, capturing three machine guns and turning them on the retreating enemy. However the enemy quickly recovered and were soon bringing down heavy and accurate fire on the consolidating British. At dusk the Scottish were ordered to secure the ground immediately west of Angre as a prelude to a further advance the next day. The Scottish casualties that day were remarkably light, only five killed and eighteen wounded. However these included Lieutenant Hyslop MM killed, the third of three brothers to die serving the Battalion, and Captain White MC wounded.

The action of the next day was, for the 1st Battalion London Scottish, the last of the war. The enemy held a strong position a mile and a half east of the Honelle river but by now were showing little disposition to fight. The 168th Brigade was ordered to attack with two battalions forward, the London Scottish on the right and Kensingtons on the left. The Scottish, who were tasked with clearing the enemy out of Angre village before advancing to Audregnies, were to advance with three companies in the first line, each on a two-platoon front. The advance was resumed at 5.30a.m. after a short but savage barrage. Initially the assault went well with only light resistance encountered, but as the river was crossed the enemy's artillery massed on the heights put down a barrage on the advancing British. C Company crossed north of Angre in touch on the right with the Kensingtons, D at Angre village, and A and B Companies to the south. D Company suffered the brunt of the German barrage and its advance across the village was checked. However, it quickly reformed and in a second assault carried the river crossing and pushed forward into the German positions. The enemy resistance disintegrated, and those who did not flee surrendered. But the Scottish quickly found themselves in a salient. To their right the 169th Brigade had been counter-attacked and driven back across the river. The Kensingtons were also forced to retire, making it necessary for C Company of the Scottish to retire in order to keep in contact. The Battalion was ordered to dig in and that afternoon was reinforced by the 4th Londons and a section of heavy machine guns in anticipation of a counter-attack. However, although the German barrage intensified the attack never came, and despite a very difficult situation the Scottish were able to hold on throughout the day. The Scottish had borne themselves well, and at a cost of eleven killed, fifty-six wounded and one missing had secured the only success of the day in that sector.

That night the 168th Brigade was relieved by a brigade of the Royal Naval Division and returned to billets at Sebourg. The men were exhausted and were allowed to sleep through the next morning, but the afternoon was devoted to cleaning the Lewis guns, rifles and other equipment. At 8.00a.m. on 8 November the Scottish were ordered to march via Roisin and Eth to the neighbourhood of Autreppe in pursuit of the retreating Germans. Rain fell incessantly and progress was further impeded by a series of large craters blown by the enemy at many of the crossroads and strategic positions. The advance continued throughout the next day, until on the morning of 10

November the Battalion found itself in billets near Blairegnies, some eight miles south of Mons.

It was here that at 7.00a.m. on the morning of 11 November the London Scottish received news from Brigade Headquarters that the Armistice had been signed late the previous evening and that all hostilities were to cease at 11.00a.m. that day. For the British the war had ended as it had begun, at Mons. The first and last rifle shots were fired within 100 yards of each other, the first and last soldiers to be killed were buried in the same cemetery.

After the Armistice

The Armistice found the 1st Battalion London Scottish at Le Dessous, near Mons, with the 56th Division, and the 2nd Battalion with the 30th Division near Marionette St Anne, on the west bank of the Scheldt, between Courtrai and Oudenarde. Early rumour suggested that the 56th Division would form part of the Army of Occupation and would shortly be moved to Cologne. However, on 20 November it was announced that the logistical difficulties of sustaining so large a force had proved too great and that the 56th Division would not now be required in Germany. Some solace was gained when three days later the Battalion moved from the overcrowded and insanitary conditions of Le Dessous to better billets at Eugies. On 27 November the 168th Brigade was transferred to the Givry area south-east of Mons, the Scottish being billeted in the village where they remained until the New Year.

The Battalion, which by now mustered 15 officers and 626 other ranks, with 7 officers and 105 men detached, embarked on a schedule of light training in which civilian as well as military skills were honed in anticipation of a speedy return to civilian life. However, on 13 January 1919 a warning order was received transferring the Scottish to the 9th Division, part of the Second Army destined for occupation of the Rhineland. The next day Brigadier General Loch, commanding the 168th Brigade, bade farewell to the Battalion, the longest serving which had been with the Brigade for nearly three years:

'Almost three years ago you joined the Brigade on its formation as a unit of the newly-formed 56th Division. During these three years you have taken part in no less than seven major operations, including the final grand offensive which culminated in the Armistice.

'Your great gallantry and unhesitating readiness to give and take punishment have been throughout of the very highest order, your cheerfulness under hardships, and excellent discipline at all times leaving nothing to be desired.

'You leave this Brigade to join a Brigade of a famous Scottish Division in the Army of Occupation, and I feel sure that the same high standard of discipline which has enabled you to overcome all obstacles in the past will help your good name in the future.

'I am profoundly grieved at the loss this Brigade suffers in your departure, and still more deeply sorry at the personal loss it means to me of many old and tried friends.

'I wish you one and all the best of luck in your new Division, with the certain knowledge that you will enhance your already magnificent reputation.

'Good-bye!'

G.S. LOCH, Brigadier General,
Commanding the 168th Brigade

At 10.30a.m. on 16 January the Battalion paraded for the last time as part of the 168th Brigade. As it began its route march to Mons from where it was to entrain for Germany it found the road lined by Kensingtons, their band playing the Regimental March as a farewell, and a little later were joined by the 4th Londons. At the next village they were met by the London Rifle Brigade, and on the outskirts of Mons by the three bands of the 167th Brigade. There could have been no better, or more genuine send-off. The German railway system had been rendered chaotic by the war, and a journey which might ordinarily have taken a few hours took two days. At Hilden, a town some thirty-two miles north of Cologne, the Scottish relieved the 1st Newfoundland Regiment. They found their stay in the town far from unpleasant, and quickly found their civility towards the local population reciprocated.

As one London Scot wrote in a letter home,

'I suppose I ought to swash-buckle as befits a conquering enemy, but, sorry and all that, it's not in me. I tell you, it positively hurts to see kiddies get the wind up and dodge off the pavement in front of you. There isn't much of that though, as they are getting used to British troops. I was talking to an old lady who spoke French, and she said that the inhabitants in general were very pleased with the quiet behaviour of the soldiers here.'

Life was relaxed for the Scottish. Detachments were provided to examine passes and control traffic crossing the Rhine, but otherwise the days were passed in peacetime military routine with three mornings a week dedicated to civilian-orientated classes. Inevitably sport came to the fore and the Battalion quickly re-established its prowess at football, athletics and boxing, Captain Newbigging MC of D Company winning the Welterweight Boxing Championship for officers.

On 13 March 1919 a soldier, in a letter home, encapsulated the pleasures of occupation:

'What did we find when we came here? A small outpost to be maintained by one platoon, which is now eagerly sought for by everybody as being more a pleasure than a duty. All the Battalion in

billets in a town cleaner and more convenient in every way than any of its size in France, Belgium, or even England or Scotland. Messrooms in restaurants with the food cooked by German women, with decent cutlery and crockery on tables. All kinds of shops, and in them articles to buy at a price at least a quarter of that in France or Belgium. Military duty consisting of a short parade in the morning, with all the afternoon devoted to sport and recreation. Who wouldn't be in the Army of Occupation?'

That day news arrived that the Battalion was to be reduced to a cadre, the balance of its troops to be either demobilized or transferred to the 2nd Battalion. On 18 March Colonel E.D Jackson DSO made his final speech to the assembled battalion which he had commanded so ably for two years, and on 29 March the final orders were received for reduction to cadre status. On 1 April, a day beloved of the British Army for change, the Scottish Rifles officially took over duties from the London Scottish. The next day a draft under the command of Captain Brown MC entrained for Etaples, and five days later the cadre remaining, now reduced to five officers and forty-eight other ranks, began their move to the Fifth Army area in Belgium. The cadre, now part of the 8th Division, was destined to spend a frustrating month in rather inadequate barracks at Ath. Fortunately duties remained light and the men were given thirty-six-hour passes to Brussels to relieve the boredom. Inevitably rumours as to the return to England abounded, and it thus came as a relief when orders were received to entrain for Dunkirk on 3 May. It is hard to imagine the views of the veterans among the cadre as their train passed through the old battle areas, still places of waste and desolation and so different to the bountifulness of Cologne.

After three days in a rest camp in Dunkirk the Scottish embarked on board the SS *Mogileef* en route for Southampton from where they entrained for Sandling. There a few days were spent returning stores and generally winding down. On 16 May Colonel Jackson and his men returned to Headquarters in London. Their arrival at Charing Cross at 3.30p.m. was marked by scenes of great enthusiasm. A pipe band including five Pipe Majors was waiting on the platform, and falling in behind it the Scottish marched out amid ringing cheers. Many old comrades who had fought in Hodden Grey proudly joined the parade as it made its short journey home. There they found the Mayor of Westminster and many comrades waiting to receive them, the galleries above crowded with many friends of the Regiment. There followed a Royal Salute to HRH Princess Louise, Duchess of Argyle, who came to bid her regiment home, speeches from Colonels Green and Greig, and a hearty meal.

Other greetings came in the form of telegrams and letters which were read out as the afternoon progressed:

From Field Marshal the Rt. Hon. Viscount French KP, GCB, OM, GCVO, KCMG

'Please convey to all members of the London Scottish who are

Arrival of the Cadre at 59 Buckingham Gate, 18 May 1919.

returning from abroad, as well as to all retired members of that distinguished Regiment, my hearty welcome and my warmest congratulations on the magnificent record they have established from the beginning of the war.

'Personally, I shall never forget the splendid service they rendered at the first battle of Ypres.'

From Colonel G.A. Malcolm, DSO, TD, to Officer Commanding
1st Cadre Battalion London Scottish, 59 Buckingham Gate, S.W.1.

'I tender to you all, Officers, NCOs and men of the 1st Batt., my sincere and heartfelt congratulations on your return to London. I regret exceedingly that absence from London prevents my being present in person to express my admiration of the glorious manner in which the traditions of the Regiment have been upheld by all ranks from the 15th September 1914, to the 11th November 1918.'

Among the most poignant was a message from the Honorable Artillery Company whose 1st Battalion had followed the Scottish to France, and who themselves saw action a few days after Messines:

To Officer Commanding London Scottish, from Major F. Charles Bell, Hon. Artillery Company:

'Permit me to offer the hearty congratulations of the Hon. Artillery Company on the magnificent manner in which your regiment has maintained traditions of the London Scottish, and at the same time tender our deepest sympathy to all those friends and relatives who must be grieving over poor chaps whose names must be inscribed on the Roll of Honour.

'Lord Albermarle, commanding the Civil Service Rifles, has also sent the heartiest congratulations of his regiment.'

No better epitaph could have been written to the officers and men of the London Scottish than that which appeared in *The Daily Graphic* in its editorial of 17 May 1919:

'"Is that all?"

'It was the voice of a small, slight, slender flapper in the crowd at Charing Cross yesterday, after the swift passing of the handful of men who represent all that is left of the brave battalion of those London Scottish, the first of the Territorial units to go out in the early days of the war.

'The speaker could have been but a small child five years ago, and for that reason her words carried no sting. But for many in the packed crowd that surged and broke out of line in their eagerness to welcome home this handful of heroes the procession was full of poignancy.

'The sons of London's great middle-class, not always of Scots descent, were once part of the London Scottish: many of them wore their khaki and blue long before the stern call came: many of them have so long ceased to wear it that mothers have laid aside their mourning garb, and keep their sadness hidden.

'Great days have come and gone since we had that early picture of the ragged remnants of the London Scottish answering the roll-call after the first gallant work. Small wonder that for some of the youngsters looking on the group of fifty officers and men who passed out of the station, headed by half as many pipers, had no meaning at all.

'But for the rest of us it was a ghostly hour, in which we saw through tears the faces of the lads we loved in days when war was undreamed of, and our hearts were burdened with no more anxieties than the dread lest our own young hopeful, newly entered on a business career, and developing a blatant taste in socks and ties, should be led astray by that zest of life which helped to make him doubly precious to our eyes.

'Very different lads they were from the men who came back. We dreaded once lest they should be facing life too frivolously. How could we dream that such a glory of pride and of suffering should be their immortal legacy?

'The bronzed group came, passed, and was lost to view in the following crowd within the space of a minute. If one were sight-seeing, it was little enough. It was only a few men looking gallant and happy, "weel pleased" with London's shouting tribute, glad to be home and accounted among the "lucky ones" in that they were able to march without fatigue on a hot day through Cockspur Street and Piccadilly, down Grosvenor Place and along Victoria Street to their yellow-flagged headquarters in Buckingham Gate.

"What went ye out for to see?"

'A very frail, elderly lady, as slightly built as the little flapper whose voice one first heard, stood on the edge of the pavement clasping the arm of an elderly man, markedly erect and stern. The group of soldiers went past the couple: and as the pipes skirled on ahead the lady raised her face, quivering like a reed shaken with the wind, towards that of her husband, who gazed at unseen things far off and dim, but moved no muscle. And one saw, rather than heard, on her lips the faintest of whispers, "Oh, my boy, my boy!"

That was all.'

Chapter Eight

PART THREE:
The Second Battalion
Early Days

The 2nd Battalion London Scottish was born of the overwhelming urge of literally thousands of men of Scottish descent to give their services to their country in time of need. The war was less than a month old when Territorial Force units were given permission to raise second battalions. The London Scottish began to recruit at 8.00a.m. on the morning of 31 August. Within a week the establishment of the new unit was complete; indeed in the following weeks it became necessary to divert 1,500 potential volunteers to the ranks of the 51st Highland Division then in billets at Bedford.

Douglas Kennedy, who had earlier served in the Battalion, was one of the many to rush to return to the Colours.

'I set off at once for the Scottish Headquarters at Buckingham Gate, where I found a long queue. Jumping this, I made my way to the Peacetime Office, which was dealing with "Rejoins," and soon found myself at a Medical Board looking into a familiar face. It was my old friend "Wurgey", now in officer's uniform and a Regimental MO. We had a chat. I recollect no medical examination, and I found myself being sworn in, and issued with a rifle and regimental number.'

The 2nd Battalion halted during a route march on Wimbledon Common: 24 October 1914.

The 2nd Battalion fixing bayonets. At this stage they were still armed with the old Lee Metford Rifle.

Others joined for sound family reasons. W. N Hendry later recalled that:

'At this time I was the proud possessor of a motorcycle, so offered my services, and my name was put down to be notified when required. Weeks after this no word came, so I went to join the OTC. Here I was asked if I had been called to the Bar, as they were only taking such gentlemen at the time. A week or two passed, and my brother Jim had joined the London Scottish, as my father had been a member in his younger days, I decided to join also. A very strict medical examination was taken and I passed half-an-inch under height, signing on November 5, 1914.'

Command of the Battalion passed to Colonel J.W. Greig, while Captain A.E. Rogers TD, who had only recently transferred to the Reserve, was

appointed Adjutant. Officers were provisionally appointed to the various companies and platoons and training began, several officers and non-commissioned officers being detailed to assist from the 1st Battalion. On 1 October it was ordered that in future officers would be appointed from within the Battalion. The Commanding Officer appointed five 'acting subalterns' from the ranks to relieve the stress. Uniquely, and highly unofficially, they were to be granted the privileges of the Officers' Mess but in all other respects were to remain private soldiers and were only paid as such. The new battalion had been in training for less than a fortnight when, on 12 September, orders were received to dispatch 200 men as a draft to the 1st Battalion, which was then stationed at Watford and which had been ordered to France.

Virtually the entire Battalion volunteered. Applicants were limited to those who had undertaken a fortnight's camp, and many a good story to gain acceptance was concocted by those who had not, but without apparent success. Due to the acute lack of uniforms only sixty-four men were ready to leave for Watford on the following evening. Of the remainder, dispatched the next day, many were sent in civilian clothes and were only fitted out by exchanging clothing and equipment with members of the 1st Battalion not proceeding to France. These men were returned to London and became the nucleus of the 1st General Service Company, which was held in readiness to form the first overseas draft. Fortuitously they contained within their ranks several experienced non-commissioned officers, a commodity then seriously lacking in the 2nd Battalion.

For the next three months training was undertaken with vigour. After the departure of the 1st Battalion, rifles were issued and the 2nd gradually gained parts of their uniform, much of it by private purchase. Training was relieved by various guards, and on 9 November 600 members of the Battalion, by then fully armed and equipped, paraded in the Lord Mayor's Procession.

None within the Battalion could have realized, as they sat down to Hallowe'en Dinner in the Victoria Station Hotel that their colleagues in the 1st Battalion were even then fighting for their lives. The Battalion history noted that,

'Though we little knew it this had been a memorable day in the history of the Scottish and of the Territorial Force. The Commanding

The 2nd Battalion on a route march passing Buckingham Palace, 7 November 1914.

Officer was at Hallowe'en when at about 10.00p.m. an officer of the Air Force came to Headquarters. He had flown from France and had been sent on from the War Office. He told the Adjutant that half the 1st Battalion and more than half the officers had been lost that day fighting near Messines. The Commanding Officer came from Hallowe'en. The news was too serious to divulge lightly and nothing was known to the Battalion till the press on Monday 2 November.'

The return of the first wounded from Messines brought a new awareness of the true realities of war to the younger members of the Battalion.

'The first casualty to enter Buckingham Gate was Lieutenant Lindsey Renton, slightly wounded in the foot,' recalled Douglas Kennedy. 'As he limped, with the aid of a stick, across the floor of the Drill Hall, a cheer broke out from the new soldiers in training. His was a superficial wound, not a real "Blighty" which, later in the war, was a wound serious enough to involve several weeks in hospital and so a probable return to England. The Regiment had taken such a shrewd knock in their first action at Messines, that it must have been thought good propaganda, and good policy, to pack all the lightly wounded home for a spot of leave.'

The story of the action at Messines had an instant effect on recruiting, and at one time the strength of the Battalion rose to over 1,500 men. A 3rd Battalion was then formed, and at the end of November all Home-Service personnel were posted to it. Lieutenant Colonel A.E. Rogers assumed command of the 2nd, or 1st Reserve Battalion as it was then known, and Colonel J.W. Greig the 3rd, or 2nd Reserve Battalion. On 17 December the 2nd Battalion was inspected on Horse Guards with other units of the Grey Brigade, and a fortnight later, on 4 January 1915, was ordered to billets in Dorking.

W.N. Hendry remembered that the Battalion was due to depart from London at 5.00a.m. and that those who could not get to the Headquarters at that time were found billets near Victoria. At Dorking the Battalion took its place as part of 2/4th London Brigade under Colonel E.W. Baird. The Headquarters was located in the church hall, the troops being billeted in a number of empty houses or with local families. Hendry was unlucky enough to be billeted in a disused stable, but it was not long before this was condemned as unsanitary and he and seven others were moved to the front basement of a draper's shop. Here, he remembered,

> 'the girls used to keep us well supplied with fruit, etc, passed through the grating, like feeding animals.'

The Scottish amply rewarded the locals for their hospitality. *The Star* reported on 2 March 1915 that,

> 'The Scottish are special favourites among the townspeople. They are for the most part billeted in empty houses, and they have entered into the furnishing line in a thoroughly businesslike way. What they have not been able to beg, borrow, or otherwise commandeer, they have exercised ingenuity in improvising from empty packing cases, with the result that they have made their quarters quite comfortable and presentable.'

The sole complaint of the Scottish seemed to relate to the monotony of their diet.

> 'When the chaplain recently gave out his text: "Man cannot live by bread alone", reported The Star, 'there came the audible response from one of the kilted ones, "nor stew neither."'

The Commanding Officer was on sick leave at the time and temporary command thus passed to Major R. Crerar. But it was the Adjutant, Captain Robert Whyte, whom Douglas Kennedy remembered as the 'dynamo, determined to charge us all with his electric enthusiasm,' who was instrumental in ensuring that a new and purposeful routine was quickly

The 2nd Battalion during a route march halted at Maida Vale, 7 November 1914.

implemented. The surrounding area with its hills proved ideal for training. Company exercises were immediately commenced, varied by Battalion drills at Cotmandene and the inevitable inspections. Of these the most memorable was an inspection by Lord Kitchener and the French Minister of War, Millerand. As the Battalion War Diary noted;

'For home service no one could wish a more unpleasant experience. Reveille was at 3.45a.m., sick parade at 4.00a.m. and breakfast at 4.30a.m. A veritable blizzard raged over Epsom Downs; the wait was long and all were encrusted with snow and half frozen,' reported the Diary. *'The Scottish, probably because fully armed, were on the right of the line. Equipment as a whole was not complete but that of the front platoons was (made so). The inspecting party arrived by motor - the "Present" brought down a deluge of snow from the crested Glengarries. Little could be seen but the red faces of the men framed in their icy panoplies.'*

After the parade it was decided not to risk the railway but to march back to Dorking. Conditions were atrocious, for it had now stopped snowing and the hot sun shining through a cloudless sky rendered the conditions unpleasantly hot for all ranks who were then marching in greatcoats.

'Our arrival at Dorking crested with snow like cockatoos,' reported the Diary, *'caused considerable amusement.'*

Lieutenant Colonel J.W. Grieg CB, VD, KC Commanding Officer 2nd Battalion, 7 November 1914.

The Lord Mayor's Parade, November 1914. Lieutenant Colonel Greig is on horse back, Captain Ford and Lieutenant Syer on foot.

Shortly thereafter the Battalion was issued with the Japanese Meiji 38 rifle in place of the outdated long Lee-Enfield rifle. Training continued, but due to the lack of a suitable range the men could not be declared proficient in musketry. Considerable tension arose when the Commanding Officer supported by the Brigadier, refused to 'sign-off' his men as fit for action due to their lack of long-range marksmanship practise. The matter was only resolved when it was agreed that the men's experience was sufficient for trench conditions, and undertakings were given that drafts for France would receive further instruction once there. On 21 February the Battalion was ordered to London to make room in Dorking for a newly-formed Kitchener Division marching through. While in London the Battalion was ordered to provide a large draft for the 1st, which had recently lost a large number of experienced soldiers to commissioning elsewhere.

A total of 383 non-commissioned officers and men were dispatched, their places being taken by transfers from the 3rd Battalion and by an almost daily acquisition of recovered wounded officers and men returned from the 1st Battalion. On 30 March 1915, after a month in London, the Scottish left for Watford. Life was relatively relaxed with plenty of leave, the Battalion's principal responsibility being the manning of road blocks at night. On 16 April the Regimental diary recorded a particularly busy night of duties when A, B and C companies were each tasked with finding twenty men for picquet duty.

> 'This was in response to an emergency order to stop and examine all motors, their drivers and passengers coming from any direction. The Brigade had to cover a fairly extended line of which the Scottish Section took in the three bridges over the Colne at Watford. At a given moment wagons were disposed across the roads in the approved fashion for barricading a mountain defile. Two sentries with fixed bayonets and pouches filled with ball ammunition stood in the road facing outwards either side of the barricade and halted the motor traffic, which could only pass when OC Picquet was satisfied. It was a strange sight in an English town, apparently so remote from war, and still stranger was the absolute "matter of courseness" with which the public, motorists included, accepted the position.'

On 17 May the Battalion relocated to Saffron Walden.

> 'We marched out of Watford one lovely spring morning with the Pipe band playing and the waving of hands by nearly all the inhabitants, who had turned out to see us off,'

remembered W.N. Hendry.

> 'We made a stop the first night at Hatfield and were billeted in the out houses and stables in the grounds of Lord Salisbury's estate. We were allowed to view the mansion and saw a fine collection of paintings, etc in the large ballroom.'

The officers were even more fortunate, being offered the hospitality of the house itself for their night's abode. Further overnight stops were made at Ware and Bishop's Stortford before the final destination was reached.

Saffron proved a popular base with everyone. Douglas Kennedy, newly commissioned, remembered that;

> 'In our own small world of Army Life in England, we found Saffron Walden to be a most agreeable place. The Headquarters and officers' Mess were at The Rose and Crown Hotel, where the food was excellent, and Robert Whyte was hard put to it, to keep our minds on war training.'

Initially Hendry was less lucky, being billeted in a small hut when most were in private billets.

> 'However, after a few days half our Company went to the Workhouse, which was very nice with plenty of hot water and a good bed each, a real good billet. After my experience here I shall not worry if I ever have to take to the workhouse.'

Although training was heavily restricted by the state of the crops much effort was expanded in honing Company drills and on musketry, while every assistance was given to the local farmers collecting in the harvest. Drafts

168

were still regularly required for the 1st Battalion, including the majority of those who had recovered from wounds sustained when serving with it earlier. Although this removed a pool of badly needed experience, it also alleviated the growing friction between 2nd Battalion and former 1st Battalion officers and soldiers on the matter of promotion. Initially it had been decided that due to their experience, preference should be given to those former 1st Battalion soldiers with combat experience. However, as the number of 'veterans' increased, 2nd Battalion 'originals', many with a year's service behind them, became increasingly resentful. The matter was finally resolved when, in the middle of July, responsibility for finding battle drafts passed to the 3rd Battalion and promotion reverted to more of an internal affair.

During the first week of August the Battalion moved from billets into camp in a pleasant field close to the railway station. Here the Battalion experienced its first sight of war when it was awakened by the hum of the first Zeppelin returning from a raid on London. At the same time the nomenclature of the force was changed from the 2/4th London Infantry Brigade to the 179th Infantry Brigade and the 2nd (London) Division to the 60th (London) Division. Early in September

Lieutenant Colonel A.E. Rogers, Commanding Officer, November 1914 to September 1915.

command passed from Lieutenant Colonel Rogers to Lieutenant Colonel Robert Dunsmore. At the end of October the Scottish returned to billets at Bishop's Stortford and began preparations for a move to Salisbury Plain. Christmas was uneventful, with leave being given to as many as possible, and on 21 January 1916, the unit left its base and moved by train to Warminster, where it took over No 9 Camp at Sutton Veney as a prelude to service in France.

A progressive scheme of training was introduced by the Divisional Commander, with everyone put through a full musketry course, mainly in atrocious conditions. Mock trenches in the area were used to practise the relief as well as the attack and the defence of trenches, while much sleep was lost to an increasing number of night exercises. Despite the conditions, and particularly the all-pervading mud, life was quite tolerable. *The Regimental Gazette* reported that;

> '*The camp is splendidly equipped, and the various buildings are well-disposed. The privates have a canteen to themselves, while the corporals (including those who carry the lance) also have a separate room in which to discuss their bestriped affairs. Military status is thus*

studied to a degree! The Regimental Institute provides the most excellent literary fare in the way of London dailies and weeklies, and a few Scottish papers.'

On 31 January Lord French, recently returned from France, inspected the Division. As the *Gazette* recalled;

'The trained men in each unit were formed up separately from the recruits, and the sick bore labels describing their fearsome diseases.'

One of the Scottish remembered meeting French before the war, and was shocked by the drastic change in his appearance.

'His shortness of stature was emphasised by a perceptible stoop, and his twelve months' direction of the campaign in France seemed to have found plenty of evidence in his careworn expression and lustreless eyes.'

Second Lieutenant H.L. Syer and Captain C.N. Ford, November 1914.

On 24 April the Battalion moved to another camp at Longbridge Deverill, about a mile distant. Four days later it received orders to proceed at 6.00a.m. the next morning for Ireland. That night was spent in issuing pay books, emergency rations and 120 rounds of ammunition per man. En route, especially at Cardiff, the Scottish were impressed by the generosity

The 2nd Battalion in Hyde Park, December 1914. Pipe Major Robertson leading Pipers Cowie, MacKinnon, Gow, Stewart, Hare, Paton, Crawford, Shand, Campbell and Wills.

The Battalion Buglers, Dorking January 1915.

of various workers from the local Soldiers' rests. As *The Regimental Gazette* later reported;

> '*These good people distributed postcards (which they afterwards collected for the post) and coffee to the men, who were keenly appreciative of these favours.*'

The Battalion spent three days at Neyland, a small Welsh fishing village, in a delightful spot overlooking the harbour. There they were favoured by the most excellent weather, of which many took advantage to swim and sunbathe, the only Regimental requirements seemingly being the occasional guard and a mandatory haircut.

On 1 May the Scottish embarked upon the *Archangel*, and after a smooth passage marred only by the necessity to wear lifebelts and take their boots

The London Scottish training in Dorking, January 1915.

A well-earned halt after a twenty-six mile route march, 19 March 1915.

off, they disembarked at Queenstown about 6.00a.m. the next morning, from where they marched seven miles to Total Island. On the next day they entrained, travelling through Cork to the small town of Bandon. Here they pitched tents just outside the town in pouring rain. During the next three nights they marched out by platoons accompanied by an officer and a policeman to various houses suspected of harbouring Sinn Fein activists. Parties of eight would fix bayonets and surround a house, demand that its occupants dress and come outside, and then search the property. On a few occasions they met minor resistance when the residents either tried to escape or refused to leave the comfort of their beds but there were no injuries sustained; indeed, there are no reports of any weapon having been fired.

On the fourth day, still in incessant rain, the Battalion marched to Cronakilty where they slept sixteen to a tent before entraining for Lassclene, where they boarded a ship arriving at Fishguard at 4.00a.m. They entrained

Ronald K Salmond, died of measles 1 February 1915; the Battalion's first casualty.

straight away for Warminster, which they had left only fifteen days earlier. W.N. Hendry was subsequently to note that it had rained throughout that period.

After a fortnight's intensive work on Divisional training the Battalion at last received its warning order for France. All were issued with balmoral hats and service kit after which the entire Division was inspected by the King. After a final medical examination the entire Battalion was given four days embarkation leave.

On The Western Front

On the morning of 21 June 1916 the Battalion entrained at Warminster, in the words of the Regimental History;

> 'in fine physical condition, and as eager as the many thousands who had preceeded them to measure themselves against the foe.'

As the train slowed for Southampton many young soldiers threw postcards out of the windows to the locals to post to families and loved ones. In company with the 2nd Battalion Kensingtons the Scottish boarded the SS *La Marguerite*, a modest and none too clean paddle steamer which had formerly run from Margate to London. Following a night of intense discomfort, compounded by the fact that all on board had to wear lifebelts and remove their boots, the party arrived at Havre at 2.00a.m., and left the boat at 9.00a.m. to march the short distance to No 1 Rest Camp where all ranks were confined to barracks for the day.

On 23 June reveille was sounded at 5.00a.m.

Private (Later Corporal) Henry Hawkes. Probably joined the 3rd Battalion in late 1916. Posted to 1st Battalion 24 July and returned to United Kingdom on 29 December 1917. Later transferred to the Machine Gun Corps.

after which the Battalion marched two miles before entraining in cattle trucks, thirty men in each, in considerable discomfort. By noon the long journey towards the line had begun, the train slowly meandering up the picturesque valley of the Seine until by dusk it had reached Rouen. As soon as the Battalion had cleared the train it marched to Abendoyt, within sound and range of the guns, which it reached at 3.00p.m. that afternoon. That night, as the young Scots slept comfortably in a series of barns and out houses, they received their baptism of fire when a number of artillery shells dropped harmlessly into the town. On 25 June the Battalion marched to Manoveal, north-west of Arras and close to Vimy Ridge. On 27 June the Scottish made their first entrance into the real trenches when working parties were supplied to the 185th Tunnelling Company, Royal Engineers

who were mining under the German lines. Their job consisted mainly of bagging earth, making fire-bays and undertaking guard duties in the sap heads. Those supporting the Royal Engineers had to pass through a sector of trenches known as The Labyrinth, where in 1915 the French had lost thousands of men in stemming the German advance. It was not long before the Battalion grew used to the sight of death and mutilation, although fortunately for them their own losses remained minimal.

On 6 July the 60th Division moved into line for instruction by battalions of the 51st (Highland) Division whom they were due to relieve. The Scottish were allocated the sector held by the 1/7th (Deeside) Battalion, The Gordon Highlanders.

Photograph of William Ernest Philpott and his fiancée May, taken on 16 September 1916. They married three weeks before William was killed at Cambrai, 24 November 1917.

'They were a fine lot of fellows,' remembered W.N. Hendry.

'Their contempt for the Hun gave us courage but perhaps too much, as we were not in the line long before some of our more inquisitive ones got sniped through looking over the top. One thing we had to watch were trench mortars of all descriptions, and if one kept an eye on the sky it was quite easy to dodge them from one traverse to another.'

Despite the overcrowding and additional duties bestowed upon them, the Gordons proved patient and excellent tutors. By the time they withdrew from the line on 12 July, leaving the Scottish in full possession, they had taught their charges a great deal about trench life and the habits of the enemy. The sector in which the Battalion found itself, and which the 179th Brigade was destined to hold for the next four months, was known as the N Sector near Neuville St Vaast and covered a front of approximately 800 yards. The front trench, known for the greater part of its length as 'Doublemont,' followed generally the line of the old farm road. It was deep, well revetted and traversed and contained the headquarters of the three companies in the line. Numerous saps led forward towards the German lines, which were generally some 250 to 300 yards distant. An important feature in the sector was the 'Paris Redoubt,' a semi-circular trench forming a salient in front of 'Doublemont.' Towards the right was the 'Argyle' crater, reputed to be the largest of its kind. The British held the western and the Germans the eastern lip, no man's land comprising a maze of disused trenches, wire and impedimenta.

Major General Bulfin employed each of his brigades in the line. The

Lieutenant A.J. Rea joined the Regiment as a private in 1916. He was promoted through the ranks becoming a Lance Serjeant on 14 February 1917. He was commissioned later that year, and wounded on 16 April 1918 when he jumped into a London Scottish trench and landed on a bayonet.

179th was disposed with two battalions forward, each with three companies in the line and one in support, one battalion in support and reserve and the remaining battalion in and around Bray village in Brigade reserve and resting. W.N. Hendry remembered that when the Battalion went out to rest, training and parades occupied most of their time.

'Water,' he complained, *'was so short at times that we could not get enough to drink for days on end. Lice were a very great enemy we had to contend with and we soon found ourselves just living with them. They got in every little crevice of our clothing and were terribly irritating, especially if one's body happened to get a little warm, now and again we managed to get clean shirts which gave us peace for a while.'*

The first tour of duty of a 'green' battalion was always fraught. Casualties became accepted but did nothing to quell the fine fighting spirit of the Battalion which continued to meet and counter all enemy moves. The 51st Division had been numerically very weak when relieved with the result that it had been wholly incapable of retaining the trenches in good condition. Work parties were therefore detailed to make extensive repairs and to carry out rewiring where required, and by the time the Battalion left the line for a period of rest on 27 July improvements were already perceptible.

In late July the Scottish received welcome reinforcements in the form of twelve officers from the 4th Battalion Cameron Highlanders. On 4 August the Battalion returned to the line, taking over from the Civil Service Rifles, and soon thereafter lost its Commanding Officer, Lieutenant Colonel Dunsmore, who was invalided back to England. Command passed temporarily to Major H.S. Cartwright, a veteran of the 1st Battalion who had been wounded at Givenchy in 1914 and who, on recovery, had been posted to the 2nd Battalion.

Trench routine continued unabated throughout the next weeks. Raiding parties were organized in one of which the Scottish succeeded in bringing back some prisoners, including a sergeant major and corporal at the cost of three killed, five wounded and one missing. In acknowledging the intelligence gained by the raid Sir Charles Fergusson, commanding the 17th Corps, wrote on 2 October:

'The arrangements appear to have been carefully worked out and the actual raid to have been carried out with gallantry and determination. The information and identifications secured are of great value.

'Please inform all concerned that their work is much appreciated and is considered to reflect credit on those who planned and carried it out.'

Each company at the front had a listening patrol consisting of one officer and two men. Their object was to get as near to the enemy as possible to discuss his identity, movements and intentions. Hendry remembered that patrols had their own ways of approaching the enemy lines. He,

'used to go out by a disused trench and over the top from one to another and from shell-hole to shell-hole.'

The patrols moved, step by step, expecting at every turn of the trench to confront the enemy.

'Our revolvers were always at the ready and we also carried bombs. Every now and again we would stop and listen for any movement. As a rule we made for a mine crater, in the bottom of which one felt a little more safe, as one could easily spot a figure moving on the skyline.'

The line at the time was fairly quiet, but on 4 September the Germans blew a mine almost immediately under the D Company post at the head of the Claudod sap. The line was quickly consolidated and held, but D Company sustained some twenty-two casualties in the action including four killed. On 1 October the Battalion went into support, being relieved by the Civil Service Rifles. When they returned to the line six days later they found that it had been all but obliterated. Redigging with the limited force available was quite impossible, and Lieutenant Colonel Ogilby, now in command, therefore ordered that only the craters in what had been the original line should be held by small posts, while another main defensive line should be organized further back.

On 20 October news came that the Division was to be relieved by the Canadians, and two days later advanced parties of the 2nd Canadian Battalion arrived in the Scottish lines. On 26 October the Battalion mustered at Bray from where it started a trek through Trevart to Montegny, where it began hard training for the Battle of the Somme. On 3 November a move was made to the hamlet of Buigny L'Abbé where the Commanding Officer was astounded to receive orders to prepare for a move to Salonika. On the afternoon of 15 November the Scottish marched to Longpré and entrained for Marseilles. After three days cramped travel in cattle trucks the port was finally reached and the Battalion marched to a fine camp called Musco. At dawn on 22 November 1916 the Scottish marched to the docks where they embarked upon the White Star liner HMT *Megantic*. The Battalion left France 39 officers and 908 other ranks strong.

Chapter Nine

The Middle East

Arrival at Salonika

Food and accommodation aboard HMT *Megantic* were excellent and the weather ideal, except for a rough sea on the 26th when passing Malta and most on board were sick. Every available minute of the voyage was dedicated to a combination of physical training, specialist training and sports, the Adjutant taking particular pride in ensuring that his runners were honed to the peak of fitness. The evenings were dedicated to the giving and enjoying of concerts, and morale was high. The ship turned north up the Aegean Sea on 28 November after which the weather commenced to get warmer. As Salonika neared the scenery was most beautiful with Mount Olympus on the left, the top of which was covered in snow, and large hills towering up all around the bay with white minarets jutting out in the sunshine.

Here the Scottish disembarked after a pleasant seven-day voyage. They marched seven miles out over atrocious roads, deep in mud and filth, their progress watched by a motley crowd of curious inhabitants. Tents were pitched on bare, muddy land close to the Monastin road and soon thereafter

Petra Pass, Greece.

MT. OLYMPVS

VIEW LOOKING SOUTH

Original panorama of the Mount Olympus area.

178

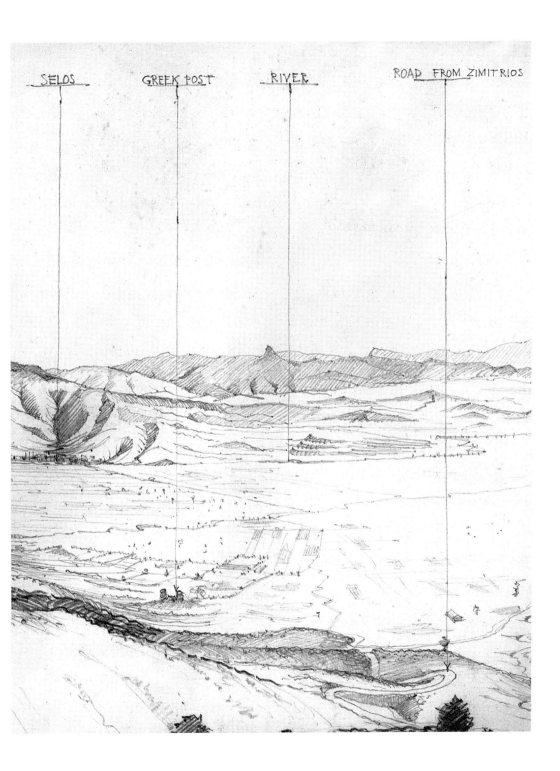

SELOS   GREEK POST   RIVER   ROAD FROM ZIMITRIOS

179

Dudular Camp, Salonika.

they commenced training. The transport was supplied with mules which had yet to be broken-in, but the rain which now fell daily helped to quieten the animals until, finally, a terrific storm flattened nearly every tent. Raging torrents coursed through the lines, the mules stampeded and were only recaptured with difficulty. When the Scottish were allowed into town they found it populated by members of every nationality including Germans, as it was well known that the city swarmed with spies.

    'Salonica is a wonderful place,'
reported a member of the Battalion.

    'It seems to be inhabited by a good many thousand tramp cyclists and equal number of sailors and soldiers of all nations. Jack Tar is there with his red bull-neck and bell-bottomed breeks. Thomas Atkins, alert and smart, talking inimitable pigeon Greek; untidy, unshaven, but wiry and workman-like Poilus; huge, stolid Russians, and vivacious Italians in a very becoming dark grey uniform with really "nutty" caps.'

Approximately a year earlier, when Bulgaria joined the Central Powers and an Austro-German army invaded Serbia from across the Danube while the Bulgarians attacked from the east, British and French forces fighting in Gallipoli made an unsuccessful attempt to assist the retreating Serbs. The Allies, weak in numbers and poorly equipped, had been forced to retire before the invaders. However, with the help of large reinforcements, mainly Italian and Russian, they had subsequently been able to organize the defence of the lower country and of the city of Salonika, converting the area into an armed camp.

    By the summer of 1916 the Allied force had been reinforced sufficiently to make the possibility of an offensive in the Balkans realistic. The rump of the Serbian Army had been re-equipped and retrained, Romania had indicated a willingness to join the Allies, and earlier fears that Greece would

180

Private Harold May joined the 3rd Battalion in early 1915. Later posted to 1st Battalion and wounded, probably on 1 July 1916. After recovery from wounds posted to 2nd Battalion in Salonika on 24 January 1917. Fatally wounded in December 1917 during the battle for Jerusalem. He died of wounds on 8 February 1918 and was buried in Alexandria, Egypt. His name is on the family grave in Teddington.

enter the war on the side of the Central Powers had abated. However, after early successes the Romanian Army had collapsed, forcing the Allies around Salonika once again onto the defensive. Further reinforcements were called for to prevent the city falling, and it was thus that the 60th Division had been called so hurriedly from France.

On 9 December the 179th Brigade was detailed for top secret duties. Relations between the Allies and King Constantine of Greece had once again deteriorated. Notoriously pro-German it was feared that he might succeed in his endeavours to bring his country into the war on the side of the Central Powers. Were he to have done so a simultaneous advance of the Bulgarians from the north and the Greeks from the south would have caused the Allies considerable logistical problems. The Greeks had only two lines of advance open to them, both leading from Larissa where the bulk of their army was reported to be concentrating. One line lay along the railway which ran along the shore of the Gulf of Salonika to the eastward of Mount Olympus, the other by the road to the west of the mountain running through the rugged Pass of Petra. General Sarrail, in supreme command of the Allied forces in the region, decided to bar both routes by occupying the town of Katerini, where the routes converged north of the mountain. As the railway which connected Salonika to southern Greece had been badly neglected, and in parts had been washed out by heavy storms, it was decided that the Brigade should proceed by sea to Vromeri, a fishing village four miles from Katerini, and from there should occupy Katerini as the advanced base of the expedition. All pack transport and artillery would proceed by route march from Salonika.

On 10 December C Company, under Major Blackie, forming the advance guard left Dudular Camp, marched to Salonika docks and embarked on the *Wave*, a small estuary paddle steamer. After a period of confusion the *Wave* arrived off Vromeri shortly after noon of the next day. C Company duly landed, secured the small and somewhat sleepy village and began to prepare to receive the main body of the brigade that afternoon. The brigade arrived in HMS *Endymion* escorted by a number of destroyers and secured a landing with some difficulty, the soldiers having to wade ashore through the surf. The Kensingtons were immediately ordered inland on outpost duty leaving the residue to work through the night, unloading stores. After a few hours sleep the Scottish left Vromeri at noon on 12 December and marched to Katerini which had been occupied by the Kensingtons earlier that day.

W.N. Hendry described Katerini as an old, dirty place with no food shops in it. The largest building was a barracks occupied by the French, who presumably had earned the dubious pleasure of liberating the town first. For their part the Scottish spent the next seven nights in some discomfort bivouacked on the muddy banks of the Pelikas river to the west of the town. Having occupied Katerini, the Brigadier took early steps to secure the surrounding countryside. The Queen's Westminsters were sent south along the line of the railway, the Kensingtons crossed the Pelikas as far as Kolokuri while an element of the Civil Service Rifles established itself in the neighbourhood of Kundoriotisa. To the rump of the brigade fell the more mundane duties of road repairs.

Piper H.W. Davidson. Joined 3rd Battalion in 1915, transferred to the 2nd Battalion and was wounded in May 1917, fighting the Bulgarians in the area of Tomato Hill. He survived and continued to serve in the post-war Battalion.

On 19 December the Scottish relieved the Kensingtons on outpost duty at Kolokuri village. The latter had worked hard and a strong defensive line had been dug. Colonel Ogilby pushed out a further two miles as he prepared to advance the line. The country in which the Battalion now found itself was as beautiful as it was unforgiving, and the Scottish quickly reconciled themselves to wet feet as they forded the many fast-flowing rivers. On the second day each company took up positions on the slopes of Mount Olympus where they passed Christmas Day in fine and warm conditions. On 5 January there was a general move forward to positions covering the village of Hani Miljas. The threat was light after France, but even so care had to be taken not to allow the Greeks, believed to be massing to the south, to take the initiative.

The weather, however, had deteriorated rendering the flimsy bivouac sheets issued to each soldier, the only shelter provided, wholly inadequate. On 13 February the Battalion again moved forward to Petra, 1000 feet above sea level, where they were accommodated in the old Turkish Guard House. Even in these difficult conditions a good deal of company and battalion training was undertaken. Hendry remembered undertaking a seven-day trek in atrocious conditions.

'On we went,' he complained, '*day after day marching in the teeth of a real icy Balkan storm over heavily rutted roads. It was a piteous sight to see men and mules lying prostrate by the roadside owing to fatigue and exposure. We just threw*

Lewis machine guns transported by mules.

> *ourselves down and slept anywhere, soaked through to the skin. The roads were littered, just like the retreat of an army. The man responsible for this should have been severely dealt with, as it was far beyond human endurance.'*

As soon as the danger from the Greek royalists was adjudged to be passed General Sorrail ordered the redeployment of the 179th Brigade to a more active part of the front. On 22 February the Scottish were relieved in the outpost line by the Kensingtons, and at 7.00a.m. on 1 March the Battalion moved off on the return march to Katerini, covering the distance of eighteen miles in less than seven hours without the loss of a single man. Not only did the Scottish now enjoy a week of rest and recreation but they were fortunate enough to be housed in the barracks, and were thus able to enjoy the benefits of roofed accommodation for the first time in a number of weeks.

On 10 March the brigade left Katerini and began the long trek northwards to the Dorian front. The journey, which took six days and was largely carried out in bad weather, proved torturous. Rarely were the advancing troops able to make more than twelve miles a day, and indeed on the first day covered only eight. The 16 March, the last day of the march, proved the most difficult. One of the participants later wrote to *The Regimental Gazette*:

> *'Scarcely had we started than it began to snow, and ere we had made two miles we were moving into the teeth of a Balkan blizzard. The Battalion will not readily forget that night, and, to crown all, it was on this of all nights that our usually perfect staff arrangements*

must needs miscarry. We reached the end of our march only to find that our guides had been taken away by the Brigade staff, and we had to wait for upwards of an hour before they could be found. The final seal to our discomfort was set when, led on to a bare snow-swept hillside, we were informed, "This is your area, you bivouac here." Well, all bad times come to an end. Somehow the night passed and with it the storm. The sun shone, the snow melted, and we found ourselves among countrymen, in the person of the 11th Battalion Scottish Rifles.'

In all the Scottish covered ninety-two miles over very bad roads or no roads at all, each man carrying in addition to full marching order a bivouac sheet and pole. Only fifteen men dropped out, two of them due to an accident and many of the rest due to sickness. One man, Private H.T. Kirby

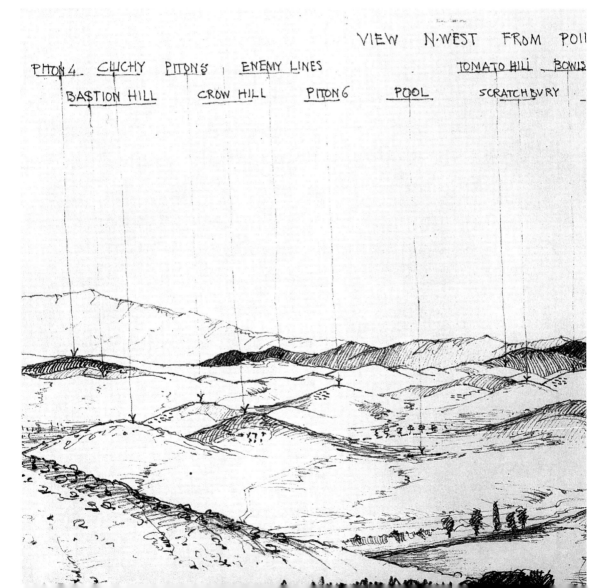

VIEW N·WEST FROM POI

PITON 4 CLUCHY PITONS ENEMY LINES TOMATO HILL BOWL

BASTION HILL CROW HILL PITON 6 POOL SCRATCHBURY

of D Company, pluckily refused to give up, and eventually fainted and died from exposure before medical aid could reach him.

On 18 March the London Scottish relieved the 11th Scottish Rifles in reserve at Dache. The Queen's Westminsters and Civil Service Rifles went in to the line, with the Kensingtons in support. The portion of the line held by the 60th Division extended from the south-western spurs of the mountainous Pip ridges westward over broken, hilly country to the valley of the Vardar, where control of the line passed to the French. The 168th Brigade sector on the left extended from the lower slopes of a hill known as Whaleback, across country to the village of Little Bekirli. The Scottish, as reserve battalion, were housed in comfortable shelters on the reverse side of the hills north of Kalinova village. It fell to the Scottish, as reserve battalion,

Original panoramic drawing of the enemy front line in the Tomato Hill area.

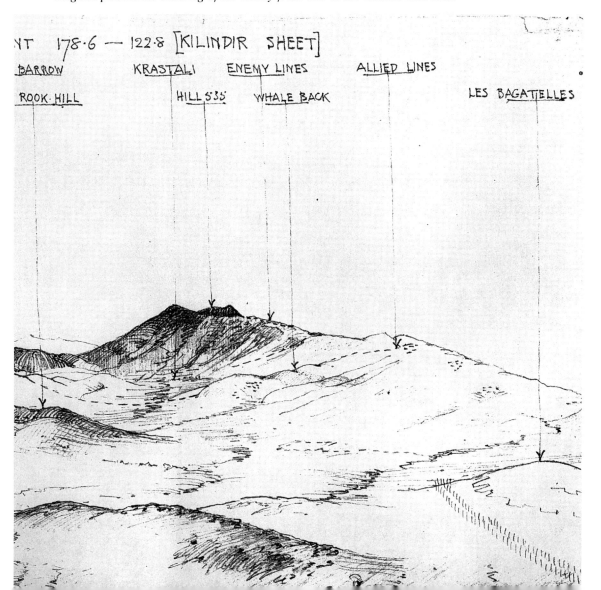

to provide the labour to construct the incomplete third line, fire and communication trenches. This proved heartbreaking as beneath a few inches of top soil the ground turned to solid rock. Despite the help of Royal Engineer blasting parties, progress was woefully slow.

Hendry recalled the presence of a large number of observation balloons in the area. One or two per day would regularly fall victim to the Bulgarian Air Force, until eventually Allied aircraft appeared on the scene and reclaimed the initiative. On 3 March the Bulgarians executed a bold and skilful raid against the Queen's Westminsters on Bowls Barrow Hill. When, a month later, the Scottish went up to relieve them they were warned to be on the alert. Although the position had now been consolidated it was overlooked everywhere by the Bulgarian trenches, particularly the observation post towering over the battlefield on top of Hill 535.

At 8.00a.m. on 4 April the Bulgarians began to shell C Company positions on the front line. Two days later, on Good Friday, their artillery laid down a larger and more comprehensive barrage, under cover of which a forty-strong raiding party attempted to advance and capture a Scottish forward patrol. Although both sides sustained fatalities, the Scottish succeeded in holding their position. Thereafter the line quietened down, and by 10 April had been consolidated into a well-dug fire-trench. Not unreasonably, British High Command, frustrated by the inferiority of their positions in comparison to those of the enemy, decided to carry the latter by assault.A preliminary bombardment began on 21 April and continued for a week. The enemy, thus warned, was given plenty of time to bring up his reserves and to strengthen the threatened sector. In anticipation of their assault, the London Scottish were ordered to move their position to the left to relieve the Queen's Westminsters. The new position consisted of two hills, 275 and P6, both well-trenched and wired, and equally well-trenched wire between.

The initial British assault, for which the 179th Brigade were held in reserve, began on the night of 24-25 April and continued for three days without success. It was then decided to extend the 60th's Divisional line forward into no man's land. This plan had little to commend it; its success would have forced the British away from their easily defended lines forward, down a slope, to a new position which would have been highly vulnerable to Bulgarian artillery. Nonetheless the attack went ahead, a preliminary attempt to seize a salient known as the Nose being undertaken by the 180th Brigade. When this was repulsed, the 179th Brigade was ordered to make its advance into no man's land. On 8 May three battalions advanced, the Kensingtons on the right, the Scottish in the centre and the Queen's Westminsters on the left. Lieutenant Colonel Ogilby had briefed his men well, and the Scottish advance went according to plan. Bulgarian forward units, appreciating that they were heavily outnumbered, retired having offered only token resistance, while their artillery, although busy, was inaccurate.

During the course of the night wire was laid and trenches dug in the new British forward positions. As dawn broke the bulk of the Battalion withdrew to its previous positions leaving detachments to hold the new line. During the course of the next night the Battalion returned to its forward positions to continue and largely complete the new line of trenches. Ironically, Bulgarian aircraft overflew the position during the course of the intervening day, but seemingly regarded the British movement as tactically irrelevant and left it largely alone. The Kensingtons to the right, tasked with taking the formidable Hill 535, failed in their endeavours. The Bulgarians had the area covered by searchlights, and as the British approached the wire illuminated them. The Londoners were driven back by a hail of lead and lost heavily.

The next day the Scottish were relieved by the Civil Service Rifles. Just before dusk the Bulgarians counter-attacked, wiping out all but one man in an advanced post of the Queen's Westminsters. The British, however, recovered the position immediately, and held it thereafter undisputed. The Scottish withdrew to Brigade reserve at Tertre Verte.

'Wild flowers were very profuse here and the hills and streams were lovely with their beautiful colourings,' enthused Hendry. *'Mosquitoes and other weird insects were quite abundant. We carried on for some time here, taking our turns in front and reserve lines, being thirty-eight days in the line altogether. At last we were relieved and set out on a real cleaning up parade, marching twenty miles. Here we had all our clothes fumigated, were given new shirts, had fine hot baths and were well disinfected - quite free from all vermin.'*

The action at Tomato Hill, as it became known, had been as masterful in its organization as it had been pointless in its conception. Much propaganda at home was made of the 'victory.' The general public were not, however, informed when a few days later the newly captured positions were abandoned and the old line reoccupied.

On 21 April the Battalion received sudden orders to relieve the Queen's Westminsters in the line close to Cdemli village. A good deal of tactical wiring was undertaken and observation posts built, but otherwise the tour was uneventful. On 3 June the Battalion was relieved by the 12th Battalion Argyle and Sutherland Highlanders, returning to its old bivouacs at Dache. On 12 June it moved from there to Kalinova station from where it turned south and marched through the night to Bergetor. Over the next few days the weary Scots continued to retrace their steps of a few months earlier to the outskirts of Salonika, where they were held in the utmost secrecy. Mysteriously battalions received orders to march into Salonika from where they appeared to disappear. Rumours abounded, but no one had the slightest indication of the fate awaiting the Battalion.

The Scottish were, in fact, the last Battalion in the Division to move. Their last days in the area were marred by a vicious sandstorm which swept over the camp one peaceful afternoon. A black menacing cloud appeared over the hills to the east, moved west and was shortly thereafter seen to approach the camp. During the ensuing storm, bivouacs were torn from the ground and personal items scattered like chaff. In a few moments the sandstorm gave way as suddenly as it had come, to a torrential downpour of rain which lasted half an hour, then perfect calm returned. The Scottish were very fortunate to be leaving the country at that time, just before the malaria season, although a number of the Battalion did suffer severe sickness, mostly of a mysterious kind, diagnosed as 'low Vardar fever.' Among those struck down was Lieutenant Colonel Ogilby, who on 24 June was compelled to retire to hospital. Command passed to Major J.H. Young.

On 30 June the Battalion paraded at 2.00a.m. and made its way to the docks at Salonika. There it embarked on lighters, and by dawn was all aboard HMT *Aragon*. Some hours later those who were able, watched the ship sail away from the coast. The next day they put into Mudros to take off members of the South Nottinghamshire Yeomanry whose transport had been torpedoed the previous day. Hendry remembered that;

'we exchanged our money into piasters and were also paid, but the canteen was poor. The weather was good and we had an ideal voyage.'

By now the Battalion knew that its destination was to be Alexandria, where it began disembarkation on the afternoon of 3 July. In the words of the Regimental History;

'Salonica was an interesting and valuable experience for the London Scottish. Abundant opportunities for training presented themselves and were taken advantage of. It was a vastly improved Battalion which went to join General Allenby's Army.'

188

Chapter Ten

Palestine

The Wells of Beersheba

The voyage to Alexandria, on board HMT *Aragon*, was uneventful, marred only by the necessity to wear lifebelts and go bare footed at all times. Nearing Egypt those on deck noticed the masts of a torpedoed steamer projecting above the water. Those watching were not to know that their own boat was to be torpedoed three weeks later with a complement of nurses on board.

Disembarkation was completed on 3 July when the Scottish embarked in comfortable carriages of the Egyptian State Railways for its slow journey to an unknown destination inland.

> *'I tried to sleep but just dozed and gradually coming to my senses I looked out of the window and perceived long white night gowns floating about in the darkness and to my surprise they came nearer,'*

remembered W. N. Hendry.

> *'I pushed down the window and found a swarm of natives in white gowns darting about laden with fruits and wine, just what we wanted.'*

Not all locals were honest. In one instance a young soldier, naive enough to leave his kit and rifle unattended in the carriage, returned to find it missing, presumably stolen by a native who had sneaked on board. A court of enquiry was convened and the soldier ordered to pay for the missing equipment from his own pocket. At dawn the next morning, after an eight-hour journey, the Battalion detrained in the town of Ismalia, and after a

Captain R. Whyte.

short march reached the camp of Moascar. Although the troops had experienced fairly hot weather in the malaria-infested regions of Macedonia, it was still considered necessary that they become acclimatized to their new environment. They therefore remained in Ismalia for approximately three weeks during which time they were put through two hours training, morning and evening, thus escaping the midday heat.

An unknown soldier, writing home, complained bitterly of his predicament.

> *'We are well up the river, cursing the flies by day and mosquitoes and sandflies by night. In addition the Arab thieves who are prowling round our camps are getting "the wind up" on us. When not kept awake by mosquitoes we are being continually roused by the guard commander reporting "Bedoos" somewhere about the camp, and therefore we are going to try a few rounds with a couple of 12-bore guns we have with us, which we think will sting the buggars fairly well, and be more effective than the rifle.'*

Hendry, on the other hand, remembered the camp as;

> *'a beautiful place at the side of the Suez Canal, with a fine big lake and splendid gardens, all surrounded by the desert'.*

Leave to Cairo was freely given and much enjoyed, it being for the majority their first release from military restraint since leaving England thirteen months earlier. The camp itself was well situated with a cinema, plenty of canteens and a large number of well-regulated native vendors. It was, therefore, with some misgivings that the Battalion received orders to strike camp, and at 5.00p.m. on 17 July marched off through Ismalia into the desert beyond. After three days of relatively gentle marching, made all the easier by nightly bathes in the Suez Canal, the Scottish reached Kantara, which from a shabby village had developed into a colossal tented camp, the

The 2nd Battalion Forage Camels, Palestine 1917. Private Groundwater in charge.

Battalion camp at Shabasi, July 1917.

largest military base in Egypt. After a sleepless night, caused by the noisy arrival of the rest of the brigade, the Battalion was given the next day off, until at 9.00p.m., headed by its pipes and drums, it marched to the military station.

After a frustrating wait of two hours the Scottish were ordered on board a series of ballast trucks provided with temporary cover to give shade from the sun. Packed like sardines and wholly incapable of lying down, they endured a thirteen-hour journey with only one stop before arriving at the coastal oasis of Dier el Belah. Here detrainment proceeded during a sandstorm, a most unpleasant experience, after which the Battalion moved off through deep heavy sand to Shabasi, where it was allotted a bivouac area on the shores of the Mediterranean. To reach the site the Scottish had to traverse about two miles of sandhills, the surface was very loose and heavy, and this, combined with the midday heat, made the going extremely trying. Nonetheless the stay of eight days was extremely enjoyable, with bathing parades the order of the day. During this period the Battalion was allotted a few, far from onerous duties including guarding a prisoner-of-war compound near the railway.

'The prisoners guarded were accommodated in the usual barbed-wire cages, and no shelter from the sun whatever was provided,' remembered Bernard Blazer. 'The poor wretches hung pieces of rag and sacking up on the wire to create a small patch of shade in which to lay their heads. They were a very mixed crowd. The Turkish cavalry were kept separate from the infantry, being considered as of a much superior class. Deserters again were kept apart from those captured in engagements.'

At the time the Turks were holding a strong line from Gaza to Hareira, forming a rough semi-circle, and from the east to the Beersheba-Hebron

The Battalion practicing an advance under an artillery barrage, Palestine 1917.

road. The line of defences thereafter ran south and east of Beersheba. The town itself stood in a wide cup-like plain surrounded on all sides by steep hills. It had been the Turkish base for their attempt on the Suez Canal, and was now an important military centre supported by a railway spur from the main Jaffa-Jerusalem line. A wide watercourse, the Wadi Ghuzze, dry in summer but carrying a running stream during the rainy season, ran inland from Gaza, first in an easterly then a south-easterly direction towards Beersheba. Initially the Turks had sought to defend the line of the wadi, but subsequently withdrew eastward to a line of hills marking the edge of the desert plain. The British were thus able to secure the valuable water supply and to construct a line confronting the Turks.

For their part the British were undergoing a complete reorganization. After the failure of the Turkish attacks on the Suez Canal in 1916 the British had assumed the offensive and had begun an advance across the Sinai Desert, following the old caravan route along the Mediterranean coast. The Turks had offered little serious resistance and the advance had thus continued as fast as the pipeline, conveying water from the Sweetwater Canal at Kantara and the railway running parallel could be constructed. By late 1916 the railhead had advanced to the Syrian frontier allowing the British to concentrate on the invasion of Palestine. The enemy barred their way at Gaza, and along the defensive line to Beersheba. Costly and unsuccessful attacks had been launched against Gaza in March and April 1917. In June of that year General Sir E.H.H. Allenby had assumed command of the Egyptian Expeditionary Force and had been granted reinforcements from Salonika, in the shape of the 10th (Irish) and 60th (London) Divisions, and by July had at his disposal a force of six British infantry divisions, mainly Territorial, one Indian division and three Colonial mounted divisions.

Allenby at first contented himself with holding the line of the Wadi Ghuzze, patrolling the line between it and the Turkish defences with his cavalry. Thereafter he ran a branch line out from the railhead at Dier el

192

Belah to the wells at Shellal, and crossing the Wadi Ghuzze at that point extended it on to Karm. The Army was then organized into three Corps, the XXth, XXIst and Desert Mounted Corps. The 60th Division was sent to the XXth under command of Lieutenant General Sir P. Chetwode, and was designated by him as his desert mounted column on the extreme right of the British position. When Major General Bulfin relinquished command of the 60th on his appointment as General Officer Commanding the XXIst Corps, his place was taken by Major General J.S.M. Shea, a highly popular and competent veteran of France since the early days of the war who had come to Palestine about the same time as Allenby.

Camels now became the only means of transport, and the Scottish had to learn the way of managing these unwieldy brutes. The Desert Column, including the London Scottish, was to be stationed to the extreme right of the line, and thus on the night of 29 July the Battalion received the order to march the seventeen miles to the Abu Sitta wells, near Sheik Nuran. The going was soft, the night hot and airless and the wire road, along which the march was intended to take place, non-existent. Dust rose in clouds in the air, choking and blinding the men, who found their first desert march a very trying experience. Abu Sitta was reached just before dawn, and the day spent in much needed rest. Towards the evening the Brigade moved off to the relief of the 159th Brigade, 53rd Division at Shellal, the Scottish relieving the 1/4th Battalion The Welch Regiment then holding the far side of the Wadi Ghuzze, covering the Shellal water-supply.

The line occupied by the Scottish enjoyed the twin benefits of strength and simplicity. A system of redoubts had been constructed some 500 yards apart, each being manned by a platoon. During the day an observation post comprising an NCO and four men was maintained at each redoubt, but at night the whole platoon stood-to, manning from four to six posts including listening posts situated at gaps in the single belt of barbed wire which protected the entire front. The deep wadi itself afforded excellent natural cover, although with the introduction of aerial observation the advantages of this important characteristic were considerably diminished. Far in the distance could be seen the hazy line of hills occupied by the Turks. The

Filling water bottles 'somewhere in Palestine'.

Turkish trenches near Beersheba.

country to the front was a barren wilderness, sparsely covered with coarse, dried-up grass. The right flank was protected by strong cavalry patrols of the Australian Light Horse and the county Yeomanries. The enemy's left flank at Beersheba was approximately fifteen miles away, the two lines converging as they approached Gaza. Life was quiet with no enemy in sight, although the intense heat, scarcity of water and all-pervading swarms of flies which intruded everywhere made sleep difficult.

Corporal R.C. Edwards, wounded early November 1917 near Beersheba.

The routine changed suddenly on 26 August when the 179th Brigade was relieved by the 180th and withdrew to a training area to the west of the Wadi Ghuzze. The Scottish, now once again under the command of Lieutenant Colonel Ogilby, was sent to El Shauth, known locally as Cactus Gardens. As Hendry remembered;

> 'we trekked to a cactus garden and bivouacked in very wide trenches the Turks had dug, so that our cavalry would stumble into them. Here we stayed for some weeks, training all the time, with exercises, drills and skirmishes in the mornings. We laid down in the sweltering heat all afternoon, or sometimes walked three miles to a canteen. On one occasion we got some bad Quaker oats which made me quite ill for two days. We used to consume a whole dixie full of this with Nestle's Milk. It was a very rare occasion when meals were really plentiful.'

While at El Shauth the Battalion entered into a new training programme laid down by the Divisional Commander. This comprised long night marches, deployment in darkness and dawn assaults. Battalion and brigade attack formations were honed and a firing range built at Al Ghabi, five miles south-west of the camp. To the joy of all it was announced that leave would be granted throughout this period of training. Cairo became the most favoured stop, and not even the discomfort of a journey by cattle truck from Kantara marred the joy of being let loose after months of toil and hardship.

Towards the end of September the senior officers were summoned and advised that the next blow was to be delivered against the Turks' left flank at Beersheba. The 60th and 74th Divisions learned that they had been selected for the attack and were ordered to make all necessary reconnaissances. The first and most important of these took place on 2 October when a strong line of cavalry was pushed forward towards the Turkish defences and the senior officers from all the attacking battalions given the chance to see the ground for themselves. Bernard Blazer was instructed to draw maps of the enemy defences, enlarging the official ones and augmenting them with the latest information obtained by aerial reconnaissance. His maps were elaborate, carefully drawn and minutely coordinated.

'*It was fascinating work committing to paper in our quiet desert home positions many miles away which we would first see in the turmoil of battle,*' he later remembered.

Allenby went to great lengths to mask his intentions towards Beersheba. Shortly after he assumed command he allowed his intelligence officer, Lieutenant Colonel Richard Meinertzhagen, to introduce a plan of deception intended to convince the Turks that a third attack was to be launched against Gaza. The plan, which took two months to implement, relied upon collateral to afford it added authenticity. Initially Meinertzhagen arranged for a known double agent to deliver a letter to the local head of Turkish espionage. The letter, which contained money and a note of thanks for services rendered, was taken instead to Turkish Intelligence. The spymaster was tried summarily and shot without being given the chance to prove his innocence.

Thereafter, a series of minor security breaches were introduced to the routine radio traffic to enable the German analysts to break one of the British codes. A series of messages was then sent using this compromised code, intimating that an attack would be launched against Gaza on 4 November. Finally Meinertzhagen rode into the desert until he met a Turkish patrol. When it fired at him he feigned injury, dropping a dispatch case while making his escape. The haversack contained the personal possessions of a fictitious officer, including a letter from his wife announcing the birth of their child. It also contained detailed plans for the attack on Gaza.

During the final stages of October, arrangements for the attack were practised and perfected. Trenches were dug in the sand near El Shauth to form a full size representation of wadis in front of Beersheba, and the brigade practised marching into its positions and deploying both by day and by night. The Divisional Commander decided to attack with 179th Brigade on the right and the 181st on the left, retaining the 180th in reserve. The Brigadier thereafter detailed that the Civil Service Rifles would assault on the right, the Scottish on the left, with the Kensingtons acting first as covering, then as pursuing forces. The Queen's Westminsters were to form the reserve.

On 21 October the Battalion set out on three days march to its brigade concentration area.

'We packed all surplus kit and articles of personal property in carefully labelled sandbags and committed them to the care of the QM's Stores,' remembered Bernard Blazer. 'Only the bare necessities were to be carried. It is a mere matter of detail that we never saw those sand bags or their contents again.'

Although the move was made as covertly as possible the Turks were not altogether unsuspicious, and on the night of 27 October made a reconnaissance in force against the Yeomanry outposts. They were however driven back and it remained the consensus that they were unaware of the impending attacks.

On 28 October the Brigade moved to Abu Ghalyun where, two days later, the Scottish received their final orders.

'Here,' Hendry later recalled, 'we had to lie doggo all day so as not to attract the enemy's attention. The Padre gave a sermon, followed by the Colonel, who urged us on by saying that he hoped we would make as good a show as the 1st Bn had on Hallowe'en 1914.'

During the afternoon, final preparations were made, each man was given two bombs and an extra bandolier of ammunition. A percentage were given coloured flare lights to be used as locating signals to aeroplanes, while others carried wire-cutters and circular saws. Two days' rations were issued, consisting of bully beef, biscuits, jam and dried fruit, together with a small bottle of tea and rum. Strict orders were given that not a shot was to be fired until dawn, only bayonets used, as the attackers did not wish to give away their numbers. At 8.00p.m. the Scottish moved off on the approach march, the Kensingtons leading the Brigade as advanced battalion with orders to drive in the Turkish patrols and thereafter protect the brigade flank during deployment. They were then to reform, and after the attack assume the role of pursuit battalion.

On the right of the Kensingtons, General Wigan's cavalry brigade (The Yeomanry Mounted Division) was to patrol the country south of the town while the Anzac Mounted Division rode east and then north to cut off the enemy line of retreat. The first five miles of the advance lay over loose sand and scrub, made easier in parts by the existence of a wire road specially constructed over a particularly heavy stretch of sand. At about 10.00p.m. the Beersheba-Khalasa road was reached and the column turned north. Conditions improved, and shortly before midnight the battalion was able to take a forty-five minute unscheduled rest before advancing to Halgon Wadi where packs were dumped, Lewis-gun mules offloaded and further ammunition issued. Bullets now started to whizz and it was not long before the wounded started dropping out. Lieutenant Colonel Ogilby led his men forward to the entrance to Scottish Wadi at which point company officers commanding proceeded to take up their allotted positions. A Company went on over the ridge to Poplar Wadi, B and C Companies went up the eastern branch of Scottish Wadi, and D Company and Battalion Headquarters into the western branch. Nothing could have worked more smoothly, and by 3.00a.m. all were in position for the dawn attack.

The men sheltered behind boulders and rocks, bullets were still purring overhead but not a sound was heard in response. Then an order came to make a meal, in which the majority quickly consumed their bottle of rum as it was a cold night. As dawn approached the machine-gunners took up their covering positions, while to the rear the artillery began pouring a barrage onto Hill 1070 to the left, which even then the 2/22nd London Battalion (Queen's) was attempting to assault. By 7.00a.m. the clouds of dust caused by the artillery were so dense that firing had to be stopped for forty-five minutes. At 8.20a.m. the bombardment was intensified for ten minutes and, as it lifted, it became apparent to those watching that the assaulting troops had succeeded in carrying their objective.

A lull now occurred while many of the guns were moved and began to register on the Turkish wire. At 12.15p.m. the assault on the main positions began, under cover of an intensified bombardment. The distance between Scottish Wadi and the Z system, the Scottish objective, was about 1,200 yards, the ground between being steep, stony and broken. The enemy defences comprised two lines of fire trenches in front of C Company, with one line elsewhere. The gunners were ordered to register on the front line for fifteen minutes after which the guns were lifted to the second line for two minutes and thereafter onto selected targets in the rear. The Lewis-gunners were pushed forward into such protection as could be afforded, and before the main assault was in position to offer covering cross-fire.

For several hours the Scottish were left without moving, hostages to their own thoughts.

'As the morning wore on the sun became very hot and we dared not drink beyond moistening our lips,'
recalled Bernard Blazer,

'for although our bottles were full we did not know when we should get them replenished. We waited half an hour, one hour, two hours, and still the word to advance was not given by Brigade Headquarters. True, the firing on the left still continued, so perhaps the Turks were counter-attacking. And yet we waited; the enemy in front of us continuing to sweep the intervening ridges with their machine-gun fire. The desire to be "up and at 'em" was general; anything but this suspense!'

The Companies finally assaulted in two waves of two lines each, each line starting in lines of half-sections in file, with orders to extend it when deemed necessary. Crossing the first ridge the attackers dropped into Poplar Wadi, passing through A Company's covering line on its eastern slope. Here B Company extended into line, while C Company preserved its original formation until the next crest had been breasted. The view of the attack was now inspiring. In the words of the *Regimental History,*

> *'From left to right, as far as one could see, line after line of khaki-clad figures, the hodden grey conspicuous in the centre, were climbing steadily up towards the line of smoke and dust which marked the enemy trenches. Their bayonets flashed in the sun; occasionally a man fell, but it seemed that nothing could have stopped that onrush of khaki and steel.'*

As the Scottish neared their objective the barrage lifted, causing the attackers to rush forward with a cheer, through the badly erected barbed wire across the front line of defence and on to the second. Resistance was light, save for a brave party of Turks who put up a token fight between the two lines and who were quickly dispatched by bomb and bullet. The Scottish paused on their objective before sending out covering screens with Lewis guns. These made excellent targets of the Turkish survivors, now fleeing towards Beersheba clearly visible some three miles away. On the Scottish flanks the Civil Service Rifles and the 2/23rd Londons had been equally successful at all points gaining with comparative ease their objectives. The Kensingtons now came up and passed through in pursuit. It might all have been over had the Turks not rallied nearer the town and succeeded in getting a battery and several machine guns into action. With these they opened a systematic fire on the troops digging in and on the supply routes behind. The enemy trenches in which the Scottish were then seeking shelter were dug in hard chalky ground, were of an average depth of less than five feet and thus offered little protection. However by dusk the remaining Turkish gunners found themselves short of ammunition causing their fire to peter out into insignificance. Shortly after nightfall, with the arrival of the cavalry, the fire ceased completely.

A London Scot, writing home at this time, allowed himself a justifiable moment of pride.

> *'I can well understand the feeling, but if you could only see the Army you would rejoice that you were British. The Tommy grouses like the devil, but he's always cheerful, and these Anzacs are grand fellows, with a soft corner in their hearts for the "Jocks." On leave in Cairo they are absolute "posh" - up the line they are hopelessly ragtime, but wonderfully practical. Their mounted patrols go out of nights in shirt sleeves and canvas shoes, but they don't forget to festoon themselves with water bottles.'*

The kilted soldier has always been held in awe by his enemies and in this instance this may have done much to minimize casualties among the advancing Scottish.

'According to a doctor we captured,' reported Hendry, *'the (Turks) had flown along the trenches to be taken prisoners by the trousered regiment, as they did not want to be captured by the skirted devils as they called us, they were given to understand that we took no prisoners.'*

Salvage parties were sent out the next day, many returning with Turkish waistcoats, scarves and woollen gloves of brilliant and various colours. At the same time the 53rd Division marched rapidly across the front of the 74th and 60th, and by 2 November was astride the Beersheba-Hebron road. The 10th Division thereafter came up on the Hareira front and the 74th and 60th wheeled to the left to bring them up to the next line of defences. On 7 November Gaza fell. The surprise attack at Beersheba had been followed by an immediate onslaught against the enemy's coastal positions. The defences were taken and the Turks forced to retreat in disorder, in the process losing thousands of prisoners to the cavalry advancing hard on their heels.

'Strange that we should start the ball rolling on Hallowe'en 1917, the anniversary of the Regiment's entry into the field,'
wrote a veteran to his family.

'Our CO, speaking to us before we attacked, commented on this coincidence, and told us he was present at 1914 and saw our first, and he was confident we should behave as well as they had done. He was not disappointed, and when later we were scrapping for three days on end, finishing with an eight-mile push clearing up the Turks, he was delighted, although he said little.'

The Advance to Jerusalem

The London Scottish remained in their positions until 3 November when they moved through Beersheba, passing close to the famous wells which were by now running dry. Their march lay over rough tracked country. At midnight they were ordered to bivouac in a depression known, with no lack of irony, as Welfare Wadi. A more inhospitable, barren and derelict place it was difficult to imagine. The hills in the area were extremely stony and chiefly composed of masses of solid rock. The pathways leading to the villages, where they existed, were naturally paved with white limestone, worn smooth by the tread of bare feet through the centuries. The camels, which still comprised the unit transport, were sadly out of their element in this environment, and Blazer remembered how sad it was to see the wretched creatures struggling up the steep slopes in the driving rain, endeavouring to maintain a firm foothold on the wet, slippery stones.

'Sometimes, one of the camels would lose its footing and, bravely but in vain trying to recover itself, would go hurtling with its load down the hillside. Several such incidents occurred...,in some cases resulting in the camels' legs being broken, when there was no alternative but to shoot the poor beasts.'

2nd Battalion Officers in Jerusalem, 1917.

General Allenby was now in a position to resume his offensive against the Turkish left. The 53rd Division and the Anzac cavalry were ordered to cover his right flank while the 74th and 60th Divisions faced the Rushdi and Kauwukah systems, with the 10th Division and a brigade of the Yeomanry on the left opposite Hareira. The XXth Corps commander ordered the 74th Division to adopt an axis of advance between Tel el Khuweilfeh and the main system of Turkish trenches covering Kauwukah and Hareira. If successful this was to be followed by an assault on the main line by the 60th Division, after which the 10th Division would carry Hareira.

Major General Shea placed the 181st Brigade on the right, the 179th on the left and the 180th in reserve. Brigadier Edwards detailed the Queen's Westminsters and the Kensingtons as right and left assault battalions, the Civil Service Rifles as support, and the Scottish in reserve. The Battalion paraded at daylight on 6 November and began slowly to proceed to its point of assembly. There it found Lieutenant Paterson with his water camels. He had been unavoidably delayed in collecting his ration, and realizing that were he to proceed to Welfare Wadi as ordered he would miss the battalion, he used his initiative and headed for the battle zone in the hope of finding

his unit.

Shortly thereafter furious small arms fire to the right told that the 74th Division had begun its attack. At about the same time the 60th Divisional artillery opened fire on the Kauwukah positions, and at 10.00a.m. the forward battalions began their advance. The Scottish moved forward to the gun positions, occupying a front of some 400 yards, companies being in artillery formation of half platoons in irregular lines of fours, later known on the Western Front as 'blobs.' From their position the Scottish were able to see the Kensingtons and Queen's Westminsters deploy forward in pairs, widely extended, line after line. Their advance seemed uncheckable and, although gaps appeared in the khaki lines, it was not long before the British were seen to disappear into their objectives. In a few minutes it was all over and Kauwukah lay in Allied hands.

The Scottish remained with the gunners that afternoon, moving forward just before dusk. During their stay they saw numerous prisoners and many wounded being taken back. Transport for the wounded was difficult in the extreme. Motor ambulances could not negotiate the sand nor cross the numerous wadis, and recourse had of necessity to be made to mule carts or camels. The carts, each two-wheeled and fitted with tyres some six inches wide, dealt with the more serious cases. The camels were each provided with two cacolets, part stretchers and part deck chairs, slung one on each side of the camel. Many patients thus carried, quickly made it clear that they would rather walk!

The Scottish spent a quiet night in bivouac in the rear of the Turkish positions, but as dawn broke it quickly became clear that the Turks had not retired far. Two miles forward of the new front line and roughly parallel with it ran the Wadi Sheria, with good wells and an all-year supply of water. The British were still being supplied from the neighbourhood of Beersheba; the supply was failing and both they and the Turks realized that it was imperative that they capture the Sheria supply as soon as possible. The 180th Brigade was ordered to advance to contact and seize the wells, but the Turks put up a stubborn defence and held them off for nearly a day. By dusk the greater part of the position had been won, but the wells remained within the range of enemy artillery, effectively preventing their large-scale use. A consolidating advance by the 179th Brigade to the left of the 180th was ordered to shift the Turks; the Civil Service Rifles attacking on the right and the London Scottish on the left.

Lieutenant Colonel Ogilby extended D Company to cover his entire front and ordered the remaining companies to follow in artillery formation. They

The German Hospice on the Mount of Olives.

were to cross the Wadi Sheria and dislodge the enemy from its northern bank, and thereafter to hold an outpost line for the night before advancing again at dawn. The Scottish moved off soon after 4.00p.m., and were at once visible to the Turks who opened fire with every gun they could bring to bear. There were, however, surprisingly few casualties, and as darkness fell D company was able to cross the wadi and begin to climb the steep bank abreast of the Civil Service Rifles. They were met with rifle and machine-gun fire at short range, yet undaunted rushed forward carrying the enemy rearguard. The Sheria water supply was assured enabling the brigade camels to draw water there that night.

Hendry, assaulting with the support companies, remembered a near shout of joy when the Adjutant's horse went down, that officer being far from popular with the men.

> *'However he got up and walked on, with his poor horse being killed outright.'*

Hendry was shortly thereafter wounded, but was able to self-administer first aid and rejoin his companions.

> *'Up we went, firing at any slight object ahead. Our machine gunners got going also and covered our advance, firing from the flank. When we arrived at the top we found the Turks had fled from their trenches, which we then occupied, firing at the retreating Turks.'*

After a brief rest the advance was resumed. The country now began to change, sand giving place to thin and then thicker scrub ending in stony, broken ground. The night was spent at the head of Tor Dimre, a narrow valley from the head of which sentries could look down upon a rolling, sandy plain in which patrols of Indian cavalry were scouring in all directions.

On guard duty at the Church of the Nativity in Jerusalem, December 1917. The photograph shows Private R. Cruickshank VC, taken by his Padre William Tomkins who was later killed by an accidental grenade explosion in his tent.

By now Allenby had completed the first phase of his campaign. In the space of nine days he had rolled up and totally defeated the Turks, who were now retiring northwards in complete confusion. He now planned to push north along the coastal plain, wheel to his right and swarm up through the hills towards Jerusalem. The London Scottish remained at Tor Dimre for two days, enjoying a well-earned if fly-infested rest. On 11 November they were ordered to Jemmameh, passing en route the village of Huj. On 13 November the Battalion moved to Nejilieh where, in anticipation of a long stay, it took steps to place the area in a state of defence and to render the bivouacs comfortable. However Allenby remained impatient to rid the area of the enemy and thus ordered XXth Corps to concentrate around the railheads to free his limited logistics for XXIst Corps now in active pursuit of the Turks. The 10th and 74th Divisions were thus returned to the Karm-Shellal area, the 53rd remained round Beersheba and the 60th was directed to assemble near Sheria.

After a short period convalescing from his wounds Hendry recalled marching seven miles to a water supply where the battalion made up for lost time and had a jolly good clean up.

'The next day we moved twelve miles and on the following day went back again to within two miles of Gaza. The railway line had already been laid through this town and a London and South Western engine was puffing fussily along with a long trail of trucks full of supplies.'

On 14 November the Scottish began a long, hard eight-day trek to Junction Station where the railway line branched to Beersheba and Gaza. By the time the Scottish reached Bab el Wad, a delightful bivouac ground situated at the foot of the Judean hills, even the veterans' feet were in a bad state. On 24 November the exhausted troops climbed the steep road from the plain of Jerusalem, and at midday reached Kuryat el Enab and ultimately the hamlet of Beit Nakuba.

The British were once again in contact with the Turks, along a line which ran from the mouth of the Wadi Auja on the Mediterranean eastward to Beit el Foka, south across the Jaffa-Jerusalem road near the village of Lifta, from there circling the Jerusalem plateau and extending eastward to the difficult terrain immediately north of Bethlehem.

The 179th Brigade took over part of the line from the 232nd Brigade of the 75th Division, the Civil Service Rifles and Queen's Westminsters going

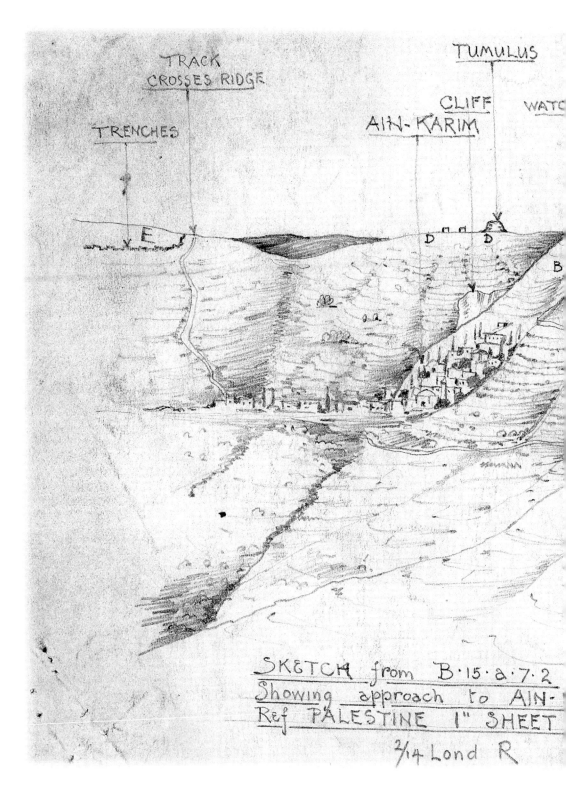

TUMULUS

TRACK
CROSSES RIDGE

CLIFF   WATC

AIN-KARIM

TRENCHES

SKETCH from B·15·a·7·2
Showing approach to AIN-
Ref PALESTINE 1" SHEET
2/4 Lond R

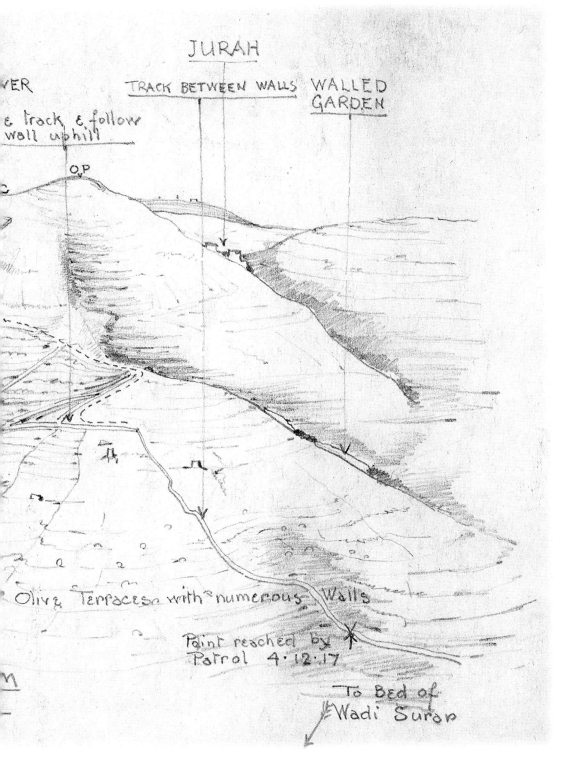

Original panoramic drawing of the Tumulus area.

into the line, the Kensingtons watching the flank at Soba and the Scottish forming the reserve at Beit Nakuba. The site, on the reverse of a steep terraced hillside, proved an excellent bivouac area, although the close proximity of a battery of British 60-pounders proved tiresome when the Turks chose to shell them. While the majority of the battalion busied itself training and road repairing, Hendry's company found itself detached.

Private I. M. Ness, wounded about 8 December 1917 in the battle for Jerusalem.

'After staying two days our company then took up a position on a very high hill some way from the rest of the battalion, doing patrols at night with the usual posts out, but things were very quiet. We found some fine herbs growing on the hillside which we used to fry with our bully beef and it made it taste like chicken.'

While patrolling, Hendry and his colleagues were able to see the roofs and buildings around Jerusalem.

On 3 December the Commanding Officer was called to Brigade Headquarters to discuss the dispositions required to take that most coveted of prizes. Jerusalem lies on top of a broad tongue-shaped plateau bound on the west, south and east by deep, steep and terraced ravines and gorges. Across the eastern ravine lies the Mount of Olives, a similarly shaped plateau with the village of Bethany at its southern extremity. The Wadi es Surar, some four miles west of the city, lies perched on the cliffs immediately above the eastern valley. From the north-west Neby Samwil overlooks the plateau, separated from it by a maze of stony hills and deep ravines. To the south of the city lies a similarly intricate country, through which the railway to Jaffa and the road to Bethlehem wend their tortuous ways.

Allenby was determined to spare the city from bombardment and was thus confined to an enveloping attack from the east and west. The British held the roads to Bethlehem and Jaffa in the south and west, but had yet to cut off the Turkish supply route from Nablus in the north. To the east of the Wadi es Surar the Turks held the hills with a line of strong defensive works, running south from Beit Iksa, crossing the Jaffa road at Ras el Alweh then passing through Deir Yesin to the hills above Ain Karim. The trenches and sangars ended near the hills known to the British as Jurah and Tumulus. From there to the Bethlehem road the country offered strong natural lines of defence, which the Turks were believed to hold in strength. The 60th Division lay opposite these defences from their southern extremity as far north as the Jaffa road. To their left the 74th Division held the line to Beit el Foka, with the 53rd Division delayed at Hebron. The initial attack was to be mounted by the 60th and 53rd Divisions from the west and south-west of the city. The 74th Division was then to attack in the flank, thereafter forming a line north of the city from Neby Samwil to Shafat. Finally the 53rd Division was to swing to the east, clear the Mount of Olives and join hands with the 74th in the area of Shafat. When it became clear that the 53rd Division's logistical difficulties were so severe that it would have difficulty in joining the main force for a number of days, Allenby found himself faced with a dilemma. He could either wait for the 53rd, or attack with the 60th Division alone. Conscious of the fact that the weather was due to break and that the heavy rains forecast would greatly increase the difficulty of his task, he elected to attack with or without the 53rd.

Orders were therefore given for the attack to commence on 8 December. Shea detailed the 179th and 180th Brigades to attack on the right and left respectively, retaining the 181st in reserve. The 179th Brigade was assigned the front from Tumulus Hill to Khurbet es Suhr inclusive, the 180th the front from the left of the 179th as far as the Jaffa-Jerusalem road. Brigadier Edwards ordered the Kensingtons to drive in the enemy patrols, seize and picket the Jurah and Tumulus Hills, and thereafter throw out patrols in an endeavour to make contact with the 53rd Division on the right. With their own right flank thus protected the London Scottish were to assault the Turkish main trenches from their left extremity to the Ain Karim-Jerusalem road. The Queen's Westminsters were to cross the Wadi es Surar further north, carry the Khurbet es Suhr system and link up with the Scottish in the rear of their objective. The Civil Service Rifles were to follow the Scottish in support.

Lieutenant Colonel Ogilby, who had been placed in command of the right column comprising the Kensingtons, London Scottish and Civil Service Rifles, detailed the Scottish to assault with A and B Companies under command of Captains Blackwell MC and Maclagan MC respectively, leaving C and D Companies, under Captains Robertson and Tinlin MC, in support. Intelligence suggested that Ain Karim was lightly held and could be taken by a support company of the Queen's Westminsters. Jurah and Tumulus Hills were said to be patrolled only, and it was therefore hoped that the Kensingtons would be able to secure both with minimum casualties.

A square stone tower, known to the British as the Watch Tower and situated approximately 1,000 yards south-west of Ain Karim, was fixed as the assembly point from which the Scottish were to assault the Turkish trenches, carrying them at the point of the bayonet it was hoped, just before dawn. The London Scottish left Beit Nakuba at 3.00p.m. on 7 December. It had begun to rain three hours earlier soaking the unprotected men who had been forced to dump their packs at Beit Nakuba, and impeding not only their advance but that of the camels who, uncomfortable on the hilly ground and wet mud, would only be goaded forward with the aid of a section of men pushing each beast from behind.

At 7.00p.m. the Kensingtons moved off, taking with them parties of Royal Engineers and Pioneers tasked with making the track passable for the pack-mules carrying the Lewis guns and ammunition. The whole column had to move in single file. The pace did not exceed one mile an hour, the going being rendered exceptionally difficult by the rain which continued to fall steadily. At 8.30p.m. the Scottish set out upon what Blazer was subsequently to describe as,

'the most sensational achievement during the whole of the late war.'

With the optimism renowned of the British soldier Hendry surmised that

'brother Turk would not expect us to attack on such a night as this.'

Later he noted that;

'the stillness was broken by shots echoing in the hills, but on we went, until things commenced to get very ugly.'

The Scottish were under orders not to fire a shot unless absolutely necessary, or until the final assault on the main trenches, and were therefore unable to respond.

As the night progressed it became increasingly apparent that the enemy's strength and alertness had both been under estimated. The Kensingtons in the lead had found strong and determined patrols around the Watch Tower itself, while their own forward elements reported that Jurah Hill was held in battalion strength. To compound the Brigade's problems it soon became clear that the Scottish would not be able to reach the Tower by the allotted time of 2.15a.m., and that any possibility of their resting before assaulting the enemy trenches was now out of the question. The Kensingtons' initial attempt to storm Jurah Hill was frustrated, and when the survivors came under sustained fire from the direction of Ain Karim matters began to look desperate.

Seizing the initiative Ogilby moved forward to the Watch Tower, which the Kensingtons had succeeded in occupying, quickly assessed the situation and ordered the Scottish forward to the Tower, disregarding the fighting on both flanks. A wedge was to be driven into the enemy centre, time was of the essence and companies were not to wait for each other, but were to push on independently and meet after daylight on the first objective. A Company was to lead, followed by B, C and D at three-minute intervals. Orders were given for three companies of the Civil Service Rifles to follow, leaving the fourth in reserve.

'As we were ascending the slope leading to the Watch Tower, creeping alongside a low wall, the enemy, by this time alive to the fact that all was not in order, commenced to fire rapidly,' remembered Bernard Blazer.

'Instinctively everybody crouched to the ground for cover, and there we lay for half an hour whilst the bullets pattered against the other side of the wall and sang overhead. During a lull we reached the sheltered precincts of the tower, where the Companies deployed, and proceeded round the deep re-entrant to attack the Turkish positions.'

By now dawn had broken affording the Turks an excellent target. A Company on the left took heavy casualties from a strong party of Turks to the front. B Company, which had been forced to cross rougher terrain, was slightly delayed, and to compound its problems also found itself under fire from a nest of machine guns positioned in an ostensibly peaceful village to the rear. C Company, following B, deployed slightly to the right and was able to help the latter secure its flank before turning its attention to the enemy dug in on Tumulus Hill. D Company followed A, which after a difficult start was now making steady progress. The hub of the battle now centred on Tumulus Hill, where C Company had nearly gained the summit before being checked by heavy machine-gun fire at short range. Cover was afforded by a convenient terrace, and orders passed for sectional rushes under covering fire.

The movement had barely started when a London Scot was sighted standing on the Turkish sangar and waving his comrades on with his helmet. This proved to be Corporal C.W. Train, commanding No. 10 platoon rifle grenade section. When the check had occurred he had found himself on the extreme right of the company. Realizing that a bold move might allow him to outflank the machine gun he at once, and at his own initiative, crawled to the flank, successfully reaching the extreme left of the enemy sangar, which was unoccupied. Creeping along behind this he came within sight of a Turkish machine gun in action. He at once fired a rifle grenade at a range of about sixty yards, and in so doing succeeded in putting most of the gun team out of action. He fired a second grenade before loading with ball ammunition and opening fire on the team. Their officer, a German, appeared and returned fire but was quickly killed. Still completely alone Train now engaged the second gun crew with grenades, forcing them to abandon their gun and flee. When C Company stormed the position they found no less than seven Turks dead by the first gun and two by the second. Corporal Train was awarded the Victoria Cross for his bravery, thus becoming the first member of the London Scottish to receive that highest award.

When Lieutenant General Chetwode visited the Battalion in May 1918 he presented the ribbon on a Battalion parade with the words,

> *'It is always a pleasure to have the privilege of looking a brave man in the face. I have that privilege today.'*

Corporal Charles William Train was invested with the Victoria Cross by King George V at 2nd Army Headquarters, Blendecques, on 6 August 1918. A veteran of the London Scottish, he had joined the Battalion in 1909 and fought at Messines and Givenchy before being wounded in March 1915. Posted to the 3rd Battalion, he was later drafted to the 2nd Battalion, joining it in Salonika.

Having gained the summit of Tumulus Hill, C Company were able to bring an enfilade fire to bear on the Turkish trenches allowing B Company to get forward again into the enemy positions. In the meantime, the Kensingtons were fighting with equal determination, and it was not long before the brigade was able to report its first objective taken.

> *'On we went to the top of this ridge and there laid down, firing as hard and as fast as we could reload, into wagons and men all hurrying away along the road at the bottom,'* recalled Hendry.

As Blazer and his colleagues gained the enemy lines a blood lust all too common in bayonet-fighting prevailed.

> *'They continued to fire at us until the very last moment, when, seeing that escape was impossible, they offered to surrender. The sight of the recumbent and bleeding forms of our comrades lying around did not tend to promote feelings of mercy, and the tactics of the Turks had so incensed us that bayonets got to work slick and sure. Turks who had been doing their utmost to mow us down were now on their bended knees; angry oaths were uttered and cries of mercy arose above the din; but no quarter was given; a few bayonet thrusts, a few shots fired point-blank, and they toppled over dead.'*

The Turkish infantry, not yet recovered from the shock of the attack, put up little resistance as the Scottish advanced to their second objective, although their gunners fired furiously causing heavy casualties among the exposed infantry. By 9.00a.m. A and B Companies had taken the second objective, with C and D close in support and the Queen's Westminsters in contact on the left. However the 180th Brigade to the right had begun its assault later and had yet to take the whole of the Dier Yesin trenches, and the Scottish were ordered to await their arrival before progressing further. Jerusalem was now in sight, and it was galling to the troops to have to wait, particularly as they had little shelter and the Turkish artillery was becoming increasingly active.

> *'They were firing from the Mount of Olives, we could see the battery clearly,'* complained Hendry. *'Our own guns could not get through to give us any support at all on this stunt. As the hours went on our nerves were getting very much shaken and already there were a good many casualties.'*

Dier Yesin fell at about 5.00p.m., after which the Scottish were given the order to advance. However the fight for Jerusalem was now over. Within minutes the Turks could be seen pulling their guns out of their pits and retiring towards the railway station. All firing from the city ceased. The day was well advanced before the Scottish could consider what arrangements could be made for the night. The men were exhausted from their previous night's exertions, yet the lack of greatcoats and bivouacs, coupled with extreme hunger, the rations having failed to arrive, made sleep all but impossible. Men not on patrol or sentry duty lay behind heaps of stones and shivered. Patrols were sent out in search of the wounded, but it was impossible to scour the entire vast area and as dawn broke the remains of several wounded men, dead of exposure, were discovered.

> *'Never was a sunrise more welcome than when, next morning, the glowing orb gradually appeared from behind Jerusalem to cheer our hearts and warm our numbed bodies,'* recalled Blazer.

The Turks had fled the city during the night, and in the morning sent the Mayor to surrender. Initial attempts to hand the keys of the city to a gunner major were frustrated when the officer reported himself as too busy. The keys were later presented to Brigadier Watson commanding 180th Brigade, but were later returned to the by now despairing Mayor to enable him to surrender a third time, in this instance to Major General Shea who accepted the keys on behalf of 60th Division. On 11 December Allenby made his official entry into Jerusalem, and the hapless Mayor was yet again ordered to participate in a formal surrender. It is reported that he was so overawed by this final occurrence that he demanded seven days leave of the British!

The Brigade was given the morning to sort out its personal administration. About noon it moved off in column of route, the Scottish leading, to enter the city. After sterling efforts, the pipers managed to tune up their instruments, many of which had fallen victim to the recent hostile climate, and played the Battalion along the white road towards the western suburbs. The skirl of the pipes, accompanied by the drums, created a great sensation among the few Arabs and Jewish pedestrians who had initially come to watch and a great crowd quickly gathered making progress difficult. In Blazer's words;

> 'December 9th 1917 was, without doubt, the greatest day known to the inhabitants of Jerusalem for many weary years. Curiously it coincided with the anniversary of the freeing of the city from the Seleucids by Judas Maccabeus two millennia earlier. Jerusalem had been under Turkish occupation for 400 years.'

The Scottish did not enter the city proper, but turned north through the Jewish quarter while still in the outskirts. They were billeted that night in the Syrian Orphanage. The building had been comprehensively plundered by the enemy, but nothing could stop the exhausted Scottish from sleeping, protected as they now were from the wind and driving rain outside. The next day the transport and baggage arrived, and in the afternoon the Battalion left Jerusalem to take its place again in the line. By now the 74th Division had swung out from the direction of Neby Samwil and the 53rd Division had caught up. The Scottish were sent to occupy the hills north of the village of Shafat, the ancient City of Nod, where they found themselves facing an enemy dug in in strength and still far from defeated.

The Turkish Counter-Attack

At 7.00a.m. on 10 December the Scottish were paraded and marched off through the narrow streets of the Jewish quarter north along the Nablus road towards the sound of firing in the direction of the Mount of Olives. Relief was effected with the 12th Battalion, The Royal Scots Fusiliers, of the 74th Division, in a sector immediately north of the village of Shafat. The Turks opposing them had retired to the north and offered little resistance, even allowing patrols to bring in the contents of an arms dump abandoned in no man's land. After six days the Scottish returned to Jerusalem where they were delighted to find themselves billeted in the Jewish school. Hendry remembers spending;

> 'a very interesting eight days, seeing all the sights and tasting all the

quaint dishes of the east, honey cakes and fig rolls were the order of the day.'

The rest was marred somewhat on 19 December when the Battalion was ordered to take part in a house-to-house search for arms. The whole city was divided into areas, of which about half of the Jewish quarter was allotted to the Scottish. As was expected, little was found, and the arms unearthed were mostly of a character fitting them for a museum rather than for actual use.

About this time major changes took place within the Battalion. Major J.H.Young left to assume the temporary appointment of Brigade Major before assuming command of the Queen's Westminsters. He was succeeded as second-in-command by Captain R. Whyte, Captain J.S.Monro assuming the duties of Adjutant. Captain W. Anderson DCM, Officer Commanding the 179th Trench Mortar Battery, was offered the appointment of second-in-command of the London Irish, but steadfastly refused to soldier as an infantryman with anyone other than the London Scottish. His request was granted, he became second-in-command of D Company, and when its Officer Commanding, Captain Tinlin, was shortly afterwards invalided home, assumed the latter's appointment.

Captain J.B. Stubbs, the Medical Officer, was himself hospitalized shortly after the capture of Jerusalem and was succeeded by Captain A. Milton RAMC. However, he returned to the battalion in time to accompany it back to France in May 1918. A new Padre, the Reverend G. Leslie joined the Scottish in Jerusalem, as did a new Quartermaster, Captain E. Farrington.

Rumour had it that the Battalion was going to spend Christmas Day in its comfortable billets, but its hopes were dashed when on the previous morning it was sent up the line to Shafat to take over from the London Irish as battalion in brigade reserve. Bandoliers of ammunition and bombs were issued to every man, a procedure which was viewed with considerable apprehension, being no part of the usual Yuletide celebrations. It was later ascertained that Intelligence had discovered that the Turks intended to put in a counter-attack on Christmas Day, and vigorous steps were thus taken to frustrate their intentions.

'There was trouble brewing for somebody,' mused Bernard Blazer,
'and Christmas or no Christmas, we were going to see to it that whoever was responsible for this untimely interference with our projected festivities would be the sufferer; to wit, John Turk.'

The 179th Brigade now lay astride the Jerusalem-Nablus road with the Queen's Westminsters deployed to its east and the Kensingtons to its west. The Civil Service Rifles were to the rear of the Westminsters and echeloned to the right, to watch the flank of the 53rd Division. The Westminsters' line included two important hills, Ras el Tawil and Tel el Ful, both commanding important positions, the latter dominating a long stretch of the road. The Kensingtons to the west joined hands with the 181st Brigade, near the village of Beit Hannina. Shortly after dusk a strong south-west wind rose, driving the heavy rain into the faces of the Turks. The hour for the anticipated attack approached amid an inevitable sense of strain, arrived and passed, the strain now overtaken by a sense of frustration and anti climax. Christmas day itself proved peaceful, but appallingly uncomfortable.

> 'We woke up to find ourselves in pools of water and soaked through, we had to get up and run about in the rain to keep the circulation up,'

complained Hendry.

> 'Rations were very bad and we had a sumptuous Christmas dinner of tea, bully beef and biscuits. This was easily the worst Christmas day we had spent in the Army.'

To compound the Scottish misfortune a consignment of turkeys, for which they had paid £60, never got beyond Deir Sineid.

The next day, Boxing Day, the rain held off. In the evening the sky cleared, and at dusk a bright moon rose. Intelligence announced that the Turks had decided to attack at 2.00a.m. on the morning of 27 December and, as if to confirm this, their gunners began to shell heavily throughout the afternoon. At midnight rum was issued, and an hour later the Battalion stood-to. As anticipated the enemy gunners opened fire at 2.00a.m., covering the advance of their infantry with a heavy bombardment. The main attack came down the line of the Nablus road and, after a series of tenacious attacks, the heights of Ras el Tawil were taken. The Westminsters, supported by elements of the Civil Service Rifles, counter-attacked at dawn but due to an unfortunate failure in synchronization, the Civil Service were practically wiped out. On the left the Kensingtons were frustrating all efforts to dislodge them. B and D Companies of the Scottish were thus released and ordered to cross east of the road in support of the Westminsters, but they were not seriously engaged as at 9.00a.m. the Westminsters counter-attacked and regained the heights at Ras el Tawil.

A lull in the battle now occurred in front of the 60th Division positions as the Turks shifted the emphasis of their attack to their right. One further attack was however launched against the Kensingtons, but was repulsed after which the Turks gave up and returned to their original lines. When darkness fell C Company of the London Scottish took over patrolling the Kensingtons' front, capturing a Turkish machine gun and crew in the process. The Turkish attempt to regain Jerusalem proved a disaster. It had led to the annihilation of one of their army corps followed by the forced withdrawal to a line some ten miles to the rear, out of sight of Jerusalem. When the 60th Division was ordered to advance on 29 December it met little resistance as it marched forward across the recent battlefield. The Scottish were halted near Kulundia, some 2,000 yards further north and a short distance west of the Nablus road. The next two days were spent in support and in light duties including road repairing. The 60th Division was now relieved in the line and ordered back to Jerusalem. On 31 December the London Scottish reached their former quarters in the Jewish school, having started from their bivouac area at dawn.

The *Regimental History* reports that,

'there was much to do and little time to do it in if the festival of Hogmanay was to be celebrated in a fitting manner. Concerts were hastily arranged, rations supplemented as far as was possible, and a certain amount of liquid refreshment procured.'

During the course of the evening orders came for the 60th Division to relieve the 53rd in the line the following day, the movement beginning at dawn. By this time, however, spirits were high, the party continued early into the morning and many a soldier awoke with a hangover. At 6.00a.m. on 1 January 1918 the Battalion moved eastwards to relieve the 1/6th Battalion, The Royal Welch Fusiliers. It reached its rendezvous at about 9.00a.m., having marched past Damascus Gate, across the brook Kedron, and up over the Mount of Olives. The sight which met them was stunning. One of those who took part in the march later recorded in the *Regimental Gazette*,

'On New Year's morn we scaled the Mount of Olives, and beheld for the first time what must be one of the most striking views in the world. At our feet lay the eastern hills of Judaea, magnificent in their naked grandeur. Brown, treeless, and desolate, twisted into all kinds of fantastic shapes, they sloped away towards the Jordan valley. To the south-east lay the Dead Sea, forbidding and sinister, and far beyond, clothed in a dim grey haze, the mountains of Moab, mysterious and defiant.'

The next five days were spent on guard or undertaking patrols. The Turks' main position was far to the east on Arak Ibrahim, where they were observed to be inhabiting a number of caves, although they did occupy the closer villages by night. Rain began to fall shortly after the relief was complete, turning the paths into familiar mud. Movement for both sides thus became difficult and, although the Turks fired on the Scottish advanced night posts as they withdrew at dawn, no casualties were sustained and fire was not returned.

On 9 January the Queen's Westminsters relieved the Scottish, who withdrew into billets on the Mount of Olives. The whole battalion was quartered in Sir John Grey Hill's magnificent stone house. The officers set up a mess in a nearby house, reputed to have been the harem of a wealthy Turk. *The Regimental History* records that,

'this gentleman had removed the ladies, but left the fleas.'

The Scottish remained in its present location until 2 February. Courses of specialist intensive training were undertaken, while large parties were constantly detailed to assist the Engineers. A range was rigged-up, and the Serjeants' Wappenshaw, a time-honoured institution, was held followed by a concert in the Mess.

The Scottish billet was close to the Augusta Victoria Hospice, ostensibly a German philanthropic institution but in reality a potential foreign home for the Kaiser. It was now occupied as XXth Corps' headquarters. Permission was granted for the Battalion to undertake a route march to the village of Bethlehem to enable its members to visit the Church of the Nativity. In small parties the entire unit was shown through the church and taken below to the crypt chapel to see the precise position of the manger. The Regiment was granted the honour of providing a sentry in the vault, on the spot which had formerly been occupied by a Turkish guard.

On 2 February the Battalion handed over Sir John Grey Hill's house to the 2/20th Battalion and moved under canvas in the same area. The move was far from popular, as the rainy season was at its height, and the period from 5th to 11th was one continuous storm, frequently made worse by gales and occasional sleet. Burns' Night was duly celebrated, with the Padre proposing the toast in the Officers' Mess, but the evening was somewhat marred when it was found that the haggis, which had been destined to form the gastronomic centre of the feast, was rancid.

It soon became clear that before a further advance could be made it would be necessary to secure the right flank. The existing bend in the line to the east of Jerusalem rendered a further direct advance impossible without first driving the enemy across the Jordan, requiring not only his dislodgement from the ridge of intervening hills but the capture of Jericho. The territory over which the forthcoming campaign was to be fought was difficult in the extreme. Jericho is only some fifteen miles from the Mount of Olives, but is some 3,000 feet lower. El Ghoraniyeh, five miles to the east of Jericho and commanding the only bridge spanning the lower waters of the Jordan, is a further 800 feet lower. The intervening terrain is wild and broken, marked by masses of steep rocky hills, covered for the most part in thick scrub. These are intersected by deep wadis, gullies and ravines many of them precipitous. A single metal road, in good repair, then lay between Jerusalem and Jericho. Numerous other tracks were only negotiable by pack transport. Roughly parallel with the road and to the north of it runs an enormously deep wadi, known in its upper reaches as the Wadi Farah and lower down as the Wadi Khelt.

On 11 February the 60th Division received orders to capture the ridge of broken hills to its front. The extreme left of the enemy's position rested on a conspicuous hill called El Muntar (The Watchtower), at 1,725 feet the highest point on the ridge. The Scottish were ordered to advance on the complete right of the Divisional line, to capture El Muntar, and then change direction left, working along the ridge to a hill named Jebel Joffet Sherif, and thereafter to close in on the centre brigade working eastwards through the hills.

Colonel Ogilby elected to approach the hill by night from the north-west, dropping one company on the north-west spur and advancing with the residue to the north spur. Here a right form was to be made, followed by an advance up the hill at dawn. The detached company was to move independently and deliver its assault simultaneously. On 18 February the whole Division moved forward among the maze of wadis intersecting the intervening country, the various battalions making for their points of deployment, entailing a long march over very rough ground. At dawn the Scottish began its advance in open order up the slopes of the hill. When half way up shots rang out and a shell from an Allied battery dropped short, many among the advancing troops began to sense a feeling of trepidation. The enemy opposition was, however, far lighter than anticipated, allowing scouts to be sent forward to ascertain more accurately the position. It quickly became clear that the Turks had no stomach for a fight and had withdrawn, leaving the hill in British hands.

The Scottish lay on El Muntar all day. From its summit the Anzacs could be seen moving round the flank between the hill and the Dead Sea. They were meeting greater opposition, and by nightfall had failed to take their objective. At 5.00p.m. Captain Buchanan received orders to move his company to Ruhm Rahif, and an hour later the rest of the battalion followed. The descent from El Muntar was accomplished with some difficulty, but by 10.00p.m. the Battalion was concentrated again near Ruhm Rahif. During the night the Turks sent out a fighting patrol, which engaged in a sharp skirmish with the centre brigade, but was soon driven off.

At dawn on 20 February a heavy bombardment announced an attack on Jebel Ekteif. This was executed by the Civil Service Rifles and Queen's Westminsters. The Kensingtons had been originally detailed as the attacking battalion, but had been unable to cross a deep wadi, and entirely at their own initiative the Civil Service Rifles had intervened, securing the hill at 3.00p.m.

The Turks were now retreating eastwards on to the Jericho plain, harried all the way by the Allied cavalry. They had little alternative but to retire across the Jordan, and seemed uncharacteristically determined to cause as much mischief as possible before doing so. At 2.00a.m. on 21 February the Scottish were ordered to clear Neby Musa, a large shrine built by the Moslems on the spot where they hold Moses to be buried, and now being used to good effect by the Turkish artillery. The position had originally been one of the objectives of the Anzac cavalry on their way round the flanks to Jericho, but they had been held up by a Turkish rearguard, and thus the Scottish were sent forward through the hills to assist in its capture. The night was particularly overcast making progress for the pack animals along the rough and steep path somewhat treacherous. Matters improved with the coming of the dawn and a race quickly developed between the Scottish and the New Zealand cavalry to see who could reach the position first, and thereby claim it as their bivouac.

'Our Colonel, readily taking in the situation, determined that we should not be outdone, and ordered the pace to be so increased that the Battalion was virtually running a race with the Horse for the right to the billet,' remembered Blazer. *'Distance and other considerations*

were in our favour, so we won, the New Zealanders having to bivouac in the open.'

The building was quite deserted, but marred by the stench and putrification left by the Turks who had hurriedly vacated a few hours earlier. The enemy now conceded defeat and retired across the Jordan by means of the El Ghoraniyeh bridge.

General Allenby having now achieved the whole of his objectives, ordered the 60th Division to retire, leaving a brigade of mounted troops to carry out patrol duties. The Scottish accordingly left Neby Musa on 23 February and undertook a trying uphill march of fourteen miles to Talaat ed Dumm. The journey the next day was wretched. Heavy rain made the road, already in a shocking state of repair treacherous in the extreme, particularly in areas where the Turks had blown up culverts. That night they reached their old camping ground on the Mount of Olives, via the famous hill of Bethany, described in the *Regimental History* as *'surely the longest, steepest and stoniest'* that the Battalion had ever negotiated.

The Scottish returned from operations in the same strength as when they had set out, not having lost a single man, a unique and highly welcome occurrence. As they marched past the German Hospice, General Sir Phillip Chetwode, the Corps Commander, stood at the gateway and took the salute.

Passage Across the Jordan

The Scottish remained for only one day on the Mount of Olives, and on 26 February marched north along the Nablus road to Er Ram where they bivouacked for the night. The next morning, in driving rain, they wound their way eastward to Ras el Tawil where they relieved the 2/24th Londons. Hardened as they were, the Scottish found this journey particularly irksome.

'Rough roads had been made by the troops who had captured the ground, but these were inches deep in mud. Camels were in a pitiful plight, slipping down at every turn, where they remained in the mud until their loads could be taken off. Some went hurtling over precipices down to their death, while others were lying about with broken legs until they could be shot, so that we were forced to rely almost entirely upon that stupid, contrary, aggravating though sure-footed beast, the mule.'

General Allenby now conceived a raid of massive proportions. He resolved to send a division of infantry across the Jordan into the Moabite hills as far as the town of Es Salt, after which the cavalry would then press forward another fifteen miles to Amman where the Turks were known to have a large supply dump. A long tunnel on the Hedjaz railway would then be blown, hindering the supply arrangements of the Turkish army in the south. This, it was hoped, would encourage the Arab irregulars then fighting with Colonel Lawrence in that area to press further north, linking up with the Allied forces.

For their part the Turks held the east bank of the Jordan from the Dead

Crossing the Jordan by pontoon bridge en route for El Haud and Es Salt.

Sea as far north as its confluence with the Wadi Auja, some twelve miles upstream. Here their line crossed to the western bank and ran along the north side of the Auja. At El Ghoraniyah the wooden bridge still spanned the river, but it was certain that the Turks would destroy it at the first sign of an Allied advance. The passage of the Jordan thus presented serious logistical problems. Blazer and his fellow cartographers were tasked with making detailed maps of the area from aerial photographs, while patrols were pushed out towards the Jordan in the hopes of locating any of the several fords which it was rumoured afforded reasonably safe crossing points at low water.

C Company, under command of Captain R.M. Robertson MC, was thus ordered to move forward to Tel el Abu Aleik, some two miles west of Jericho, *'a small dirty place,'* according to W.N. Hendry, *'with just the one street through it.'*

> *'On the 28th we moved down to the plain by a narrow winding road,'* reported Hendry. *'It began to get very hot and by the time we got to our camping ground we were soaked through and not a breath of air about. It was just a dry, dead heat, and we were now 1,300 feet below the Mediterranean...The plain consisted of small, steep, treacherous sand hills, so we had to find the well-trodden paths and this was no easy matter until a native was found wandering in the vicinity. He was silent at first until a little persuasion in the proper place made him lead the way through the hills to the lower valley where we reached the river.'*

Matters were made no easier when a pontoon bridge constructed by the Engineers across the Jordan broke loose in the strong current. Patrolling was not without its dangers. A six-man watching patrol under the command of

Second Lieutenant Ware was rushed by the enemy and five of its number taken prisoner. It was thought by some that the prisoners might break under interrogation and reveal the British intention to cross the river. But that was not the Scottish way, it was subsequently discovered from Turkish prisoners that all had refused to answer any questions on the subject.

On 10 March C Company rejoined the Battalion on Kuruntul, where not only did the troops find the breezes and cooler air comforting, but were bolstered in the knowledge that their peers had spent the previous days in the uncomfortable pursuit of road making. Four days later a conference was held at which the plan of attack was disclosed and the objectives given. It was intended to cross the river in the region of El Ghoraniyeh and from there to make good use of the metalled road which led across the plain and into the Moabite hills towards El Haud. The position itself completely commanded the road, and it quickly became obvious that no advance would be possible while it remained in enemy hands. It was therefore proposed that, once the Jordan was crossed, the hill should be seized and held. Major General Shea ordered the 180th Brigade to force a crossing of the river, the 179th Brigade to assault El Haud and retained the 181st in reserve. Brigadier Humphries, who had recently assumed command of the 179th Brigade, ordered the London Scottish to deliver the main attack on El Haud, with the Westminsters covering their left flank. Ogilby ordered C Company to make the main attack, with B Company in support and A and D companies in reserve.

All attempts to ford the Jordan were now abandoned and suitable bridging sites sought. Pontoons and other bridging material were taken down by night and concealed in the broken hills close to the scene of the proposed operations. Meanwhile, the troops were warned that there would be a great deal of hard marching before them, and to render them as mobile as possible were ordered to return their packs and entrenching tools to battalion stores while committing their greatcoats and blankets to the camel train. At 7.00p.m. on 21 March the Battalion moved from Kuruntul down into the plain. Blazer remembered it as a close and oppressive night, dark and overcast. The Scottish halted some three miles from the Jordan where the mules were off loaded and a rest ordered while the river crossing was secured. When it became clear that enemy fire from the further bank was so fierce that the 2/17th Londons (Poplar and Stepney) would have difficulty in securing a crossing, D Company of the Scottish was ordered up to El Ghoraniyeh in support. At 5.00a.m. news was received that all efforts to cross at that point had failed. Attempts to construct barges of tarpaulins stretched over wooden frames had been frustrated when they had been pierced by bullets and had become waterlogged and unmanageable, in many instances drowning their crews.

At 8.00a.m. came news that the 2/19th Londons had met with greater success at Haljah. They had first effected a landing by roping a number of their strongest swimmers together and letting them forge over at a spot where the stream was very deep and in consequence less swift. On the east bank they had managed to secure a rope to which a number of their stronger colleagues had been able to secure themselves while crossing. The Australian Engineers meanwhile had brought up pontoons and had succeeded in constructing a bridge over which the Auckland Mounted Rifles had crossed at dawn.

The 179th Brigade, by now at Wadi Khelt, was ordered to cross the Jordan and establish a bridgehead without further delay.

'As we were approaching the river a large motor-car passed us, travelling in the opposite direction,' Blazer was later to recall.

'In it sat the Commander-in-Chief. His presence on the very scene of operations at such a critical time showed a fine example to the troops, and evoked general admiration.'

That evening the Scottish crossed the Jordan.

'In passing over the swaying, trembling pontoons, with the swollen waters rushing underneath, it seems hardly credible that this can really be the great Jordan River,' mused Bernard Blazer, yet it was and with its crossing passed the last great obstacle to victory.

Having cleared the hills and gained the eastern plain the Scottish turned north and marched towards El Ghoraniyeh, reaching their objective the next morning. Rest was ordered in the shelter of the Wadi Nimrin, save for the luckless C Company who were sent out on outpost duty in the direction of El Haud. The day was somewhat disturbed by the Turkish gunners who were searching the line of the wadi, and it soon became clear that C Company had the best of the deal. The enemy to their front were demoralized in the extreme, some seventy surrendering after no more than a token fight.

At 9.00a.m. the infantry emerged from the Wadi Nimrin and advanced across the plain towards its battalion objectives, the Scottish towards El Haud. C Company, already to the fore, was extended across the entire 900 yard front, the remainder following in artillery formation. The land ahead of the Scottish comprised scrub dispersed with acres of fine green barley, with the occasional stunted tree among it. The scrub ended abruptly some 800 yards of flat, stoney ground short of the point where the hills rose steeply from the plain. The Battalion halted at the far end of the scrub, the last available cover, where the Lewis-gun mules were off loaded. B Company was ordered to the right of C Company, and after ten minutes the advance was resumed. The assaulting companies moved in two waves, of two lines each, the men deploying in the now familiar pattern of half-sections in file.

Despite sporadic enemy machine-gun fire, most of it directed at B

Bridge over the Jordan built by the London Scottish.

Company, the advance continued comparatively unchecked. C Company clambered up the re-entrants of Spectacle Hill, while B Company took the lower ground. As C Company halted to reorganize on the top of Spectacle Hill it became clear that a deep re-entrant lay between them and the main mass of El Haud. B Company kept up its momentum, and quickly took some forty prisoners in the low ground. Thereafter C Company was ordered to double over the crest of Spectacle Hill and into the dead ground beyond. The few enemy brave or foolish enough to show any resistance were quickly picked off by the Lewis gunners now on Spectacle Hill. The more realistic chose to surrender, including a party of three German officers and thirty-three men from the 203rd Regiment of Infantry.

For the Scottish the incident now developed into a mountain climbing expedition up El Haud. As darkness fell the Turks could be seen retiring in disorder, the 180th Brigade in pursuit. That night C Company was ordered to form an outpost line round the summit of El Haud, A and B Companies were ordered to bivouac in Wadi Arseniyat, while D Company and Battalion Headquarters located themselves about halfway to the base of the hill. During the night the weather changed for the worse, and heavy rain added to the logistical difficulties. The troops on the hill were ordered to move at dawn to join the Battalion in the wadi. There were no tracks, and many of the mules, losing their footing on the slippery grass, rolled or slipped hundreds of feet down the slope. Morale was restored, however, when it was found that the cooks, against all the odds, had lit fires and made tea.

As Blazer remembered,

'Rations and water were issued, and we snatched a hasty meal of our staff of life, bully beef and biscuits. This finished, everything was again packed up, loads once more put on the pack animals, and in single file the whole Brigade set off to Es Salt, prepared for any eventualities.'

Mile after mile, ever upwards, the Brigade plugged away, the Kensingtons in

Ariel photographs of the El Muntar area showing clearly the unforgiving nature of the terrain.

the lead and Scottish in the rear. At 2.00p.m. a halt was ordered, but after an hour the march resumed into the night. As darkness fell the animals began to give trouble. One by one the mules and donkeys stopped, refusing to go any further. Men began to drop in their tracks from fatigue while the camels fell further behind. The sound of rifle fire heightened tensions somewhat, until it was discovered that it emanated from local Arabs rejoicing at the arrival of their Allies. At last, at midnight, the Scottish were ordered to halt. Having closed up as one, regardless of the sea of mud surrounding them, they fell and slept.

As they awoke on the morning of 26 March the leading soldiers saw the town of Es Salt lying in a deep valley some 800 yards below. The Battalion was moved to better and dryer ground and given a full day's rest. The Queen's Westminsters and Civil Service Rifles were then holding the line to the north while the Kensingtons provided guards and pickets for Es Salt. The town itself, with its hybrid population of Christians, Circassians and particularly warlike Bedouin was considered too volatile for leave, and the Scottish were thus confined to camp.

'All the natives here carry revolvers, rifles and knives of all descriptions - a very bloodthirsty looking crowd,' reported Hendry.

During the course of the morning rest was interrupted by a German aircraft which flew four times over the position taking photographs. Orders were given to erect machine guns, and when the aircraft returned thirty minutes later, again flying very low, it was shot down and its pilot captured. As the Scottish rested the cavalry continued to probe the Turkish lines, sending back large numbers of prisoners in the process. Their progress was, however, halted just outside of Amman by a large body of the enemy and they were thus unable to do mortal damage to the railway by blowing the tunnel. They did, however, destroy a bridge together with large parts of the line before retiring.

On 27 March the Scottish received orders to move back from Es Salt to El Howeij bridge on the main road. The Battalion took full advantage of the fine morning by marching through Es Salt, its band at the fore. At the sound of the pipes the whole population turned out to discover the cause of the unfamiliar commotion, and many followed the Scottish for miles along the road until, after about six miles, they bivouacked by the side of a picturesque river where a swim was enjoyed by all those not on duty.

Just as they were beginning to settle for the night word came that they were to prepare to move in twenty minutes and return to Es Salt. A Turkish force of 5,000 to 7,000 was said to be marching on the town from the north-west and the Scottish were required to bolster its defences. The cavalry was by now pinned down by superior forces and the Divisional Commander had found it necessary to send the 181st Brigade with two battalions of the 180th north to extricate them, leaving scant reserves for the defence of Es Salt and the lines of communication.

'We reached the town in the small hours of morning after a forced *march, and found everything quiet and still,'* reported Blazer.

'Passing through the silent and deserted street we mounted the hill by a rough track and halted at the Headquarters of the 15th Battalion.'

The Commanding Officer of the 15th Battalion being on home leave, Colonel Ogilby assumed control of the sector, and sent A and B Companies forward in support. The next morning the Turks advanced against his position in large numbers but in a half-hearted manner, allowing the Australian Light Horse on the left flank to execute a brilliant counter-attack. Two machine guns and 120 prisoners were taken before the remaining Turks fled.

By 1 April the troops withdrawing from Amman had reached Es Salt, and that evening, having blown up the Turkish ammunition dumps, Colonel Ogilby prepared to withdraw his force. At 10.00p.m. the roll was called in muffled whispers and every man accounted for. The front line platoons quietly left their positions and joined the main body and shortly thereafter the Scottish began the long march down the Wadi Arseniyat. Caution mixed with the adrenalin of fear as the Scottish, the last troops to leave Es Salt, pressed on in silence, conscious of the fact that, were the Turks to have been alerted to their intentions and have attacked, the results would have been catastrophic. Hendry remembered it as a very hard march, in pitch darkness.

'I may say,' he noted, *'we soon beat it down here in half the time it took us to get up, knowing the enemy were following on our heals.'*

'With every yard we gained confidence,' recalled Blazer. *'The exigencies of the occasion were a sufficient incentive to urge us on, and in spite of the difficulties of the ground we made fair progress.'*

The moon rose shortly after midnight making the going easier and at 6.00a.m. the Battalion emerged on the Jordan plain where it proceeded to

Marching out of Es Salt, 1918.

Marching out of Es Salt, 27 March 1918. Brigadier Humphries, commanding 179th Brigade, can be seen on the right.

feed. The river was re-crossed by midday, from where the march continued to a point some three miles north-east of Jericho, where bivouacs were pitched in the scrub. All that day hundreds of fugitives came across the Jordan, friendly Arabs, many of them Christians, who, having received the British so openly, dared not wait the return of the Turks. They were disarmed as they crossed the Jordan, discarding their various weapons in heaps by the bridge.

After a good rest the Battalion went up the hills again to Talaat ed Dumm where they rested for the night, and on 6 April marched up the long terrible hill to Bethany once again where, instead of returning to Sir John Grey Hill's house as hoped, they continued along the Nablus Road and bivouacked on the side of a terraced hill.

By now the weather had generally improved and the hills were covered once more with prolific vegetation, providing a refreshing relief from the barrenness of the Jericho plain. It was the height of the orange season, and wherever the Scottish went they were besieged by a small army of natives selling their wares for twopence each. After two days' rest, the Scottish again marched up the Nablus road, and on 11 April, with the rest of the 60th Division, took over the line from the 10th Division. The line consisted of a series of strong points along the forward slope of a commanding range of hills. The Turks held the hills some 2,000 yards to the north, and between the two forces ran the deep Wadi Gharib. The Turks shelled occasionally, and their aeroplanes bombed at times, but on the whole it was a peaceful front.

The 18 April brought an unexpected relief when the 5th Inniskillings took over the line from the Scottish who moved out to El Jib, where they had the opportunity of enjoying excellent entertainment from the Divisional Concert Party. The wonderment increased when on 21 April the Battalion moved south again, their destination being announced as Jerusalem. Four days marching to spend eight days in the line seemed excessive. As one man tersely put it, *'if they didna think o' ma feet, they might a' thocht o' ma buits.'*

The return trip was made by easy stages, two days spent at Jufna and three at Balua Lake. At this stage the reason for the return became apparent, the Battalion was to attack El Haud again! Colonel Lawrence and his Arab irregulars were making good progress on the other side of the Dead Sea, and it was thought possible that if the British were to hold the railway for a little, the Arab troops might be able to make contact from the south.

The Jordan was crossed again on 28 April, this time at El Ghoraniyeh which now boasted three bridges each capable of handling artillery. The Scottish bivouacked before dawn in the Wadi Nimrin. All bivouacs had to be camouflaged and movement was banned as it was essential that the enemy aircraft flying overhead be kept in ignorance of the fact that two brigades of infantry had crossed the river during the night.

Colonel Ogilby and his company commanders spent the morning in reconnaissance. The site which met them was salutary in the extreme. The Battalion had been weakened by months of fighting and privation and each company was now no more than eighty strong. The Turks on the other hand had strengthened the defences of El Haud enormously while Spectacle Hill now bristled with newly dug sangars. The Royal Air Force reported that the Turkish positions were defended by a force estimated at 5,000 bayonets and thirty-two guns. This proved to be an under-estimate.

As the earlier assault on El Haud had proved so successful it was resolved to use the same tactics. In this instance, however, in deference to the stronger Turkish dispositions, it was planned that the assault would take place along a three battalion front; the Queen's Westminsters on the left, the Scottish in the centre and the 2/20th Londons (Blackheath and Woolwich) on the right. While the infantry attacked the El Haud positions the mounted troops were to move north from El Ghoraniyeh and then eastwards via a hill track to Es

Bivouacs near Es Salt, 1918.

Salt. This would bring them into the rear of the Turkish positions cutting off their line of retreat. Confronted by the British to their front, the cavalry to their rear and the Arab irregulars to the south, it was even hoped that the whole enemy force might then surrender.

It was decided to execute a moonlight assault at 2.30a.m. on the morning of 30 April. C Company were to take Spectacle Hill, B Company were to seize the Turkish works on the lower ground to the right, A Company were to follow in support and D Company form the reserve. The Scottish broke camp at 6.45p.m. and by 10.00p.m. had reached the front line.

At 2.30a.m. the lead battalions set off for their objectives, but on this occasion almost immediately encountered heavy enemy rifle and machine-gun fire.

Private Jasper Hawkinson attached to the Transport Platoon; taken at Cairo, April 1918.

> '*Stealthily advancing in artillery formation we crossed the plain, and at a certain point opened out in extended order,*' remembered Blazer. '*Long before reaching the foothills the enemy had discovered our approach, and a line of bright flashes warned us that they were not to be taken by surprise this time.*'

Onward into the unrelenting fire B and C Companies made their bloody way.

> '*As we got nearer the bullets began to find their victims. Here and there men were hit, some falling in a crumpled heap to cry out for the last time, others writhing in the agony of their wounds.*'

Captain Maclagan MC, leading B Company from the front, fell mortally wounded, but not until he had the satisfaction of seeing a few of his men enter the enemy forward positions. Command passed to Lieutenant MacDougall who continued the advance, until he too was killed. By now the position facing B Company was critical. CSM Martin and Lieutenant Edgar succeeded in forcing the line forward until the entire first line of Turkish sangars was in Scottish hands, but further than this they could not go.

C Company fared slightly better. They did not come under heavy fire until they were within 100 yards of the foot of Spectacle Hill. At this point a tremendous fusillade was opened on them. Luckily the foot of Spectacle Hill provided dead ground. Half the company thereafter climbed the hill on the left, half on the right while Serjeant McRostie led a small team against the centre. The stratagem proved surprisingly successful, even though the Turks above threw hundreds of bombs down among the rocks. Hendry saw the man next to him fall dead, a bullet through his pith helmet, while another went through the butt of his own rifle. There was fierce and confused bayonet work as C Company breasted the hill, but in a few minutes the peak was in Scottish possession. Some seventy-six Turks were taken prisoner, many of them suffering from bayonet wounds.

Steps were then taken by B Company to link up with C on its right. These were successful, but the Company was by then so badly mauled that it was unable to take any further serious part in the battle. A Company followed through the B Company positions, pushing forward on the right, but almost at once suffered heavily from machine-gun fire.

It was by now almost daylight, and the coming of dawn enabled the situation to be better understood. Flanking Wadi Arseniyat, the Westminsters now held the foothills as far south as the base of Spectacle Hill. The Hill itself was held by C Company, the London Scottish, the remains of B and A Companies lying in the low ground south of Spectacle Hill. The 2/20th on the Scottish right had yet to take their crest.

The Scottish had now, in effect, driven a salient into the enemy line, and it seemed unlikely that further ground could be gained until the right came forward. Nonetheless, Colonel Ogilby decided to try to swing forward on the battalion right to clear the low ground giving access to the lower slopes of El Haud, and with this object in view ordered D Company, still in reserve, to move to the right and reconnoitre a line of advance. Captain Anderson in command elected to push his men forward over a low ridge in an endeavour to dislodge a nest of enemy machine guns skilfully posted among the rocks and holding up the advance. His leading platoons almost immediately came under a withering fire reducing their numbers to a mere handful.

A volunteer was called for to take back a message to Company Headquarters, and Private R.E. Cruickshank at once responded. He rushed up the side of the wadi, but as he neared the top was hit and rolled back. Regardless of his wound, he at once made a second attempt, but was again

Captain J.S. Munro, Adjutant Palestine 1918.

Water-carrying camels, Palestine 1918.

hit, and again fell back into the shelter of the wadi bed. This time he agreed to have his wounds dressed, but then insisted on making a third attempt. He was again hit, and now unable to stand, was forced to abandon his efforts.

'*He displayed the utmost valour and endurance, and was cheerful and uncomplaining throughout,*' stated the official record of the occasion. Cruickshank was awarded the Victoria Cross, and invested by King George V at Buckingham Palace on 24 October 1918.

Anderson decided not to squander even more lives and therefore declined to commit his two remaining platoons to the carnage. That evening they went forward in an attempt to recover their dead.

'*Each lifeless body was lifted into the wagons,*' mourned Blazer, '*ten, twenty, thirty and more, the very best of fellows; men with whom we had lived, with whom we had laughed, men with whom we had discussed the past and planned the future, now all covered with blood and dust, tattered and disfigured - dead. It was a horrible sight.*'

The artillery at last moved forward, and heralded the coming of dawn with a heavy bombardment of El Haud. No further advance was ordered, however, save on the right where the London Irish, who had relieved the 2/20th, made efforts to take the high ground to their front. The infantry were now ordered to consolidate while the cavalry, riding round the flanks, attacked Es Salt. It was felt certain that this would force the Turks to retire from El Haud, yet little could have been further from the truth and they never faltered in their hold on the hill. Indeed, Turkish reinforcements approaching from the north very nearly succeeded in cutting off the cavalry and forced the Horse Gunners supporting them to abandon nine of their guns.

After dusk on 2 May the Westminsters were relieved by the Kensingtons, and the London Scottish by the Civil Service Rifles. The Battalion, now just over 200 strong, went into brigade reserve. The next day, just as the light was fading those who were able paraded, marched to the Wadi Nimrin and to the plaintive wail of *The Flowers of the Forest* buried their dead. Three officers and thirty men had died in the abortive assault and over a hundred has sustained wounds. Even the pack animals had not escaped punishment, the Turkish artillery had discovered their shelter and had shelled it mercilessly.

On 4 May the Scottish withdrew down the Wadi Nimrin and bivouacked near the bridges. At 4.30a.m. the next morning they recrossed the Jordan and from there marched to their former bivouac ground just east of Jericho, reaching it by 9.00a.m.

Rumours of a heavy reverse pervaded, and the very scantiness of information seemed ominous. An air of sadness reigned over the camp, for wherever the survivors looked they were faced with a plethora of reminders of their grief. The officers did all they could to lift morale and on the first afternoon organized Battalion games, but these brought only fleeting relief. The first raid across the Jordan had met with doubtful success, the second was undoubtedly a failure. True the Scots had gained their objective and captured about 150 prisoners, but at forty-eight per cent their losses had been extraordinarily heavy.

After two days the Scottish began the return march to Jerusalem, but this time were conveyed by motor lorries, and in them made their last journey up the infamous Bethany Hill. On 7 May Major General Shea inspected the Battalion at Shafat. Here the Scottish learned that the 60th Division had been ordered into Corps reserve, and that as a battalion they were now to enjoy a well-earned and lengthy period of rest. The next day they moved to Kefr Akab, and on 9 April passed through Ram Allah en route to a delightful bivouac spot between Ain Arik and Deir Ibzia. There they met General Allenby, who congratulated them warmly on their recent achievements. Parcels from home now arrived and, as the companies were so thinned, each man had about three parcels, many making themselves sick on the excesses.

As the *Official History* recalls,

> '*tents were available for all; companies were well spread out, the location was pleasant, the prospect cheerful.*'

Preparations were made for a long stay and a stage dug out of the hillside. Training was limited to three hours a day, with beer a ready inducement for any job well done. On one occasion Hendry remembered a race in which the participants had to run up to the top of a hill, drink a bottle of beer and return. The officers, he recalled, had a race on donkeys which brought forth great laughter and mirth. On 25 May the Battalion marched to Ram Allah where they were again addressed by General Shea. Rumours of an armistice were shattered when he bade the Scottish farewell and advised them that they had been recalled to France. On 28 May they began the long trek from the hills to the coastal plain, finally arriving at Ladd. Here they entrained in cattle trucks for Kantara where each man was awarded four days leave. The adventurous visited Cairo, the exhausted simply slept.

On the evening of 15 June the Battalion entrained in open trucks for Alexandria, the first part of their journey through the desert being accomplished on a glorious moonlit night. The next morning they embarked

Somewhere in Palestine, 1918.

on the SS *Canberra* which two days later sailed. The 60th Division had shared with the 52nd Division the honour of being the best-known fighting Division in Allenby's Army. The London Scottish had fought without rest for over six months. With the single exception of Kauwukah they had been at the fore of every engagement and had never once been found wanting.

The campaign as a whole was aptly summed-up by Major H.C. Palmer, writing from his sick bed.

> '*It has not been by any means a picnic, and in doing what has been done we have had some extraordinary heavy fighting. The Turk is a beggar to shift, and out here has certainly lived up to his reputation as a splendid fighting man on the defensive. However, we have been winning all along and knew it - that makes a world of difference.*'

Chapter Eleven

Ordered to France

The U-boat threat in the area of the eastern Mediterranean was now considerable, indeed the previous two convoys had each lost a troop ship. Accordingly the authorities took no chances and for 100 miles or so from Alexandria the convoy was escorted by sloops, a sausage balloon and aeroplanes, besides its escort of ten Japanese torpedo-boat destroyers. The troops were allowed to remain on deck and, as Hendry later recalled, many a lingering eye turned backwards as the land of Egypt receded from view. Within sight of the Italian coast an attempt was made to torpedo one of the convoy. The alarm was immediately given, and 'boat stations' sounded, which allowed the troops to witness a thrilling episode of sea warfare. Like a flash, two of the escorts turned outwards and dashed with great speed in the direction of the sighted periscope, giving rapid fire as they advanced. When over the spot where the U-boat had been seen to submerge, they dropped several depth charges and remained to cruise in the neighbourhood. Later, they were able to report oil floating on the surface, a certain indication of a U-boat paying the penalty for its audacity.

The troopships made for the safety of Taranto harbour, where they disembarked on 22 June. There they remained in hutted accommodation for two days rest before entraining for a seven-day journey back to the Western Front. Despite the many stops en route the journey was far from uncomfortable, the troops being billeted six to a carriage which allowed them to sleep two either side and two on the floor. A long stop at Castellamare, on the shores of the Adriatic, gave the Scottish an initial indication of the beauty of the Italian countryside, particularly when

2nd Battalion at a French farm shortly after their return from Palestine.

The Battalion Pipe Band in France, 1918.

compared with the bareness of Egypt. The next stops for rations were Ancona, Faenza and Palma, where free food and chocolate was supplied. Voghera, San-Pierre and Genoa were passed, and on 27 June the Battalion was able to bask in the beauty of the Riviera as the train continued along the coast. The next morning the train passed through Marseilles, and three days later, on 1 July, finally drew into a siding at Audruicq, some ten miles north-west of St Omer.

Here the Scottish learned that they, in conjunction with the 2nd Civil Service Rifles and the 2nd Queen's Westminsters, long-term friends from Palestine, were to form the 90th Brigade of the 30th Division. Originally a New Army division recruited in Lancashire, the 30th had borne the brunt of the German offensive of 21 March 1918, and after an heroic stand had been reduced to a mere cadre. After a short period of training the new American troops then flooding into France, it had been moved to St Omer to re-form. The veterans of the 90th Brigade were thus particularly welcome, even though when Major General Williams, the new General Officer Commanding, expressed his belief in young company commanders Colonel Ogilby had to admit that his had an average age of forty,

'aggregate years of service in the Regiment, eighty.'

After a twelve mile march to Recques, and thence to Brigade Headquarters at Serques, the Battalion began at once to train for warfare on the Western Front. The tranquillity of the village, quite untouched by the war, was somewhat marred when an influenza epidemic struck, but even this inconvenience was alleviated when it was announced that home leave was to be granted. The veterans of Salonika and Beersheba had not set foot in Britain for two years, and few had not lain awake in the wilderness of the Middle East yearning for home and wondering if they would ever see it again. No wonder Hendry described his leave as;

'the most enjoyable holiday I have ever had and ever likely to.'

On 8 July the Division began a general move towards the line, where it was to come into Corps reserve. Divisional Headquarters moved to Cassel, the 90th Brigade Headquarters to St Sylvestre Cappel. The Scottish were sent to

234

the little village of Eecke, where for the first time in weeks they came once
again into the range of the enemy guns. The position in France at this time
was critical. In what transpired to be a final desperate act the Germans had
thrown their entire resources into an offensive. They had driven massive
salients into the Allied front, had crossed the Lys, had taken Mount Kemmel
and were once again at the outskirts of Ypres. The whole line was gripped
with the certain knowledge that a further German attack would shortly be
launched. It was felt that Prince Rupprecht had twenty-four Divisions at his
disposal and would inevitably launch an attack in the direction of the
Channel Ports. Intelligence reports suggested that the attack would take
place on 18 July. During the preceding nights the Scottish underwent night
training with particular emphasis on the counter-attack, and on the night of
the anticipated assault went silently into the line. After a night of fear and
frustration during which the enemy made no attempt to leave his trenches,
the Scottish withdrew in the morning amid a dual sense of relief and
frustration.

During the next few days the Battalion received reinforcements from the
Gordon Highlanders. So close was the relationship of the two battalions
that the Gordons were permitted to retain their kilts, a consideration which
was greatly appreciated. During its stay at Eecke the Battalion marched to
St Sylvestre Cappel for inspection by General Plumer, then in command of
the 2nd Army and arguably the most able commander in the British Army.

On 27 July the Scottish were ordered up to the line to relieve the 18th
Highland Light Infantry, members of the 31st Division. Initially the
battalion occupied a reserve position at Moth Farm, but three days later
relieved the Civil Service Rifles in the front line. Their new position was
unenviable, the trenches were neither continuous nor properly dug, and
were in full view of the enemy positions on Mount Kemmel. Movement in
daylight would have proved suicidal, so much so that all the chores of front
line living; evacuating the wounded, bringing up rations, water and stores,
had to be undertaken in the hours of darkness.

While the Battalion was being relieved by the Queen's Westminsters on
the night of 1-2 August the enemy became suspicious and illuminated the
area with star shells. A brisk barrage followed, in which five Scottish were
killed and nine wounded. It had originally been planned that the 31st
Division would reduce the salient to its front by taking Wakefield Wood, but
a combination of the weather and logistics caused a postponement. The
legacy was handed over to the 30th Division when it returned to the line on
9 August.

Elsewhere the tide of war was turning against the Germans. To the south
Foch had delivered a highly successful counter stroke on 8 August, causing
the Germans to rush reinforcements from Flanders. This gave Plumer an
excellent opportunity to take the initiative. Orders were therefore given for
the destruction of the salient and the formation of a new line from Locre
Hospice on the north-east to the British line south-east of Koudekot.

HM King George investing Serjeant Charles William Train with the Victoria Cross gained on Tumulus Hill on 8 December 1917. The presentation was made at Second Army Headquarters on 6 August 1918.

Mobray and Wakefield Woods, two large, well-grown plantations both forming considerable hindrances to the advance, were pivotal to the attack. The ground over which the advance was to be made was heavily cratered with shell holes, well wired, and in places water logged. Fallen trees and the remains of hedges and ditches formed additional impediments.

All three brigades of the 30th Division were to participate. On the left two companies of the 1/6th Cheshires were to advance from Angle Trench and connect with the Scottish at Locre Hospice. The Scottish, in the centre, were detailed for the longest advance, from Prose Farm, through Wakefield Wood to Locrehof Farm, which was to be seized and held. The Scottish right, just east of Romp Farm, was to link up with the 2nd South Lancashire Regiment. Three companies of the latter were to carry Mobray Wood and continue to Romp Farm. To their right the 7/8th Inniskilling Fusiliers were to complete the line between the South Lancashires and Koudekot.

The role of the Scottish, in the centre, was crucial to the success of the entire enterprise. Colonel Ogilby detailed three companies to assault: A under Captain Burn on the right, B under Captain Noble in the centre and C under Lieutenant Jones on the left. D Company, under Captain Anderson, was to remain in reserve. The attack was scheduled for 2.00a.m. on the morning of 21 August and was to be covered by a creeping barrage of machine guns, lifting at the rate of 100 yards per four minutes. The Scottish advance was to be made in their favoured formation of two waves, each of two lines, the men moving by sections in file.

In his subsequent report to Brigade Headquarters Ogilby wrote,

'In accordance with your Operation Order No 179 I assembled for the attack on the DRANOUTRE Ridge and reported all in position and ready to move forward at 1240 midnight 20/21.'

In his notes Lieutenant Jones, reporting on the fate of C Company, was even less emotive.

'Assembly: This was carried out quietly and without mishap.'

Hendry was more expansive.

'We were all given instructions and each carried a spade across our backs. Each section had a bottle of rum. In the early night hours of August 20 we moved down the slopes, with the usual machine-gun bullets pattering away, and a volley of shells bursting around.'

Hendry's section was hit and several men wounded.

'We bound them up as best as possible in the time we had and had to leave them to find their way back as best they could, not a nice position to be in on a night like this, because as soon as we attack the Germans would flood the area with shells.'

At approximately 1.00a.m. a mist came down and hung until nearly 10.00a.m. that morning. It gave the attackers the advantage of extra time in which to complete consolidation, but also covered the enemy preparations for counter-attack. At 2.05a.m. the British barrage descended, the infantry rose from their shell holes and trenches, and began their advance. The

2nd Battalion The London Scottish, December 1918.

artillery had given considerable thought to the barrage; their heavy guns selecting targets in the rear, their field guns creeping forward with the infantry and the trench mortars and machine guns firing from forward positions. The German outposts were swamped and had no chance to recover from the bombardment before the British infantry were upon them. On the flank an enemy machine gun somehow survived and came into action, virtually annihilating the right hand platoon of the Scottish line. Serjeant Wiles got a party together, rushed and captured the machine gun, but was killed almost immediately thereafter. Touch with the South Lancashires was thus lost at an early stage but, save for this incident, the advance proceeded without a check. Wakefield Wood was difficult, but the pace of the barrage had taken this into account and the men were able to keep up with it despite the perplexing character of the ground.

The German artillery counter was both feeble and inaccurate, and the Scottish were thus able to attain their objective in less than an hour. The second wave thereafter brought up stakes and wire, and the leading line was soon digging in and wiring. Lieutenant Jones, commanding C Company, noted in his battle report that,

> 'The attack was completely successful; the objective being reached as per timetable. The barrage moved steadily forward and our line kept fairly close to it. Some distance was lost crossing through WAKEFIELD WOOD but was made up again immediately the wood was crossed. There was a little machine gun fire from the enemy but this only lasted for a short time and gave no trouble.'

In the darkness, and obscured by the mist and smoke of exploding shells, many men felt themselves alone and had to call upon reservoirs of tenacity coupled with training to survive. Hendry remembered that;

> 'the ground was swampy and it was hard to keep in touch having to climb over tree trunks brought down by shells, and jump trenches and shell holes to say nothing of the barbed wire. No one could have

made an obstacle race more difficult. I soon lost sight of my pals and didn't give a damn for anyone after such a rum ration as I had.'

He proceeded to confront a group of figures crouching ahead,

'and instantly fired at the same time jumping behind a tree and followed this quickly with a bomb. I then crawled behind a fallen tree towards them and found four Boche groaning.'

The 6th South Wales Borderers (Pioneers) followed up the attack and did some wonderful digging on the ridge. While the Scottish consolidated their outpost line, the Borderers dug a line of resistance further to the rear. Only on the right flank was there a hint of weakness. As Ogilby subsequently noted in his report to Brigade,

'I proceeded immediately to consolidate, and on reaching the new line I found my Right was well in the air, and though consolidation had started I thought it advisable to pull it back so as to conform with the unit on my right. This meant a considerable loss of ground, but owing to the density of the mist and the time so short before dawn, it seemed the most practical way of making certain of the ground gained.'

At about 8.00a.m. the mist suddenly lifted exposing the Scottish positions to view from Mount Kemmel and making further movement impossible. At about that time a terrific rain of shells fell upon the Scottish defences as the enemy were noted doubling up in single file along a hedgerow. Their audacity was met by rapid fire from the Scottish positions, but the German onslaught was such that one by one it became necessary to withdraw the outpost lines and fall back. Lieutenant Jones, with C Company, fell back further than intended and immediately counter-attacked. He succeeded in clearing Locrehof Farm, capturing five machine guns and reaching his original objective with a serjeant and three men, but came under heavy machine-gun fire and was forced to withdraw. Corporal Davis, however, remained in the farm and was able to deny it to the enemy.

Throughout the day the German artillery, chastened by its previous inactivity, kept up a continual bombardment of the Scottish trenches. In B Company Captain Noble in command was severely concussed, and all his officers killed or injured. Lieutenant Paterson from D Company was sent up to take over command. That night, after a gas shell attack, the enemy counter attacked twice, but both endeavours were easily repulsed before reaching bombing range, despite the fact that they were made by special *Sturmtruppen* brought up in motor buses for the purpose. B Company alone accounted for eighty-nine dead, while the battalion as a whole took seventy-two prisoners. During the night of 22-23 August the Scottish were relieved and withdrew to shelters on the western side of Mont Rouge. Their losses sustained were 2 officers and 27 other ranks killed, 5 officers and 120 other ranks wounded and 5 missing.

The fight on the Dranoutre Ridge was one of the most successful minor actions of the war and boded well for the newly-reformed 30th Division.

The Scottish in particular acquitted themselves well. Colonel Ogilby was later awarded a bar to his DSO, and other honours gained in the Battalion were two Military Crosses, two Distinguished Conduct Medals and two Military Medals. Major Crawford, commanding 302 Battery RFA, paid the Battalion a signal compliment when he penned the message,

> 'We all thank the SCOTTISH most heartily for their yeoman service both yesterday and more especially this morning.'

On 27 August Brigadier Stevens wrote to the Command Officer:

> 'Dear Ogilby, The last air photo, dated 25th, which I have received, discloses a very fine bit of consolidation by your Battalion. Will you congratulate all those concerned on their good work? Really the whole show from start to finish was most excellent.'

Soon after the action, the retirement of the enemy rendered it possible to walk over the battlefield in safety. The dead bodies of many Scots lying well beyond the objective proved conclusively their dedication. Their bravery was made the subject of a special Divisional order by Major General Williams.

The Scottish suffered continuous shelling during its four days in support at Mont Rouge, but the dugouts were deep and few casualties were sustained. Hendry later recalled being detailed to take a party of stretcher bearers back to the front to recover some of the dead. He set out with fourteen men and made a bee-line for the woods. Having collected his grisly loads he and his team set off back, but quickly found that transporting dead men over tree trunks and shell holes was no easy chore in the pitch black. He was rewarded upon his return with a large glass of whisky, which, he proudly recalled, he 'swigged like an old veteran.' The Battalion was relieved by the Westminsters on 24 August and withdrew to the security of Moth Farm where it remained for a further four days until returning to support on Mont Rouge. Plans for the Scottish to relieve the Westminsters on the night of 30-31 August were frustrated when, during the night preceding, large fires were seen in the German rear area denoting their intention to withdraw. Under the circumstances the battalions in the line were ordered to remain in readiness to follow up and harass the enemy's retreat as soon as it should begin.

On the 30 August the Germans withdrew followed closely by the British probing for weaknesses. A stand was made in the old British trenches between Daylight Corner and Neuve Eglise. The 89th Brigade, following a brilliant advance by the South Lancashires and Inniskillings, succeeded in wresting Neuve Eglise from the demoralized 'Boche', and after doing so handed over the line to the 36th (Ulster) Division.

The Scottish began their slow advance from Mont Rouge early that afternoon. They left the road at Locrehof Farm and cut across country to the shoulder of Mount Kemmel, where they enjoyed a long halt until dusk. Major Whyte, in temporary command in the absence of Colonel Ogilby, was ordered to Brigade Headquarters where he was advised that 90th Brigade

2nd Battalion Officers, December 1918.

had been tasked with clearing the area in the neighbourhood of Wulverghem. The Scottish were to advance, covering the entire Brigade front, in four 'bounds'. They were to move at night through Wulverghem in the general direction of the Messines ridge, the last 'bound' being to the line of the road connecting Messines with Wytschaete. The War Diary reported that the Scottish had been scheduled to relieve the 7th Royal Irish Regiment in daylight but this had proved impractical, hence the delay at Mount Kemmel. Meanwhile the 7th Royal Irish Regiment. supported by the 2/23rd Londons launched another daylight attack. Matters quickly became confused, and by the time the Scottish were in a position to enter the fray the forward dispositions of the lead battalions were far from clear.

It was initially thought that the earlier attack had been halted, and D Company was thus sent forward to relieve the old line and make contact with the 2/23rd on the left. However after two platoons had gone forward a report was received that the 2/23rd had taken Wulverghem and were now forward in a dangerously isolated position. A Company was immediately dispatched to their assistance while D Company was ordered forward towards Frenchman's Farm. The right flank remained dangerously open but the enemy were in no state to exploit this uncomfortable fact; indeed, when the lead companies of the Scottish began to advance in the morning they met with little resistance. C Company, which entered Wulverghem, found it unrecognizable as a village. Weeds grew forlornly among the ruins and only a battered sign remained to advise the Scottish that they were on the site of the 1st Battalion's first great encounter with the enemy almost precisely four years earlier.

A Company, passing through C, pushed forward some 600 yards until it was held up by a strong defensive line on the ridge east of Wulverghem. C Company remained watching the flank from the village while B Company moved over in support of D. The enemy still held Hill 63 from which they were able to bring enfilade fire to bear, and it quickly became clear that no further advance could be made until the 36th (Ulster) Division came into line on the right. This they did with tenacity and bravery, regardless of heavy loss. The Germans now contested every inch of ground, and before any further appreciable loss could be made, the Scottish were relieved by the Civil Service Rifles.

The Scottish withdrew to reserve at Donegal Farm where two miserable days were spent. The area was devastated and provided no shelter at all. The enemy shells were dropping around all day long, and one of the battalion cookers caught a direct hit. Fortunately there were few casualties, but even so the Battalion breathed a collective sigh of relief when, on 8 September, they were withdrawn to Divisional reserve at Mount Noir. The Scottish spent the night at Starling Farm, described in the *Official History* as '*a loathsomely dirty and muddy place,*' and the next morning moved to Mount Noir. There they found the area overcrowded, the best positions having been taken by support troops of the Divisional Headquarters, Gunners or Engineers. It seemed to the Scottish that these men had been allowed to wander around the Divisional area seizing billets at will. Not for the first time, they felt that the infantry coming from the line had been left to fend for themselves, often in conditions which were uninhabitable. Nor could the Scottish seek cover in the former German dugouts for fear of delayed action bombs.

It had become clear to the High Command that the final stages of the war would take on an entirely different perspective. Veterans of the trenches would have to be taught the subtleties of fire and movement if they were not to be cut to pieces in the open. On 15 September the 90th Brigade went forward again, the Scottish moving to Ulster Camp near Dranoutre. Here they remained in support of the 21st Brigade for four days, occasionally suffering bombardment by long-range enemy artillery. One section per company was constantly on duty in the line in the area of Daylight Corner and losses were inevitable. Tragically Second Lieutenant R. A. Brown, a recently joined young officer and the son of Colour Serjeant H.B. Brown, one of the oldest members of the Regiment, was killed. He now lies in Westoutre British Cemetery near Heuvelland, to the south-west of Ypres.

At this time Brigadier Stevens took some well-earned leave. Colonel Ogilby assumed command of the 90th Brigade, and in the absence of Major Whyte on Base duties, command of the Scottish passed to Captain R.M. Robertson. On the night of 19-20 September the Scottish moved from the support area to the front line east of Hill 63 and relieved the 9th Battalion, The Royal Inniskillings, part of the 36th (Ulster) Division. The line held extended from Hyde Park Corner on the right, over Hill 63 to a point some 150 yards northward of the River Douve, where it linked with the 21st Brigade. The Civil Service Rifles were in support, the Westminsters in reserve. B Company was tasked with holding the line on the right, A Company, less two platoons, the centre, and C Company the left. D Company, under Lieutenant Geddes, with the remaining two platoons of A Company, formed the reserve.

Battalion Headquarters enjoyed the luxury of a deep-tunnelled dugout situated on the extreme north-western corner of Ploegstreete Wood, which boasted no less than 115 wire beds. The lack of communication trenches, coupled with the German habit of smothering the line with trench mortars, led to inevitable casualties. On the night of 23 September a raid was made against the C Company front, but was easily driven off. Later a four-man patrol from the German 167th Regiment of Infantry was taken prisoner without a fight, and afforded ample evidence of the plummeting state of morale now pervading the enemy. Later a fourteen-man patrol from B Company carried out a raid against a troublesome machine gun posted in the chateau to their front. One prisoner was taken, nine enemy killed and the machine gun destroyed in exchange for one member of the patrol missing and three wounded. Hendry, a member of the patrol, recalled that nothing was subsequently heard of the missing man, although the area was thoroughly searched.

On the morning of 24 September the Battalion was relieved by the Queen's Westminsters and moved down the Ravelsberg road to Bailleul where the cellars of a ruined asylum were allotted to them. Throughout their tour of Hill 63 the Scottish were able to see the ruins of Messines. Colonel Ogilby made no secret of the fact that he regarded it as the Scottish prerogative to retake the village and contrived to have them in the front line when the assault on its ruins was scheduled. However, the Germans frustrated his intentions by weakening their hold on the line. The attack was brought forward from early October to 28 September at which time the Scottish were still in Bailleul, and had perforce to act as the support battalion.

Colonel Ogilby resumed command on 27 September, and at 1.15a.m. the next morning left Bailleul with the Battalion to move east up the Ravelsberg road in support of the Civil Service Rifles and Westminsters who were forming the attacking line for a 4.00a.m. assault. The march was made in broad moonlight and went smoothly until, just outside Neuve Eglise, a German aeroplane came over flying low. It circled, yet astonishingly no orders were given to the troops below to take cover. The pilot dropped five bombs in quick succession, straddling A Company and causing a number of wholly avoidable casualties. The survivors continued on towards Wulverghem where they halted for refreshment. By now the grand attack had started along a twenty-four mile front. Everywhere guns and supplies were pressing forward, while prisoners were passing sullenly to the rear. For their part the Civil Service Rifles on the left and the Westminsters on the right attacked astride the Wulverghem-Messines road. The Scottish moved slowly forward in support, and by 3.00p.m. that afternoon were lying in and around Messines.

Inevitably, as the battle progressed and the advance went forward, reliable information became scarce. Colonel Ogilby, in Messines, realizing the necessity for hard intelligence, went forward to find the lead battalions still making steady progress, but by now disorganized by reason of casualties and the difficulties of the ground they had to traverse. It became clear that the 30th Division's right flank, which should have been linking with the XVth Corps, was now dangerously exposed. The Scottish filled this void, and at dusk they moved off in heavy rain through Messines and on eastward down Huns Walk. Ogilby quickly ascertained that the Civil Service Rifles were holding a line between a point west of Houthem and the Kortekeer Beck to the south while the XVth Corps were approaching Warneton. The Scottish were therefore ordered to fill the gap between the right of the Civil Service Rifles and Warneton by pushing out patrols to the bank of the River Lys and into Warneton town. Hendry remembered the area as strewn with concrete pillboxes all containing a plethora of souvenirs; thirteen guns and three machine guns were found bogged in the mud, as were two British tanks abandoned in an earlier action.

A patrol under Lieutenant S.A. Paterson penetrated into Warneton and found the bridges across the Lys destroyed. During the day the enemy shelled a great deal, causing some casualties and making a further daylight advance impractical. On 3 October the 30th Division was withdrawn, the place of the Scottish being taken by the 29th Battalion Durham Light Infantry, 14th Division. Many of the Durhams were only class 'C' men whom the shortage of manpower had sent to the line again. Not a few were still suffering from unhealed wounds, and all had physical disabilities of one sort or another.

> 'The sight gave me seriously to think of the "gentlemen in Britain" now tucked in their comfortable beds, who should have been in their places,'

complained Hendry with some justificaton.

The Scottish were ordered to withdraw to an area around Gun Farm, a mad place for rest, destitute of dugouts or shelter and lying in full view of the German observers across the Lys. Within twenty-four hours the Battalion had been spotted and was frequently shelled. On 6 October it was at last ordered further back, this time to L'Enfer Hill, an area hallowed in London Scottish Regimental tradition by reason of its association with the original fighting for Messines.

Although losses for the month of September had not been great - Lieutenant Brown and four other ranks killed, Lieutenants Jones and Conacher and forty-five other ranks seriously injured and one man missing - months of attrition had inevitably taken their toll. The Battalion strength had been reduced to 33 officers and 789 other ranks, of whom no more than 75 men per company were fully fit. Two days of strenuous training in open-warfare formation was put in at L'Enfer, and on the evening of 10 October orders came through for another move to the line.

By early October 1918 the German army was reeling under the Allied onslaught. The front before the 30th Division formed a huge salient pressing into the flat, desolate country between the Messines Ridge and Menin. The Scottish were ordered to relieve the 7/8th Royal Inniskilling Fusiliers on the south side of the salient between Gheluwe and Wervicq, and on the morning of 11 October assembled at Pick House, on the Wytschaete-Messines road. Their journey to the front line, already onerous, was compounded by ill-luck. From the outset the transport limbers became hopelessly bogged down, and only after superhuman efforts by Lieutenant S. G. Wilson, the Transport Officer, were they able to rejoin the column. Not for the first time guides failed to materialize on time, yet the Scottish were forced to continue 'blind' in the general direction of their goal, as the Civil Service Rifles were following and any enforced halt would have caused chaos.

When one of the guides did find the Battalion he was suffering agonies from gas poisoning. With his dying gasps he was able to report that earlier that day the Inniskillings had sustained a heavy gas shell bombardment, and that most of the Irishmen were already casualties. Inevitably, before long, the Scottish also began to suffer. Major Whyte, in temporary command, attempted to relocate his headquarters, but with his Intelligence Officer and many of the forward party suffering the effects of gas he was unable to relay his orders to the main party following. The Battalion blustered forward, lost, but in the general direction of America Corner, until they encountered a machine-gunner who told the lead elements that they were within 600 yards of the front line, in an area held by the 2/17th Londons. The column, still closed-up in column of route and offering an ideal target for enemy artillery, turned about at once and, led by the Civil Service Rifles, retired to safety. At last the correct road was found, and at midnight the Scottish were able to relieve the exhausted Inniskillings.

The line was fundamentally different from anything the Scottish had experienced before. The area was devastated with no trenches. Hedges, ditches and shell-holes afforded some cover but only those in the rear were able to enjoy the real protection of well-constructed pillboxes. D and C Companies were pushed forward, each with three platoons, on average comprising only eighteen bayonets in front, and one in support. Duty in the line was unexciting, but relatively safe. Gas and high explosive shells occasionally landed on the front line, but the weather was far more disconcerting than the enemy. It rained constantly. Sentries stood knee deep in water in their shell holes and ditches and ration parties frequently failed to reach their goals. In the words of one unknown but perceptive Scot,

'It's no' the Army they're needin' here. It's Admiral Beatty and the bloody Navy.'

On 13 October it was announced that a full dress attack was to take place the next morning. Major Whyte, suffering badly from the effects of gas, was too ill to lead the attack. Companies were to assault as they lay in the line, with D Company on the right and C on the left. The Civil Service Rifles were to assault on the right of the Scottish, the 7th Cheshires on the left. B Company was detailed to mop up and supply support to the lead companies, A Company to act as reserve. The objective was to be the Menin-Wervicq road, 2,400 yards ahead. A creeping barrage was promised, to begin some 300 yards ahead of the line and to lift at the rate of 100 yards every 90 seconds. As was then the practice, at the fifteenth lift the barrage was to remain stationary for fifteen minutes to enable the infantry to consolidate, and thereafter to continue until it had attained a point 200 yards beyond the objective. Machine guns were to cooperate with overhead fire, and the Corps heavy artillery were to fire on selected targets in the rear.

The night of 13 October was a busy one. Hendry remembered being issued with *'good hot stew and rum'* after which he felt ready for the fray. The assault was timed for 5.35a.m., and by 4.00am all was reported ready. Ten minutes later the men moved forward to the jumping-off line, marked by the Royal Engineers the night before with crossed tapes at intervals, and at 5.35a.m. the swish of hundreds of shells announced the off.

The rain had by now stopped, but the five per cent of smoke shells fired by the gunners gave some degree of protection to the advancing infantry. The German outposts, demoralized and dazed by the intensity of the barrage, capitulated at once, but the machine-gunners behind them showed more spirit and began to cause serious casualties. The wire was sporadic, but where it existed was effective causing inevitable pauses in the line. A wooded area with many pillboxes was reached. Some of the garrison offered resistance, others surrendered at once. Those who resisted found the Scottish in no mood to be trifled with. A very large number of the enemy, who far outnumbered the attackers, were killed.

Hendry reported that;

> *'on my right was a large high mound and the machine-guns soon opened up from here causing us many casualties, but we pressed on and got round this, where we soon made these gunners pay the penalty.'*

By 7.35a.m. the objective had been attained. Although the barrage had now lifted, smoke still hung in the still morning air causing confusion among the by now scattered Scots. When Captain Robertson advanced with his signallers and a runner to meet the Cheshires, he instead found a group of German machine-gunners who at once surrendered. When suddenly a light wind lifted the smoke the Scottish, by now digging in, became easy targets for the Germans who had retired to a hedgerow some 500 yards away. However a short, sharp duel with the Lewis gunners forced the enemy to withdraw further, after which, save for intermittent shelling, the Scottish were left unmolested.

Casualties for the day among the attacking and support companies were about twenty per cent. The War Diary reported that 220 prisoners were taken and a large number of the enemy killed. Officialdom, ever an ill bedmate of the front line soldier, now intervened. The signallers had been ordered to carry baskets of pigeons forward with them as a means of contact with Division. Battalion Headquarters became involved in a voluminous correspondence when a signaller, against standing orders, discarded his basket of pigeons in order to use his bayonet!

The advance of 14 October was one of the most successful operations of the latter stages of the war. The Germans fell back everywhere, surrendering territory from the coastal fortresses of Ostend and Zeebrugge on their right, to Lille in the centre and La Bassée in the south. For their part the Scottish had done well, but were the first to admit that their successes would not have been so great had it not been for the Gunners. In the words of the *Official History*,

> *'their barrage work was perfect. It is the custom of many infantry Regiments to boast of the prisoners they have secured. In this case the London Scottish can gracefully acknowledge that a great number of the 400 taken by them were captured as a result of the prowess of the Royal Regiment of Artillery.'*

During the course of the night the lead and reserve companies swapped. The next afternoon the Battalion was ordered to advance to the line of the River Lys. The move began just before dusk but the line had no sooner settled down than orders came for the relief of the two companies in front by A Company, from reserve, who were to take over the whole front. Captain Burn brought his company forward at about 2.00a.m., at which time D and C withdrew into billets at Quest and Quiet Farms respectively.

The Scottish rested in reserve until the afternoon of 16 October when they moved east across the river. Earlier in the day the Civil Service Rifles had effected a passage at Bousbecque, after which the Royal Engineers had erected a pontoon bridge. Once across the bridge the Scottish began to occupy Bousbecque as Brigade reserve, but were almost immediately ordered forward in relief of the Civil Service, and at 10.00p.m. reached Roncq, a fairly large town some four miles south-east of Bousbecque.

> *'This was the first large town we had seen for a long time that was practically untouched by shells,'* remembered Hendry.

> *'All the inhabitants had been evacuated and everything removable had been carried off. Here we went into fine, dry billets and I got into a room with a real bed in it, so we had a jolly good sleep here for a few hours.'*

Before dawn the advance eastward was resumed, with the Scottish in reserve. The enemy, now in full retreat, was pursued all morning, until at about midday contact was made with his rearguard near Triloy. When it became clear that the enemy determined to make a stand, B Company, under Lieutenant C.L. Tennant MC, which was covering the entire Scottish front of some 1,300 yards, was ordered to advance in open order. Hendry remembered it as, *'very open'* the Company having by then been much reduced. The German right quickly capitulated but its left held, and it was only when two platoons of D Company joined the fray on the Scottish right that the enemy was finally dislodged.

The advance continued into the early morning of 18 October. C Company, now reduced to seventy-six all ranks, was extended on a front of 1,000 yards to a depth of 1,500 yards. The support of a battery of 18-pounders was sought and promised, and it was agreed that the Queen's Westminsters would advance simultaneously on the left. Due to a misunderstanding, the artillery barrage failed to materialize and the assault was thus postponed until 3.10a.m. There followed a furious fight in and around the village of Aelbek, but elsewhere the enemy disengaged without a fight. With the dawn came scenes of indescribable joy. Hendry remembered the face of a woman peering out of her back door.

> *'When she saw it was the British she flung open the door and in great excitement shouted to her companions, who were hiding under the house. They came crawling out one by one.'*

Elsewhere in the villages of Elebeke and Sterhoek, church bells were rung, bunting displayed and the Scottish welcomed with open arms. At 8.00a.m. A Company passed through the outpost line and took up the running. It continued to advance steadily throughout the day until at 5.00p.m. it made contact with the enemy east of the village of Tombroek. The next morning D Company was ordered to continue the advance to the River Scheldt. C Company on the right and B on the left were to be in support, A was to re-form and fall into reserve. The Queen's Westminsters were to advance on the Battalion left, and the 20th Middlesex, from the 43rd Brigade, on its right. The terrain rather than the Germans now proved the greatest enemy, and the Westminsters found themselves falling far behind when forced to negotiate a heavily wooded hill astride their route of advance. Darkness found the three lead companies of the Scottish in Pijpestaat. During the night the Westminsters, assisted by the 1/6th Cheshires, cleared the offending hill and the line of the Scheldt was won. Advance to contact remained an alien, nerve-racking form of warfare to the veterans of Palestine and the trenches, yet the Scottish pace never wavered. Indeed, D Company was so resolute in its advance that its actions brought forth a letter of unstinting praise from the Divisional Commander.

During the afternoon of 21 October, the 90th Brigade was relieved by the 89th and the Scottish marched back to billets in Tombroek. The usual reserve routine of kit inspections, company and specialist training and parades was frustrated on 24 October when Spanish influenza struck. Men succumbed at the rate of twenty or thirty per day, the field ambulances were unable to cope and battalions were put into isolation. The Scottish took over a school, in which their medical officer was much assisted in nursing by nuns from a neighbouring convent.

Hallowe'en was celebrated at Tombroek, after which, at dusk the next day, the Battalion left to return to the line. The Scottish took over from the 6th Hampshires in an area in which daylight movement was severely restricted due to the excellence of the German observation positions. Night patrolling was active, but in all other respects the period was quiet with few casualties. On the morning of 4 November the Scottish were relieved for the last time by the Westminsters and the 7/8th Inniskillings and that night withdrew to billets at Geuzenhoek. The Battalion, now commanded by Colonel Ogilby back from leave, returned to the line on 9 November to find the Germans in full retreat. Attempts were made to bridge the Scheldt without success when, on the morning of 11 November, the Armistice was announced. In the words of the *Official History*,

> *'There was little or nothing in the way of demonstration at the good tidings. Feelings were heartfelt but restrained, for through the sense of deep unutterable thankfulness that the horror and tension were over there pressed forward insistently but inevitably their memories of cherished comrades who had made the great sacrifice.'*

It had at one time been hoped that being in Plumer's Second Army, which was one of those ordered forward to the Rhine, the 2nd London Scottish might have had the privilege of entering enemy territory. This was not to be. The Xth Corps was transferred to the Fifth Army while training was reduced to the bare minimum. On 26 November a Brigade parade was held near Marcke after which the Battalion began a slow march westward. After a period of discomfort, compounded by the unsympathetic attitudes of the local population, the Scottish moved into comfortable accommodation at La Lacque, where among other duties they assumed responsibility for prisoner of war handling.

On 3 January 1919 the Scottish began to wend their slow way to Etaples. Five days later Captain Robertson, who had been seconded as Commanding Officer to the 2nd South Lancashires, returned to the Battalion, and Major Whyte being absent, assumed command from Colonel Ogilby when the latter was forced to return to England for a serious internal operation. Demobilization began on 20 January and proceeded at such a pace that on 11 February the 2nd London Scottish were obliged to accept a draft of 10 officers and 200 men from the 1/4th Gordon Highlanders who remained until 27 March. On 5 April they were joined by a draft of 15 officers and 223 men from the 1st Battalion, London Scottish, by then reduced to cadre strength.

On 19 May a King's Colour was presented to the Battalion by Major General Jefferys, commanding the 60th Division.

> *'The weather was gorgeous and all that one could wish for during a military spectacle of this nature,'* reported the Regimental History.

> *'The Battalion, under the command of Lieutenant Colonel R Whyte MC, was formed up on three sides of a square, the Colour Party consisting of Lieutenant Gibson, Company Serjeant-Major Williams,*

DCM, and Quartermaster Serjeant Grape being in the centre.'
The Major General spoke of his having met the 1st Battalion at Zillebeke Woods in 1914, and of the high regard in which he held them. He went on to say that hostilities had ceased but that the war was not quite over, that mundane duties remained but that he was sure that the Scottish would undertake these with their usual zeal and alacrity. He was not to be disappointed.

The rump battalion continued guard and administrative duties throughout the summer. On 1 August Lieutenant Colonel Whyte was demobilized, his place as Commanding Officer being taken by Lieutenant Colonel Colson of the Hampshire Regiment. Towards the end of August the Battalion was relieved by the 20th Hampshires from England and, on 15 September, moved to Boulogne, crossing to England two days later.

Orders for final demobilization were received in the middle of October and the disbandment of the 2nd London Scottish was completed by the first week of November; the last man to receive his papers being Captain L.G. Brown MC.

In April 1919 the *Regimental Gazette* published a letter from Walter E. Webb:

'Dear Sir

'It is good to be assured, as we are in the letter in your December issue, that the future of the London Scottish is in the thoughts of past and present members now at home.

'Judging from what is to happen in the case of the Regular army, it cannot, I should say, be imagined that the Territorial Force will cease to exist after demobilization, and it appears to be taken for granted that the original Battalions, certainly of the London units, will be continued, though probably under different conditions in some respects.

'As regards the London Scottish, the experience of this war has fully justified the many-sided activities of the Corps since 1859, as engineered from its London Head-Quarters. The Scottish entered the war with a foundation of physical fitness and esprit de corps, which still lives, and which has carried the three Battalions successfully through a severe a test as it is possible to apply to non-regular soldiers and units...'

He would have been pleased to know that, today, the London Scottish survives as A Company, The London Regiment.

The Menin Gate at Ypres commemorates British and Commonwealth soldiers with no known graves who died on the Ypres Salient between 1914 and 1917. It contains the names of approximately 100 London Scots. Those who died later, including at Passchendaele, and who have no known graves, are remembered at Tien Cot.

APPENDICES

ONE: BATTLE HONOURS

1914
Ypres
Givenchy

1915
Neuve Chapelle
Festubert
Loos

1916
Gommecourt
Somme

1917
Salonika
Vimy
Arras
Ypres
Cambrai
Beersheba
Sheria
Jerusalem
Shafat

1918
Jordan
Es Salt
El Haud
Arras
Dranoutre
Cambrai-St Quentin
Menin
Mons-Maubeuge

TWO: AWARDS FOR HONOUR

List of Honours and Awards won by the London Scottish throughout the war:

VC	2
CM	2
CBE	1
DSO	19
OBE	3
MBE	1
MC	60
AFC	1
DCM	41
MM	156
MSM	25
Albert Medal, 1st Class	1
Croix de Guerre *(French)*	6
Medaille Militaire *(French)*	6
Croix de Guerre *(Belgian)*	1
Officier l'Ordre de Leopold	1
Cross of the Order of St George *(Russian)*	1
Medaille Barbatie si Credenta, 3rd Class *(Romanian)*	1
Order of the Nile, 4th Class *(Egyptian)*	2
Mentioned in Dispatches	104
TOTAL:	437

THREE: BATTALIONS OF THE LONDON REGIMENT

1st   Royal Fusiliers
2nd   Royal Fusiliers
3rd   Royal Fusiliers
4th   Royal Fusiliers
5th   London Rifle Brigade
6th   City of London Rifles
7th   City of London Battalion
8th   Post Office Rifles
9th   Queen Victoria's Rifles
10th Paddington Rifles
11th Finsbury Rifles
12th The Rangers
13th Kensingtons
14th London Scottish
15th Civil Service Rifles
16th Queen's Westminsters
17th Poplar and Stepney Rifles
18th London Irish Rifles
19th St Pancras
20th Blackheath & Woolwich
21st 1st Surrey Rifles
22nd The Queens
23rd 23rd London
24th The Queens
25th Cyclists
28th Cyclists

N.B. 26th and 27th - HAC and Royal Yeomanry - did not form part of the Regiment.

FOUR: BRIGADE ORDERS OF BATTLE FIRST BATTALION

1 May 1915 - 1st Division
1st Guards Brigade
1st Coldstream Guards
1st Scots Guards
1st Black Watch

1st Cameron Highlanders
1st London Scottish (T.F.)

25 September 1915 - 1st Division
1st Infantry Brigade
1st Black Watch
1st Cameron Highlanders
1st London Scottish (T.F.)
10th Gloucestershire
8th Royal Berkshire

February 1916 - 56th (London) Division
168th Infantry Brigade
1/4th London Regiment (Royal Fusiliers)
1/12th London Regiment (Rangers)
1/13th London Regiment (Kensingtons)
1/14th London Regiment (London Scottish)
168th Machine Gun Company
168th Light Trench Mortar Battery

SECOND BATTALION

June 1916 - 60th (London) Division
179th Infantry Brigade
2/13th London Regiment (Kensingtons)
2/14th London Regiment (London Scottish)
2/15th London Regiment (Civil Service Rifles)
2/16th London Regiment (Queen's Westminster Rifles)
179th Light Trench Mortar Battery

July 1918 - 30th Division
90th Infantry Brigade
2/14th London Regiment (London Scottish)
2/15th London Regiment (Civil Service Rifles)
2/16th London Regiment (Queen's Westminster Rifles)

90th Light Trench Mortar Battery

INDEX

255